Pathways in Ethics: Justice – Interpretation – Discourse – Economics
Beyers Naudé Centre Series on Public Theology

Published by SUN MeDIA Stellenbosch under the SUN PReSS imprint.
www.africansunmedia.co.za
www.sun-e-shop.co.za

All rights reserved.

Copyright © 2016 Stellenbosch University, Beyers Naudé Centre

No part of this book may be reproduced or transmitted in any form or by any electronic, photographic or mechanical means, including photocopying and recording on record, tape or laser disk, on microfilm, via the Internet, by e-mail, or by any other information storage and retrieval system, without prior written permission by the publisher.

First edition, October 2016

ISBN 978-1-928357-15-5
ISBN 978-1-928357-16-2 (e-book)
DOI: 10.18820/9781928357162

Set in 10/12 Palatino Linotype
Cover photograph by Johannes Richter
Typesetting by SUN MeDIA Stellenbosch

SUN PReSS is an imprint of SUN MeDIA Stellenbosch. Academic, professional and reference works are published under this imprint in print and electronic format. This publication may be ordered directly from www.sun-e-shop.co.za

Printed and bound by SUN MeDIA Stellenbosch, Ryneveld Street, Stellenbosch, 7600.

Volume IX in the Beyers Naudé Centre Series on Public Theology

PATHWAYS IN ETHICS

JUSTICE – INTERPRETATION – DISCOURSE – ECONOMICS

Piet Naudé

DEDICATION

*I dedicate this volume to Heinrich Bedford-Strohm:
ethicist, bishop, public theologian and friend.*

ACKNOWLEDGEMENTS

PART ONE – ETHICS, JUSTICE AND HUMANITY

1. Globalisation and the challenge of cultural justice

   2007. The challenge of cultural justice under conditions of globalization: Is the New Testament of any use? In Breytenbach, Cilliers; Thom, Johan C; and Punt, Jeremy: *The New Testament interpreted. Essays in honour of Bernard C Lategan*. Leiden: Brill, 267-287.

2. In defence of partisan justice. An ethical reflection on "the preferential option for the poor"

   2007. In defense of partisan justice? An ethical reflection on "the preferential option for the poor". *Verbum et Ecclesia* 28/1, 166-190.

3. Between humility and boldness: Explicating human rights from a Christian perspective

   2007. Menschenrechte: Enige systematisch-theologische Überlegungen. *Ökumenische Rundschau* 56, Heft 1, 3-18.

   2007. Between humility and boldness: Explicating human rights from a Christian perspective. *Nederduits Gereformeerde Teologiese Tydskrif* deel 48, nommers 1 & 2, 139-149.

4. "Am I my brother's keeper?" An African reflection on humanisation

   2011. "Am I my brother's keeper?" An African reflection on humanization. In Len Hansen, Nico Koopman & Robert Vosloo (eds.): *Living theology. Essays presented to Dirk J Smit on his sixtieth birthday*. Wellington: Bible Media, 496-512.

PART TWO – ETHICS AND INTERPRETATION

5. Toward a post-disciplinary interpretation of theology, ethics and the sciences

   1996. Is God hovering above the nineteenth floor? *Inaugural Address D38*. UPE: Port Elizabeth.

6. Why is a multiplicity of confessional interpretations particular to the Reformed tradition?

   2014. Why is a multiplicity of confessions particular to the Reformed tradition? *Acta Theologica,* Suppl 20, 35-49.

7. Can we still hear Paul on the agora? An outsider perspective on the ethics of South African New Testament scholarship

   2005. Can we still hear Paul on the agora? An outsider perspective on New Testament scholarship in South Africa. *Neotestamentica* 39 (2), 339-358.

8. "But you, who do you say I am?" How the Christian faith can turn into an ideology of power

   2009. "But you, who do you say I am?" A homily on ideological faith from the Gospel of Mark. In Andreas Schuele and Günter Thomas (eds.): *Who is Jesus Christ for us today? Pathways to contemporary Christology*. Louisville, Kentucky: WJK, 134-149.

PART THREE – ETHICS AND MORAL DISCOURSE

9. What has Accra to do with New York? An analysis of moral discourse in the Accra Confession

   2008. What has Accra to do with New York? An analysis of moral discourse in the Accra Confession. *Nederduits Gereformeerde Teologiese Tydskrif* deel 49, nommers 3 & 4, 206-216.

10. Is prophetic discourse adequate to address global economic justice?

    2011. Is prophetic discourse adequate to address global economic justice? *HTS Teologiese Studies/Theological Studies* 67 (1) Art. #1014, 8 pages. DOI:10.4102/hts.v67i1.1014.

11. Virtue and responsibility: Economic-ethical arguments in the work of Etienne de Villiers

    2012. Virtue and responsibility: Economic-ethical perspectives in the work of Etienne de Villiers. *Verbum et Ecclesia* 33 (2), Art. #737, 6 pages.

12. Models of how we speak about "happiness" – A South African perspective

    2011. Modelle von Glückseligkeit. Eine Südafrikanische Perspektive. In Heinrich Bedford-Strohm (Hrsg.): *Glück-Seligkeit. Theologische Rede vom Glück in einer bedrohten Welt.* Neukirchen-Vluyn: Neukirchener Verlagsgesellschaft, 119-127.

    2011. Models of 'happiness' – A South African perspective. *NGTT* 52, 3&4, 465-471.

PART FOUR – ETHICS, BUSINESS AND ECONOMICS

13. Ethics education in Accounting: An outsider perspective

    2008. Ethics education in accounting: An outsider perspective. *South African Journal of Accounting Research*, volume 22, number 1, 1-17.

14. Transparency and corporate social responsibility: A South African perspective

    2011. Transparency and corporate social responsibility: A South African perspective. In Gotlind Ulshöfer und Beate Feuchte (Hrsg.): *Finanzmarktakteure und Corporate Social Responsibility. Ordnungspolitik – Transparenz – Anlagestrategien.* Wiesbaden: VS Verlag, 193-204. (with Willem Fourie).

15. Fair global trade: A perspective from Africa

    2010. Fair global trade: A perspective from Africa. In Geoff Moore (ed.) *Fairness in International trade.* London: Springer, 99-116.

16. Economic policy and theological reflection in South Africa: An overview and reflection after 20 years of democracy

    2014. Economic policy and theological reflection in South Africa. An overview and assessment after twenty years of democracy. *International Journal of Public Theology* 8, 445-470.

CONTENTS

DEDICATION iv
ACKNOWLEDGEMENTS v
FOREWORD ix

PART 1 – ETHICS, JUSTICE AND HUMANITY

1.1 Globalisation and the challenge of cultural justice 3

1.2 In defence of partisan justice 21
    An ethical reflection on "the preferential option for the poor"

1.3 Between humility and boldness 41
    Explicating human rights from a Christian perspective

1.4 "Am I my brother's keeper?" 53
    An African reflection on humanisation

PART 2 – ETHICS AND INTERPRETATION

2.1 Toward a post-disciplinary interpretation of theology, ethics and
    the sciences 65

2.2 Why is a multiplicity of confessions particular to the
    Reformed tradition? 79

2.3 Can we still hear Paul on the Agora? 91
    An outsider perspective on the ethics of South African New
    Testament scholarship

2.4 "But you, who do you say I am?" 107
    How the Christian faith turns into an ideology of power

PART 3 – ETHICS AND MORAL DISCOURSE

3.1 What has Accra to do with New York? 123
    An analysis of moral discourse in the Accra Confession

3.2 Is prophetic discourse adequate to address global economic justice? .. 133

3.3 Virtue and responsibility 149
    Economic-ethical perspectives in the work of Etienne de Villiers

3.4 Models of how we speak about "happiness" 159
    A South African perspective

PART 4 – ETHICS, BUSINESS AND ECONOMICS

4.1 **Ethics education in Accounting** 169
An outsider's perspective

4.2 **Transparency and corporate social responsibility** 185
A South African perspective

4.3 **Fair global trade** 195
A perspective from Africa

4.4 **Economic policy and theological reflection in South Africa** 211
An overview and assessment after 20 years of democracy

SUBJECT INDEX 233
NAME INDEX 235

FOREWORD

The publication of these essays brings to a close a three-year project that commenced in 2014. At the invitation of the Beyers Naudé Centre for Public Theology, a collection of my essays in theology was published in 2015 with the title *Pathways in theology: Ecumenical, African and Reformed* (Sun Press, edited by Henco van der Westhuizen). It was decided to collect my essays with an "ethical" focus in a separate volume. The result is this, the second volume, which could be read separately, although it will make richer sense if viewed in tandem with the first collection.

Like the first volume, these essays were not originally written to form part of a coherent collection. Though this volume may not be as well-structured as a book that one normally plans and writes in one movement, it was possible to collect these essays under four broad headings: justice, interpretation, discourse and economics. Each subsection consists of four chapters and the collection as whole covers a fairly wide (some would say: eclectic) spectrum of "ethical" reflections. Topics covered include analysing concepts of cultural and distributive justice, reading biblical texts and scholarship from an ethical perspective, advancing ethical discourse analysis, and attempting to make sense of global and local economic policies whilst also providing a rationale for ethics education in the (quite powerful) accounting profession.

This wide range of topics is rooted in theology and the Christian tradition, but some essays were written for professional journals or as chapters for books not directly related to theology. This reflects my own academic biography: I have worked in Faculties of Art, Education and Economic Sciences and at one point set up an inter-disciplinary Centre for Ethics. I was challenged to reflect on matters in business and economics due to my previous and current involvement in Business School education. I therefore argue (see Chapter 4.4) that the link between theology and economics is vital for ethics in the 21st century, in the same way that philosophy and the natural sciences are traditionally key dialogue partners for theology.

The topics addressed in this volume augment my earlier work on the ethical challenges of HIV/AIDS, gender discrimination, restorative justice and poverty as contained in *Neither calendar nor clock. Perspectives on the Belhar confession*, published by Eerdmans in 2010. Like most theologians who attempt to "do" theology in different publics, written records and formal research are but a slice of our theological work. I am honoured to interact with business, church, political and civil society structures on a regular basis in seminars and projects where we combine our best efforts for the sake of a greater public good and a more ethical society.

Back to this volume: Some editorial changes were made, but the essays are published very close to their original form and content. Chapter 2.1, a substantially revised version of my inaugural address at the University of Port Elizabeth, has not been published in peer-reviewed books or journals before. There is no attempt to "bring the strands together" or write inter-linking passages between chapters. The essays are simply collected for others to read and hopefully make sense of a small sample of ethics reflections by a middle-class, white male person in South Africa in a crucial period of our post-apartheid history.

I decided to keep the "pathways" of the first volume in the title and would like to provide some explanation for this:

"Pathways" expresses the fact that I never intended to write "a systematic theology" or develop "an ethical approach" in the traditional sense. Instead of a "high-way" – a comprehensive system of thinking – I, like many other South African theologians and ethicists – do most of my work in response to invitations or reacting to events in church and society. My thinking was never premised on a grand design or overarching construct, and then developed along the trajectories flowing from such a design.

The "pathways" in the two volumes are, nevertheless, not simply a chaotic "following of leads". They are constructed along a few vital contours:

My commitment to an ecumenical Christian tradition with a socially engaged Reformed focus; an acute contextual awareness shaped primarily by events in South Africa and on the African continent, seen from a global perspective; advancement of what one could broadly call humanisation and justice, with a specific heart for socially marginalised people and the natural environment, which has no voice of their own; an inter-disciplinary approach that makes room for synergy among theology, philosophy, hermeneutics, and – later in my writings – economics and business. All this work was done – for better or for worse – with the intellectual instruments provided by Western academic discourse, strongly influenced by German and (to a lesser extent) American scholars, but interpreted for and in dialogue with our African context and local scholarship.

Apart from this methodological consideration, there is the matter of the nature of theology. If theology is "faith seeking understanding", this may lead one to see theology as contemplation on God as revealed in Scripture. If the beginning of wisdom is the fear of the Lord (Proverbs 1), then the Old Testament image of following the right path to know God comes to mind. Psalm 1 – perhaps a prologue to the Psalter as a whole – makes clear that there is the pathway of foolishness and the pathway of wisdom. Wisdom is the fruit of those who delight in the law of the Lord and who meditates on his law day and night. Wisdom, personified as a woman, calls out. "At the highest point along the way, where the paths meet, she takes her stand" (Proverbs 8:2). Those who heed her call, and follow her on this pathway, receive insight and knowledge.

This tradition is set forth in the New Testament. Christ is our wisdom (1 Cor 1:30). He reveals the truth and is the (path)way to knowledge of God (John 14:6). Those who see him have seen the Father. No wonder the earliest Christians, witnesses to Jesus Christ, are called "people of the way" (Acts). And no wonder that the Christian life is often depicted as a journey, following in the footsteps of Christ (1 Peter 2:21), being transformed into his image as we grow in sanctification and love through the work of the Holy Spirit, the Spirit of wisdom.

Theology is faith seeking to understand God through Jesus Christ and the Spirit, by following the pathways of Scripture, interpreted anew for every age and context, so that we may grow in wisdom.

I remain immensely grateful for the Beyers Naudé Centre for publishing this work. The Centre is slowly building a valuable collection of historical and contemporary public theologies and ethics in South Africa. It is an honour to be part of this. My sincere appreciation to the professional colleagues at Sun Press who assisted me in finalising the text and index, specifically Johannes Richter and Edwin Moose.

My collaboration with the Stellenbosch Faculty of Theology (led by Nico Koopman) and, since late 2014, the Faculty of Economic and Management Sciences (led by Stan du Plessis), provides a fruitful environment in which to reflect. The University of Stellenbosch Business School, my current academic home, has developed a vibrant research culture, as well as a commitment to participate and influence public policy and debate in South Africa and on the African continent. I thank my colleagues for their open conversations and for providing the platforms on which we can collectively pursue ethics in public life.

Those closest to us – away from the public eye – make enormous sacrifices to create the space in which we can do research. I herewith express admiration for my wife, Elize, for her love and for her example of a Christian life marked by integrity and commitment.

Some might ask: What is our deepest motivation to do academic work? The injunction that strikes me as most appropriate is: "Love the Lord your God with all your mind".

Piet Naudé
Stellenbosch
June 2016

PART 1 –
ETHICS, JUSTICE AND HUMANITY

1.1 GLOBALISATION AND THE CHALLENGE OF CULTURAL JUSTICE

In a recent article entitled "Globalisierung in wissenschaftlich-theologischer Sicht" Michael Welker gives an interesting brief description of globalisation: "Globalisation means: the development of an increasingly solidifying network of connections and interdependences between people and cultures. In this process, tensions, conflicts and collisions between cultures, between politico-economic interests and systems of laws and values can be highlighted" (Welker 2008:368, my translation).

He then explains how the ecumenical church and academic theology participate in and contribute to the closer interconnection of the world, but warns that we should maintain "a healthy scepticism towards general images of globalisation" (372). The reason for this scepticism is that the ideal of closer connections and communication in the world does not usually materialise in practice. In fact: "The image of the 'global village', the world as a village in which everyone communicates in harmony with everyone else … completely neglects present implementation opportunities in real space-time" (372). Welker bases this sober conclusion on concrete experiences in building a truly global theological network that attempts to be as inclusive as possible, but which time and again falters as a result of the vast differences in academic infrastructure, competencies and support in various parts of the world.

Based on the updated and detailed overview of ecumenical literature on globalisation by Konrad Raiser (2009) and others,[1] it is clear that the predominant focus is on the ethical and theological challenges related to the impact of a global neoliberal market economy and its concomitant "ökologische Brutalismus" ("ecological brutalism", Welker 2008:375). A prime example is the Accra Confession,[2] which depicts the current global system as an evil empire that destroys not only the lives of people but also the earth.

An emerging theme – and the focus of this essay[3] – is the issue of globalisation as a powerful **cultural force**, shaping personal and national identities, social cohesion and human coherence "at the intersection of trans-national forces, cross-cutting the local

---

1   Konrad Raiser, Globalisierung in der ökumenisch-ethischen Diskussion, *Verkündigung und Forschung* 54. Jahrgang, Heft 1 (2009): 6-33. See also Raiser's excellent literature references. For a summary of views up to about 1990, see Aart van den Berg: *Churches speak out on economic issues. A survey of several statements*. Geneva: WCC, 1990. See also *Christian faith and world economy today* (Geneva: WCC, 1992); articles on "technology" and "culture" in the *Dictionary of the Ecumenical Movement*; Julio de Santa Ana (ed.) *Sustainability and globalization* (Geneva: WCC, 1998), and *The Ecumenical Review* 52/2, 2000, which was devoted to the issue of "economic globalisation".
2   The Accra Confession (AC) was adopted by the World Alliance of Reformed Churches during its 24th General Council held in Ghana, Africa. For a summary and discussion, see Raiser 2009:11-13.
3   This paper is an updated version of Piet J Naudé, "The challenge of cultural justice under conditions of globalization. Is the New Testament of any use?" In Cilliers Breytenbach, Johan C Thom & Jeremy Punt (eds.) *The New Testament interpreted. Essays in honour of Bernard Lategan*. Leiden: Brill, 2006, 267-287.

and the global" (Chidester 2003: vii). It is noteworthy that Welker's description[4] of globalisation includes a specific mention of cultural networks and tensions between cultures, and that Bedford-Strohm has recently reminded us that "cultural processes also have to be considered under the heading of 'globalisation'" (Bedford-Strohm 2009:2, my translation). Whereas the economic face of globalisation raises issues related to distributive and ecological justice, the cultural-technological face raises issues related to cultural and aesthetic justice, and the values that shape identity formation (see Kwenda 2003).

1. GLOBALISATION AS CULTURAL FORCE IN IDENTITY TRANSFORMATION

There are as many definitions of culture[5] as there are social scientists. For the sake of our discussion here, two notions of culture will be put forward.

The first is by Clifford Geertz, who espouses a semiotic view based on his interpretation that "man (sic) is an animal suspended in webs of significance he himself has spun (and) I take culture to be those webs." Culture therefore consists of "interworked systems of construable symbols" in which social events can be intelligibly described (Geertz 1975: 5, 14). These symbols form – through their inter-relations – a cultural map within which people negotiate their identities.

In a publication on social cohesion Chirevo Kwenda takes a shorter route and sees culture merely as "our way of life" and "what people take for granted". In other words: "It is that comfort zone within, and out of which, we think, act and speak. If it is our 'mother culture', we do all these things without having to be self-conscious about what we are doing" (Kwenda 2003:68, 69).

Both culture and identity are fluid and hybrid notions. On an individual level, we live in overlapping social territories and migrate between different social roles constructed on the basis of who we are and who we are becoming. On a group or national level, this is equally true: cultures and identities are constantly negotiated between "what is taken for granted", between what is an assumed network of significance and a changing environment that might seek to disarrange our symbolic cultural maps.

In an ideal world such identity negotiations may occur peacefully, in a symmetrical power relationship and over an extended period, so that natural assimilation and

---

4   See Welker's references (2008:368, footnotes 5 and 6) to the work of S.P. Huntington on the clashes of civilisation and the cultural dimensions of globalisation as discussed by A. Appudurai.

5   I am not an expert in anthropology or cultural studies, but have found the following sources very helpful (without fully integrating them into this paper): Simon During (ed.): *The cultural studies reader* (1993) is an excellent collection of ground-breaking essays by authors such as Adorno, Horkheimer, Barthes, Foucault, Lyotard, Cornel West and others. See specifically Part IV for its relevance to this paper. The somewhat older collection, *Ideas of culture* (1976) by Gamst and Norbeck, has a strong sociological focus with contributions by *inter alia* Durkheim, Parsons and Malinowski. Maartin J Gannon in his *Understanding global cultures* develops an interesting analytical instrument, namely significant social actions as metaphors for analysing local and global cultures. See Chapter 16 on the Nigerian marketplace for an example from the African continent. I am deeply aware of my limitations in this exciting field of study.

hybridisation enrich this "meeting of cultures" and evolving of identities. But we have ample examples in history and the contemporary world that such processes derail more often than not. "We know that for these four words, 'our way of life', people are often prepared to kill or be killed. In such instances, it becomes clear that there is a very small step from 'a way of life' to life itself. Thus, a threat to a people's culture tends to be perceived and experienced as a personal threat" (Kwenda 2003:68).

The dichotomies represented by contending factions such as Israelis versus Palestinians, Hutsis versus Tutsis, Catholics versus Protestants, Serbians versus Croatians, Americans versus Islamic fundamentalists are the violent consequences of derailed identity negotiations coupled with cultural acts of threats and resistance. There are also less violent, but nevertheless intense, processes of interchange among, for example, Nigerians in France, Turks in Germany, Mozambicans in South Africa, Aborigines in Australia and Hispanics and Chinese in America (and the list can go on and on).

These regional cultural negotiations are both intensified and 'mondialised' (*le monde*: French) by the Janus face of cultural globalisation. Like all globalisation processes, this one is equally ambiguous[6] and even contradictory: **The globalisation of culture is on the one hand a huge process of homogenisation, whilst at the same time fostering, on the other hand, a celebration of cultural difference and fragmentation.**

In this regard one may point to the hybridisation of culture as "a global phenomenon that happens locally" through interesting cultural mixes of music, art, literature and architecture. For example, the post-colonial discourse on "creolisation", ambivalence and multiple identities is a way of "writing back" in response to a hegemonic global culture (see Gerle 2000:159) and related to a process of identity transformation.

But the romantic idea of multiculturalism is betrayed by a globalising process that creates an illusion of differentiation, but in fact is a comprehensive force toward "Vereinheitlichung" ("unification", Raiser 1999: 37). In this earlier work Raiser (1999:32ff) points out three central challenges facing the ecumenical church in the 21st century: a life-centred vision (*lebenszentrierte Vision*) to replace a destructive anthropocentrism; the acknowledgement of plurality; and facing the inner contradictions of globalisation. He expresses one of these contradictions as the simultaneous process of "unification of lifestyles and cultural forms" and the "strains" caused by a defence of "native cultures, religious traditions (and) ethnic and racial identities" (Raiser 1999:37, my translation).

Globalisation moves slowly toward creating a depersonalised mass society typified by "mass communications, mass consumption, homogeneity of patterns of life, mass culture" (De Santa Ana 1998:14). The process is driven by mega-cultural firms "based on the commodification of Anglophone culture with the aid of the electronic highway" (Louw 2002: 79). Samuel Kobia writes from an African perspective and depicts the situation of this continent as being subject to both economic and cultural colonisation, and such cultural hegemony is in part imparted by modern Western

---

6   See Bedford-Strohm's reference to "die Ambivalenz der Globalisierung" ("the ambivalence of globalization", (2009:2) and Welker's call that we should not be naïve about the interconnectedness of the world, as globalisation has both "Licht- und Schattenseiten" (literally: "light and shadow sides", 2008:372).

capitalism (Kobia 2003:138). Here the economic, technological and cultural intersect in a deadly asymmetrical negotiation: "You can survive, even thrive, among us, if you become like us; you can keep your life, if you give up your identity". With reference to Levi-Strauss, "we can say that exclusion by assimilation rests on a deal: we will refrain from vomiting you out (anthropoemic strategy) if you let us swallow you up (anthropophagic strategy)" (Volf 1996:75).

Globalisation – seen in this way – acquires an ideological nature as *la pensee unique*, aspiring to be the only valid view, "imposing itself as the paradigm to which all other cultures should be adjusted" (De Santa Ana 1998:16). Where previous forms of cultural subjugation were spatially confined and time-bound, the commercial homogeneity of a consumerist culture expands itself with the aid of the newest and fastest technological communication (itself an ambiguous blessing in the 21st century!).

2. THE ETHICAL ISSUES

One might ask: What are the ethical issues? In the ebb and flow of history many cultures and civilisations have come and gone. Globalisation is just a new and more potent cultural force that speeds up this process of assimilation, subjugation and eventual extinction. The museumisation of the "indigenous" cultures of yesteryear is the same as keeping fossils and mummies for the (possible?) attention and curiosity of future generations.

It is not that simple, though. Enough work has been done on the ethical issues related to the casino economy[7] of digital capitalism. In this essay I wish to argue the case for **cultural justice** and outline the ethical issues in terms of the following two broad themes: first, the moral significance of cosmological stories in shaping identity and values; second, the unequal burden of suspending or surrendering "what is taken for granted".

2.1 Cosmological stories and narrative moral identity

Let us accept with Peter Berger (1967:152ff), Ninian Smart (1973) and David Tracy (1981:159) that the role of religion is to construct a comprehensive view of the world by framing parts of reality within the context of that which transcends reality (i.e. ultimate reality). Let us accept with Larry Rasmussen that "we are incorrigibly storytellers" (1994:178) and concur with Thomas Berry that religious cosmologies are designed to answer identity questions like: Who am I? Who are we? Where are we going? "For peoples, generally, their story of the universe and the human role in the universe is their primary source of intelligibility and value" (1998: xi).

On the basis of these assumptions one could argue that globalisation in its cultural garb usurps and misplaces the role of religion by constituting its own cosmological narrative. We have here, writes Welker (2008:376), a clash of value systems where justice, compassion and care for the weak are endangered by an Olympian or Nietzschean ethos. What is at stake, is not merely the physics of our information

---

7 "Like any casino, this global game is rigged so that only the house wins" – Fidel Castro in a speech to the South African parliament. See Chidester 2003:10.

age, but its metaphysics, "its significance to individual and social morality ... and its consequences for the formation, maintenance and alteration of personal identity" (Arthur 1998:3; see Smit 2000:15). Homogenisation takes on the proportions of an autonomous force governing the lives of individuals and communities (De Santa Ana 1998:19).

To a certain extent globalisation as comprehensive cosmology reflects the moral tendencies of both modernity and post-modernity. According to Zygmunt Bauman, globalisation – as an autonomous force against which you apparently can do nothing but be swept along – does "shift moral responsibilities away from the moral self, either toward a socially constructed and managed supra-individual agency, or through floating responsibility inside a bureaucratic 'rule of nobody'" (Bauman 1995:99; see Volf 1996:21ff). But as in some forms of post-modernity, globalisation creates a climate of evasion of moral responsibilities by rendering relationships "fragmentary" and "discontinuous" (or should we say "virtual"?), resulting in disengagement and commitment-avoidance (Bauman 1995:156).

We have learnt from various forms of narrative ethics (from Richard H Niebuhr to Stanley Hauerwas): *Agere sequiter esse*. What we do, is a result of who we are. And who we are, is determined by the narrative communities in which we are formed. From a moral perspective "it is possible to argue that the real challenges embedded in globalisation concern not so much what we **do**, but who we **are**, who we are becoming ..." (Smit 2000:15, original emphasis). The mass culture of a globalising world is a powerful narrative agent that contributes significantly to moral formation. Its values become **the** values, the way things **are**, the way **everybody** acts.

This analysis might provide some clue to answering the vexing question: Why do societies in rapid transition (e.g. from so-called non-Western cultures – be they Islamic, African or Eastern European – to being "Westernised") so often exhibit a partial or total collapse of values? The answer might be that societies in transition undergo a collective identity crisis as they move from the known to the "not yet". It is because they cannot yet adequately answer the question 'Who are we?' that they are unable to exercise responsible and virtuous options.[8] In a situation of transition a "contraction of time" occurs that instinctively cuts off the past (nobody wants to return to an oppressive past), but cannot yet conceptualise the future ("a journey into unchartered territory without safety equipment"[9]). In this way life becomes a continual "collapsed present", driven by emotional, physical and economic survival in which clear moral ideals and ethical visions are difficult to uphold or sustain.

---

8 Two distinguishing features of societies in transition are a marked increase in socio-economic inequality and a significant rise in violence and criminality. This is true of countries as diverse as Russia and South Africa. In the latter case, the new government resorted to a moratorium on the release of police statistics in a desperate bid to contain the images of a "violent" new democracy. See Addy and Silny (2001:505), who state that in some cases Eastern European areas experienced a 400% rise in criminality over a ten-year period.
9 A comment from Addy and Silny (2001:503) to describe the transitions in Eastern Europe.

It is into this situation of confusion and *anomie*,[10] where people find themselves "in between stories"[11] and in a situation of *Heimatlosigkeit*,[12] that the globalised consumer culture moves to provide a viable alternative, "the only answer", **the moral story**. It works so well because consumerism ("We want more for less!")[13] sustains itself precisely by creating constantly changing demands that have to be satisfied instantly, thereby creating an ever-shifting "hedonistic present", closed to both the past and the future.

The notion that what Africa (or Eastern Europe or Latin America or Iraq and Afghanistan) needs is more development aid and physical infrastructure – however important these may be – is fatally flawed and may in practice result in the intensification of resistance and loss of hope in "democracy". What needs to be restored and cultivated is a culturally mediated reconstruction of the self in a personal and collective sense. In political terms the African Renaissance, for example, is as much about economic development as it is about a post-colonial restoration of cultural pride and selfhood "to counter the excesses of European modes of being-in-the-world" (Comaroff & Comaroff 2002:80).

The crucial insight – missed by most development agencies – is that restoration of being not only precedes economic restoration, but – at least in an African situation – is **the precondition** for economic survival. Being precedes bread (Balcomb 1998:71). Why? Because in a situation of scarce resources, one needs a view of identity that resists economic greed and self-referential individualism. **What you require is a notion of identity as identity-in-community, which underpins redistribution patterns that in turn guarantee physical and economic survival. One needs the survival of (the) community instead of the survival of the fittest.**

---

10 This term stems from Emile Durkheim in his ground-breaking study on social cohesion and suicide: "When society is disturbed by some painful crisis or by beneficial but abrupt transitions, the collective conscience is momentarily incapable of exercising restraint. Time is required for the public conscience to reclassify men [sic] and things. So long as social forces thus freed have not regained equilibrium, their respective values are unknown and so all regulation is lacking for a time. The state of de-regulation or anomie is heightened by passions being less disciplined precisely when they need more disciplining" (*Suicide,* 1897/1951:252-253).

11 "It's all a question of story. We are in trouble just now because we do not have a good story. We are in between stories." Previously, with the old story (whether my own or the clear story of an oppressive regime) "we awoke in the morning and knew where we were. We could answer the questions of our children. We could identify crime, punish transgressors. Everything was taken care of because the story was there…" (Berry 188:123).

12 See Fischer's discussion in a different context of how the mode of knowledge emanating from the Enlightenment enabled humankind to make the world so habitable, so transparent, that it exactly loses its character as *Heimat*. "Der ärgste Feind der Verantwortung ist die Gleichgültigkeit. Gleichgültigkeit aber ist die Folge **existentieller Heimatlosigkeit**" ("Indifference is responsibility's worst enemy. However, indifference follows **existential rootlessness**." My emphasis and translation). He then pleads for a process of *Beheimatung* to restore responsibility (Fischer 1992:124).

13 See Welker's critical reference to a speech by American industrialist, William Timken, who states that the core of a consumer society is expressed by this dictum, which is the engine for economic growth (Welker 2008:374).

But then a cosmological story and other local narratives are required precisely to sustain such communities in which moral formation can take shape. If not, globalisation in the name of "development aid" will shape moral formation.

Perhaps the following case study – reconstructed from actual events – conveys this journey of identity and life "in between stories" in a way that arguments are unable to do.

> My brother Sipho and I grew up in a rural village in the Limpopo province of South Africa. My father was a farm labourer and my mother a domestic worker. They were both functionally illiterate, but had a keen sense that the education of their children was of paramount importance. By the time we reached high school age, the whole extended family contributed to send the two of us (one year apart) to a former model C school in Pretoria. After matriculation we both attended university – again with the material and emotional support of the family. This support was not so much a contractual as a familial, moral issue. It was a form of "donation" that everybody tacitly knew would one day return – though in no exact manner like in written contracts – to assist parents in their old age and make the same possible for other siblings after us.
>
> The eventual graduation festivals were huge family affairs with praise singers, pap and slaughtering of goats.
>
> We both were excited to land our first jobs – I with my degree in humanities in the academic administration of the university in Port Elizabeth, Sipho with his B Commerce degree at an international consulting firm in Johannesburg. We never openly spoke about it, but took it for granted that we send a monthly amount "back home" and visit at least once a year.
>
> After about eighteen months Sipho's contributions dried up. The next year he did not return for his annual visit. What is more, when my grandfather passed away he did not attend the funeral. I took the courage to talk this over with him and soon realised that he had embraced the yuppie lifestyle of Egoli, the City of Gold: designer clothes (from Carducci to Billabong and Man about Town), a red BMW 318i and a townhouse in Fourways.
>
> He now traverses a different world. He has embraced different values. We feel not so much a sense of betrayal, but of sadness to have lost him. He has become a different person. Though, in the eyes of most, he is a highly successful person; a sign that the new South Africa is really opening opportunities to create a new black middle class.
>
> And I am not sure that he would ever want to return to our village. Due to its location in the mountains, it is called Tshilapfene, "the place of the baboons".

2.2 Surrendering what is taken for granted

In a perceptive essay referred to several times above the historian of religion, Chirevo Kwenda (2003:70), explains the notion of cultural (in)justice as follows:

> Where people live by what they naturally take for granted, or where the details of everyday life coincide with what is taken for granted, we can say there is cultural justice – at least in this limited sense of freedom from constant self-consciousness about every little thing. Cultural injustice occurs when some people are forced, by coercion or persuasion, to submit to the burdensome condition of suspending – or more permanently surrendering – what they naturally take for granted, and then begin to depend on what someone else takes for granted. The reality is that substitution of what is taken for granted is seldom adequate. This means that, in reality, the subjugated person has no linguistic or cultural 'default drive', that critical minimum of ways, customs, manners, gestures and postures that facilitate uninhibited, unselfconscious action.

The injustice lies in the unequal burden and stress of constant self-consciousness that millions of people carry on behalf of others without gaining recognition or respect. In fact, they are objects of further subjugation and humiliation that vary from physical violence to subtle body language that clearly communicate that you are stupid and do not know "the ways things are done or said here".

On a regional and national level these forms of exclusions (Miroslav Volf reminds us) range from domination and indifference to abandonment and ultimately elimination. From the "inside" this exclusion results from being "uncomfortable with anything that blurs accepted boundaries, disturbs our identities, and disarranges our symbolic cultural maps".[14]

The "fall of the Berlin wall" or "end of the apartheid regime" are ways of designating the way that many societies moved from oppressive political systems to achieving greater civil liberties after 1989. What is sometimes underestimated is the massive identity renegotiation processes required in the "post-liberation" period, often leading to an upsurge in ethnic violence and loss of social stability. As we saw in the previous section, questions of culture and life-in-community then arise with great urgency. This is because it takes tremendous courage and political wisdom to assert (for the first time?) "what we take for granted" and to act unselfconsciously after decades of suspension and suppression of identity.

Shortly after the first democratic elections in South Africa that ended 46 years of minority rule, African theologian Tinyiko Sam Maluleke, made the following incisive observation:

> Issues of culture are again acquiring a new form of prominence in various spheres of South African society. **It is as if we can, at last, speak truly and honestly, about our culture.** This is due to the widespread

---

14 Volf 1996: 78; note also the interesting debate about the wearing of Muslim head scarves in European schools, as well as the heated debate about "European identity" in the light of Turkey's possible entry into the EU. These are all interesting examples of disarranging cultural maps!

> feeling that now, more than at any other time, **we can be subjects of our own cultural destiny**. ... The reconstruction of structures and physical development alone will not quench our **cultural and spiritual thirst**. On the contrary, the heavy emphasis on the material and the structural may simply result in the intensification of black frustration. We do not just need jobs and houses, **we must recover our own selves** (Maluleke in Balcomb 1998:70, my emphases).

Whereas the struggle against apartheid or communism or imperialism or Americanism forced and still forces a kind of uniformity of resistance, and is aimed at **the right to be "the same"**, the post-liberation struggle aims at a restored subjectivity and agency with **the right to be different.** In the ethical terms of this section: **the right to live unselfconsciously.**

This was echoed from a different perspective by Miroslav Volf:

> In recent decades the **issue of identity** has risen to the forefront of discussions in social philosophy. If the liberation movements of the sixties were all about equality – above all gender equality and race equality – major concerns in the nineties seem to be about identity – about the **recognition of distinct identities** of persons who differ in gender, skin color, or culture (Volf 1998: 23, my emphasis).

Let us make this argument about culture and distinct identities more concrete. I found it quite remarkable to see how much emphasis is placed on **language** in the process of identity renegotiation.

On a first level, language itself plays this exclusivist role. I will turn to this in the next paragraph. On a second level, a "language of exclusion" is created by naming or labelling the other in a manner that takes the other outside "the class of objects of potential moral responsibility" (Zygmunt Bauman as quoted by Volf 1996:76). This does not only justify exclusion, but in fact necessitates it. "The rhetoric of the other's inhumanity **obliges** the self to practice inhumanity" (Volf 1996:76; original emphasis). Like supporters of the linguistic turn, one could state that exclusion is equally mediated by language. Words do kill.

But in a more subtle way, language itself – as in "mother tongue" and "foreign" language – plays an exclusionary role. In a remarkable essay, "Aria: A memoir of a bilingual childhood", Richard Rodriguez recounts how he grew up in Sacramento, California, in a Mexican immigrant home in a predominantly white suburb. During his first few years in school he struggled with English, but managed to move between the language of the public sphere (English) and the private language of the home (Spanish). "Like others who feel the pain of public alienation, we transformed the knowledge of our public separateness into a consoling reminder of our intimacy" (Rodriguez 1982:23). He eloquently describes life in two linguistic and social worlds:

> But then there was Spanish: **español**, the language rarely heard away from house, the language which seemed to me therefore a private language, my family's language. To hear its sounds was to feel myself specially recognised as one of the family, apart from **los otros** (the others). A simple remark, an inconsequential comment could convey that assurance. My parents would say something to me and I would

> feel embraced by the sounds of their words. Those sounds said: I am speaking with ease in Spanish ... I recognise you as somebody special, close, like no one outside. You belong with us. In the family. Ricardo (Rodriguez 1982:22-23).

But this juxtaposition of a double identity was shattered by a simple request from the teachers (nuns at the Catholic school) that, in order to improve their academic performance, English should be spoken at home. This led to an ambivalent outcome: a growing confidence in public, but a devastating silence at home:

> There was a new silence at home. As we children learned more and more English, we shared fewer and fewer words with our parents. Sentences needed to be spoken slowly ... Often the parent wouldn't understand. The child would need to repeat himself. Still the parent misunderstood. The young voice, frustrated, would end up saying, "Never mind" – the subject was closed. Dinners would be noisy with the clinking of knives and forks against dishes. My mother would smile softly between her remarks; my father, at the other end of the table, would chew and chew his food while he stared over the heads of his children.

What followed was first a "disconcerting confusion" (29). Then, as fluency in Spanish faded fast, a feeling of guilt arose over the betrayal of immediate family and visitors from Mexico (30). This was followed by an understanding that the linguistic change was a social one where the intimacy at home was traded for the acquisition of fluency and acceptance in the public language. "I moved easily at last, a citizen in a crowded city of words" (31).

But the ambiguities remain. This is evident from the end of the essay, where Rodriguez describes the funeral of his grandmother:

> When I went up to look at my grandmother, I saw her through the haze of a veil draped over the open lid of the casket. Her face looked calm – but distant and unyielding to love. It was not the face I remembered seeing most often. It was the face she made in public when a clerk at Safeway asked her some question and I would need to respond. It was her public face that the mortician had designed with his dubious art (35).

It was – in the terms set out above – the burdensome face of someone who constantly had to surrender what is taken for granted. You can keep your life, if you give up your identity. You can keep your culture, as long as you hold its values and customs, its "things taken for granted", with diffidence. This cultural diffidence is a disposition that causes people either to be ashamed of their culture or to simply ignore it as irrelevant in the modern world (see Kwenda 2003:71).

These powerful images from a single life and immigrant family is a metaphor, a simile, a parable of national and trans-national processes of cultural injustice. In *The political economy of transition* Tony Addy and Jiri Silny (2001) reflect on the changes that occurred in Central and Eastern Europe in the ten years from 1989-1999. They make the interesting observation that the "market Bolsheviks" (economic advisors who advocated the move to a full market economy in one jump) not only harboured a blind faith in policy prescriptions from "the West" to be applied unaltered to "the East", but also showed "little respect for indigenous knowledge and practice" (2001: 503). The rapid privatisation of former industries was carried out "in a way which did not respect positive cultural and ethical values within the region. Under conditions of globalisation, the process tended to block creative responses" (2001: 505).

In a bizarre example of exclusion by elimination (cf. Volf), the application of rigid market rules meant the literal closure of what Addy and Silny call "cultural industries": "For example, rich traditions of film-making were lost and historic theatres, orchestras and other artistic companies were decimated. It would take a great deal of time and money to rebuild such industries and cultural assets" (2001:505).

Would it therefore be justified to include **aesthetic justice**[15] as an integral part of cultural justice? I think so, because the symbols of national identity (statutes, flags, books, artefacts, photographs, histories and language) are normally the first casualties of war. The subjugation of the other is completed with the removal or destruction of identity-confirming symbols. And in the context of globalisation, this war is mostly fought without military ordnance, in a faceless silence, and in the name of advancement and consumerism.

3. GLOBALISATION AND CULTURAL JUSTICE: A FEW BIBLICAL PERSPECTIVES

I have argued that globalisation as a cultural force poses two ethical challenges: first, the challenge of a competing cosmological story with its effect on identity and value formation; second, the challenge of cultural justice with its effect on community-in-diversity and the freedom of an unselfconscious life. A full biblical-ethical response is not possible within the scope of this essay. What follows are a few suggestions drawn from select passages[16] that may provide some direction in addressing these challenges.

3.1 Globalisation: The challenge of who is Lord

By constituting a cosmological narrative and providing **the** alternative normative "story", globalisation enters the age-old realm of the battle of the gods, the battle for ultimate loyalty, for the ultimate frame of reference within which to interpret the self and life-in-community.

It is common knowledge that the period reflected in New Testament writings was dominated by two forces:[17] the residual influence of Hellenistic culture, and of Roman political rule since the occupation of Palestine in 63 BCE and its incorporation into the province of Syria. I will follow up only on the issue of Roman political authority here.

---

15 This process of being subject to the aesthetics of "the other" is a vivid reality in the lucrative global tourism industry. See the illuminating analysis by Sandra Klopper in which she highlights the marginalisation effect on local communities of turning the City Bowl area of Cape Town into an international tourist destination (2003:224ff).
16 All references below are to the New International Version.
17 See the very simple but informative discussion in Roetzel 1985:1-23.

Although Roman rule allowed relative local religious freedom to occupied territories, its growing usurpation of religious power (in a time that had not yet seen the modernist division of the spheres of life), brought local Christian communities into growing conflict with the Roman state. There is no room here for an extensive treatment of a complex[18] topic. For the sake of my overall argument, I refer to three New Testament passages to illustrate what became a battle for ultimate loyalty, and for the guiding orientation point in constructing a moral identity and community.

First. In Mark 12:13-17 the sensitive question of imperial tax is of great religious significance. The *dinarius* for which Jesus asks referred clearly to the emperor's apotheosis: the laurel wreath symbolised divinity, reinforced by the inscription "Emperor Tiberius, venerated son of the venerated God" and "high priest". The pericope reaches its climax in what can be read as an ironic parallelism or perhaps even as an antithesis: "Render to Caesar the things that are Caesar's, and to God the things that are God's." Jesus does not here contest the legitimacy of the state, nor does he denigrate what belongs to Caesar. But in a time of the total interpenetration of politics and religion, this saying "effectively secularises civil authority and removes it from the realm of ideology" (Schrage 1988: 113).

Second. The well-known (and often misused[19]) Pauline passage in Rom 13:1-7 forms part of the paranetic section which is introduced in chapter 12:1-2. The former could be read as the public practice of love – a theme followed through from 12:21 to 13:11-14. The significance of this passage for my argument here does not lie in a (futile?) reconstruction of a "doctrine of the state", but the clarity and apparent ease with which Paul shifts the origin of state power from the gods (however perceived) to the Christian God. "There is no power (*eksousia*) that is not from God" (*hupo theou*) in 13:1 can therefore be construed as implicit critique of a self-divinised authority that later required the confession that Caesar is lord.

Third. By the time that the notion of the Apocalypse was articulated – specifically Rev 13 – the emperor cult had been established and vigorously enforced as state religion.[20] Here the Roman empire (by now established as *imperium* in the technical sense of the word with a uniform supervisory authority over the whole Mediterranean region) is described as the incarnation of Satan's power upon earth and as a caricature of Christ. The issue at stake is ultimate loyalty, the battle of the gods, because the state demands what is appropriate to God and to Christ alone. "In making these demands, the state is from the devil. It is not satanic because it is imperfect, but because it is totalitarian. It does not have too little authority, but too

---

18 There is – as with most "topics" in the New Testament – a wide variety of witnesses to the relation between the faith community and the state. See the clearly apologetic nature of Lukan views in the Gospel of Luke and Acts; the sayings attributed to Jesus; the varied responses in the Pauline corpus; and the obviously radical opposition expressed in Revelation. For cursory discussions and further literature, see Schrage 1988:107ff, 157ff, 235ff and 342ff.

19 In South Africa's recent history this passage was the subject of a severe hermeneutical struggle between those who cited this in support of subordination to the apartheid government that claimed to be Christian and thus worthy of support, and those who (in 1985) called for a prayer for the fall of the government precisely because it did not fulfil the "criteria" for a godly government put forward in this passage.

20 See, for example, Domitian, who claimed the divine honour of *dominus ac deus*.

much, authority over 'every tribe and people and tongue and nation' (13:7). It is demonic in its **totalitarian deification**" (Schrage 1988:345, my emphasis).

The political impotence of early Christian communities made only "passive" resistance possible. But the simple confession of Christ's Lordship was, especially in the Eastern regions of the empire, in fact a public, active political act as it represented – from a Roman perspective – both "atheism" and anarchy. In the face of martyrdom, the faith communities are reminded that God has set a limit to the rule of the dragon (forty-two months according to 13:5), that they are blessed if they die in the Lord (14:13) as their names are entered in the book of life (13:8).

Although there are varied responses in the New Testament to the growing totalitarianism of an increasingly comprehensive global empire, there is enough textual evidence to state at least the following: as moral communities,[21] the early Christians were confronted with the question of what will serve as ultimate reference point, as principle in the narrative, symbolic arrangement of the Christian life. They simply chose the person of Jesus, confessed as *kurios*, and derived direction from their memories of him, against the deified, global power of the day.

The conclusion is clear. Insofar and where globalisation assumes the character of a religion, it needs to be resisted, confronted and where possible transformed with a "Christ-centred" ethics. The implication for the people of God is a renewed vision of Christ's Lordship as constitutive for their very existence as a community, and as identity-confirming narrative in times of change and transition. Where loyalties shift to other gods, or where the cosmic pre-eminence of Christ is compromised,[22] or where the "gospel of Jesus Christ" is no longer faithfully transmitted in word, liturgy and (especially) a life *coram Dei*, there identity and moral orientation are lost. Into this vacuum so-called "global values" move as an alternative moral and identity-forming story.

Welker (2008:382) is right to warn against reducing the biblical traditions about money and God to a simple dichotomy of "God versus Mammon". There is no way that moral formation which hopefully leads to real action[23] can take place in a vacuum of "anti-ökonomischen Manichaismus" ("anti-economic Manichaeism") or by a simple-minded "ökonomisches Analphabetismus" ("economic illiteracy"). Jesus' own ministry and the life of the early church testify to discipleship in the realities of that time, challenging the then dominant political, social and ethical paradigms whilst living in the world.

This brings us to the ecclesiological challenge of cultural justice in the world today.

---

21 See the recent attempt by Allen Verhey (2002) to reconstruct a New Testament ethics on the basis of the early church as a remembering and instructing community. He takes Rom 15:14 as point of departure and aligns himself with eminent ethicists such as James Gustafson, Larry Rasmussen and (the more controversial) Stanley Hauerwas to develop the idea of early churches as communities of moral discourse.
22 See the clear "cosmic" bias of passages such as the prologue to John, the exaltation in Eph 1:3-14, the hymnal in Col 1:15-20 and the depiction of the cross as cosmic battle in Col 2:6-15.
23 See Dirk Smit's overview of African contributions to the globalisation debate where he emphasises that "der wahre Prüfstein schliesslich die Praxis [ist]" ("praxis (is) ultimately the real proof", Smit 2009: 65).

3.2 Globalisation: A challenge to households of life-in-communion

Challenged by the processes of globalisation, a very important reinterpretation of *oikoumene* (the whole of the habitable earth) and *oikodome* (building up of community) has occurred in ecumenical circles. This came about as the former ethical concerns of Life and Work ("ethics") and the ecclesial concerns of Faith and Order ("church unity") converged in a number of studies[24] which emphasised that the core challenge of globalisation is the nature of the household or households we create and belong to. And in this regard, the churches "as central players of a worldwide civil society" play an important role (Bedford-Strohm 2009:5, my translation). Whereas the first ethical challenge above relates to the sovereignty of God (and the concomitant moral claim of God on our lives through Christ), the second relates to the types of communities we build in the midst of the claims that we now live in a "global village".[25]

This is expressed in no uncertain terms by the Johannesburg delegation (see footnote 24):

> Moral issues, formerly seen as having to do mainly with personal conduct within stable orders of value, have now become radicalised. They now have to do with life, or the death, of human beings and of the created order in which we live. **Before we can even speak of a 21st-century 'global civilisation' life together on this planet will need shared visions and institutional expressions for which we have few really relevant precedents.** As Christians we speak of an *oikoumene*, or inclusive horizon of human belonging, offered by God in Jesus Christ to the human race. Following the scriptures we call this a 'household of life', a 'heavenly city' where justice, peace and care for creation's integrity prevail (Best and Robra 1997: 51-52, my emphasis).

This moves the focus to ecclesiology. The challenge is for the church to be one such "precedent" or "institutional expression" of a life-centred spirituality and ethics (Raiser 1998: 34) and of a moral community known for true *koinonia*. How could the church – in the light of cultural injustice and the burden of unselfconscious living – be such a moral community? The answer is deceptively simple – by following Christ.

---

24 See, for example, the publications and later comments related to the well-known "three costlies" emanating from three conferences: costly unity (Ronde, Denmark 1993), costly commitment (Jerusalem 1994) and costly obedience (Johannesburg 1996). The three final statements were published in 1997 as *Ecclesiology and ethics* edited by Thomas Best and Martin Robra. "The titles (of the three consultations) reflect **a progression of ecclesiological reflection and deepening of moral concern**: from realising that 'the unity we seek' will turn out to be **costly unity**; through recognising that 'a **costly unity** requires **costly commitment** to one another' as Christians and as churches: to admitting that it is, finally, not a matter of programmes and institutions, even ecumenical ones, but of a **costly obedience** to our calling to be one and, as one body of Christ, to serve all humanity and creation" (*Ecclesiology and ethics*: ix, emphases in original).

25 As noted by Welker above, the notion of a "global village" is deeply ambiguous. On the one hand, it depicts the reality of a world shrunken through global communication and virtual closeness such as you would find in a traditional rural village; on the other hand, this village is highly exclusionary (think of the digital divide!) with false senses of belonging and imbued with asymmetrical power relations.

As the early hymn recounts, Christ did not cling to his nature of being God and did not harp on his equality with God, but was humbled in self-donation, even to the death on the cross (Phil 2: 5-8). Those who are in Christ consider whatever is to their profit as a loss (Phil 3:7); they are new creations (2 Cor 5:17); they have been crucified with Christ and no longer live, but Christ lives in them (Gal 2:20).

It is only because Christians no longer take their natural identity dead seriously and instead find their new consciousness in Christ and his self-donation that a community of (cultural) justice becomes a possibility. The Pentecost as birth of the church is not without reason described in the book of Acts as an event in which the well-mannered Spirit, in search of cultural justice, enabled a speaking in the diverse known languages of those gathered in Jerusalem! For our purpose here, let us examine the view expressed in Gal 3:26-29.

In the context of the argument that faith in Christ liberates from the curse of the law, the writer nevertheless emphasises the permanence of the promise to Abraham, fulfilled in Christ.[26] Through faith Jews and Gentiles are now sons of God. Through baptism all have been clothed with Christ. Therefore: "There is neither Jew nor Greek; slave nor free, male nor female, for you are all one in Christ Jesus. And if you belong to Christ, then you are Abraham's offspring (*sperma*), heirs according to promise" (Gal. 3:28).

This "egalitarian" view of the religious community corresponds in a contradictory manner to Jewish formulae in which the threefold distinction is upheld by men, who thank God for not being created a Gentile, slave or woman. This is not so much rooted in "discrimination" as understood today, as in the disqualification from religious privileges that were available to free Jewish males. Whether this passage is a remnant of Thales (6th century BCE, see Bruce 1982:187), or derives from fanatical circles (Schrage), or is a fragment of an early baptismal formula (Scroggs), it remains a powerful witness to a community that enables what was described as "cultural justice" above.

This community both transcends cultural, economic and gender identities and simultaneously affirms these identities in a manner that enhances unity and avoids the "-isms" of ideology and exclusion.

That this had tremendous social implications at the time is evident from New Testament witnesses to the struggle with regard to circumcision for Gentile converts (Gal 2, Acts 15), the contradictory position of women in the early church (Acts 2; 1 Cor 11), and the status of slaves after their conversion (e.g. Onesimus in Phm 16). That it has and – wherever realised – will have tremendous social significance as "precedent" community in a global world today is certain.[27]

---

26 As can be expected, and following the context of this passage, Luther in his commentary places heavy emphasis on the social implication of justification by faith alone: "As in Christ no partiality for the Jewish movement applies, thus no other partiality is found in Him. It is a sign of human and legal righteousness that one splits oneself into sects and differentiates according to works" (Luther 1968:160, my translation).

27 An example of such communities in Africa is the so-called African Independent Churches, where tribal, cultural and class distinctions are transcended in communities that represent far more than a mere "religious affiliation" to include economic partnership and holistic healing as well.

We can therefore conclude that, theologically speaking, cultural justice is not so much the result of re-claiming minority or indigenous rights, as the vision of a Christ-like household, "where fully realized human identities and values, far from being forgotten, meet in search of graciously shared abundance of life. This household welcomes all the different human cultures, identities, and interests, including our own" (Mudge 1998:140).

This is the vision of the African-rooted Belhar confession,[28] borne out of a situation of radical cultural injustice; under conditions of pluralism gone wrong; and in the face of an oppressive, homogenising socio-political system. Following the teaching of the Heidelberg Catechism about the communion of saints, Belhar believes that, as a result of Christ's reconciliation, "the variety of spiritual gifts, opportunities, backgrounds, convictions, as well as the variety of language and culture, are opportunities to reciprocal service and enrichment in the one visible people of God" (Belhar Confession: Statement 2, my translation from Afrikaans).

I close with two magnificent biblical passages where the idea of the household of God extends beyond the people of God and the church to all of creation. Here we reach a confluence of various forms of justice: economic, cultural and ecological. These passages confirm the "usefulness" of the Scriptures to address the issue of cultural justice in a globalised world.

Under severely depressive spiritual conditions, about 40 years before the fall of Samaria, proto-Isaiah sees a vision of the peaceable kingdom. Divisions and life-threatening enmities based on natural identities (wolf-lamb; leopard-goat; calf-lion) are overcome through a radical transformation of those very identities (lions eat straw and children put hands in the viper's nest). There will be neither harm nor destruction, "for the earth will be full of the knowledge of the Lord as the waters cover the sea" (see Isaiah 11:6-9).

Under conditions of persecution and a seemingly hopeless situation for the second-generation Christians, the apostle John sees a vision of a truly global community (truly global and truly in communion) before the throne of God: "After this I looked and there before me was a great multitude that no one could count, from every nation, tribe, people and language, standing before the throne and in front of the Lamb ... and he who sits on the throne will spread his tent over them. Never again will they hunger, never again will they thirst" (Rev 7: 9, 15).

Whilst we live in the midst of the ambiguities of a globalising world – marvelling at its opportunities, but at the same time despairing at its consequences – we nurture these visions as narratives of a radically other world made possible by the knowledge of the Lord.

---

28 The confession was adopted in 1986 by the then Dutch Reformed Mission Church after acceptance of the ecumenically endorsed *status confessionis* on apartheid. For the English text (original in Afrikaans) and initial explication, see Cloete and Smit, *A moment of truth* (1982).

BIBLIOGRAPHY

Addy, Tony and Sinly, Jiri. 2001. The political economy of transition. *The Ecumenical Review* 53/4: 501-508.

Arthur, Chris. 1998. *The globalisation of communications*. Geneva: WCC.

Balcomb, Tony. 1998. From liberation to democracy: Theologies of bread and being in the new South Africa. *Missionalia*, 26/1, April: 54-73.

Bauman, Zygmunt. 1995. *Life in fragments: Essays in postmodern morality*. Oxford: Blackwell.

Bedford-Strohm, Heinrich. 2009. Zu diesem Heft. *Verkündigung und Forschung* 54. Jahrgang, Heft 1:2-5.

Berry, T. 1988. *The dream of the earth*. San Francisco: Sierra Club Books.

Best, Thomas F and Robra, Martin. 1997. *Ecclesiology and ethics. Ecumenical ethical engagement, moral formation and the nature of the church*. Geneva: WCC.

Bloomquist, Karen L. 2001. Engaging economic globalisation as churches. *The Ecumenical Review* 53/4: 493-500.

Bruce, FF. 1982. *The Epistle to the Galatians. A commentary on the Greek text*. Exeter: Paternoster.

Chidester, David, Dexter, Philip and Wilmot, James. 2003. *What holds us together. Social cohesion in South Africa*. Cape Town: HSRC Press.

Cloete, D and Smit DJ. 1982. *A moment of truth*. Grand Rapids: Eerdmans.

Comaroff, John L & Comaroff Jean. 2002. On personhood. An anthropological perspective from Africa. Pages 67-82 in *Die outonome Person - Eine Europäische Erfindung?* Herausgegeben von Klaus-Peter Köpping, Michael Welker, Reiner Wiehl. München: Wilhelm Fink.

De Santa Ana, Julio ed. 1998. *Sustainability and globalization*. Geneva: WCC.

During, Simon ed. 1993. *The cultural studies reader*. London: Routledge.

Fischer, Johannes. 1992. Christliche Ethik als Verantwortungsethik? *Evangelische Theologie* 52, Heft 2: 114-128.

Gamst, Frederick C and Norbeck, Edward eds. 1976. *Ideas of culture. Sources and uses*. New York: Holt, Rinehart and Winston.

Gannon, Maartin J. 1994. *Understanding global cultures. Metaphorical journeys through 17 countries*. London: Sage.

Geertz, Cilfford. 1975. *The interpretation of culture*. London: Hutchinson and Co.

Gerle, Elizabeth. 2000. Contemporary globalisation and its ethical challenges. *The Ecumenical Review* 52/2: 158-171

Klopper, Sandra. 2003. Global tourism, marginalised communities and the development of Cape Town's City Bowl area. Pages 224-241 in Chidester et al.

Kobia, Samuel 2003. *The courage to hope. The roots for a new vision and the calling of the church in Africa*. Geneva: WCC.

Kwenda, Chirevo V. 2003. Cultural justice: the pathway to reconciliation and social cohesion. Pages 67-80 in Chidester et al.

Louw Daniel J. 2002. A practical theological ecclesiology of relocalisation and globalisation from below: toward a viable African renaissance. *Journal of Theology for Southern Africa* 112 (March): 69-87.

Luther, Martin. 1968. *Kommentar zum Galaterbrief*. Hamburg: Taschenbuch (Band 10 der Calwer Luther–Ausgabe).

Raiser, Konrad. 1999. *Ernstfall des Glaubens. Kirche sein im 21.Jahrhundert*. Göttingen: Vandenhoek und Ruprecht.

Raiser, Konrad. 2009. Globalisierung in der oekumenisch-ethischen Diskussion. *Verkündigung und Forschung* 54. Jahrgang, Heft 1:6-33.

Rasmussen, L. 1994. Cosmology and ethics. Pages 173-180 in *Worldviews and ecology*. Edited by ME Tucker and JA Grimm. New York: Maryknoll.

Smart, Ninian.1973. *The phenomenon of religion*. London: Mowbrays.

Tracy, David. 1981. *The analogical imagination. Christian theology and the culture of pluralism*. London: SCM.

Rodriques, Richard. 1982. *Hunger of memory: The education of Richard Rodriques*. Boston: Godine.

Roetzel, Calvin, J. 1985. *The world that shaped the New Testament*. London: SCM.

Schrage, Wolfgang. 1988. *The ethics of the New Testament*. (Original: *Ethik des Neuen Testmanents*, 1982) Edinburgh: T&T Clark.

Smit, Dirk J. 2000. Living unity? On the ecumenical movement and globalisation. Paper read at a joint consultation by EFSA and the Evangelische Akademie in Tutzing, Germany on "Consequences of globalisation for Germany and South Africa", 5-7 June 2000.

Smit, Dirk. 2009. Schreie nach Leben. Eine (süd-)afrikanische Stimme. *Verkündigung und Forschung* 54. Jahrgang, Heft 1: 59-69.

Verhey, Allen. 2002. *Remembering Jesus. Christian community, Scripture, and moral life*. Grand Rapids: Eerdmans.

Volf, Miroslav. 1996. *Exclusion and embrace. A theological exploration of identity, otherness and reconciliation*. Nashville: Abingdon.

Welker, Michael 2008. Globalisierung in wissenschaftlich-theologischer Sicht. *Evangelische Theologie* 68. Jahrgang, Heft 53: 365-382.

1.2 IN DEFENCE OF PARTISAN JUSTICE

An ethical reflection on "the preferential option for the poor"

When lady justice is depicted, we see her with the scales of justice balanced carefully in her hands, often while she is blindfolded. The notion of "blind" justice attempts to express our moral sentiment that equal treatment of all people under the law is a cornerstone of fairness and democracy.

This common sense notion of justice can, however, under conditions of inequality, lead to undesirable outcomes. A case can therefore be made for partisan justice, which implies – against the notion of "sameness" – a differential treatment of some individuals or nations.

This essay argues for such a preferential or differential or partisan justice and is developed in four sections. The first section briefly sketches a profile of the different theological arguments underlying a preferential option for the poor, particularly as developed by Gustavo Gutierrez and other Latin American liberation theologians, and later accepted in wider ecumenical circles.

The second section outlines philosophical arguments for a position of "prioritarianism" which seems to support such a "preferential option". This is undertaken through a discussion of two influential books by the well-known American political philosopher, John Rawls, namely his *A theory of justice* (1973), and *The law of peoples* (1999).

The third section discusses the popular work of economist Joseph Stiglitz in the light of his argument for a global trade regime where poor nations receive differential treatment.

Section four concludes the essay by demonstrating the synergy between these views from theology, philosophy and economics, and by pointing out – in a provisional way – the important consequences of such a "preferential" or "partisan" view for guiding ethical reflection on local and global socio-economic relations.

1. PARTISAN JUSTICE FROM A THEOLOGICAL PERSPECTIVE: GUSTAVO GUTIERREZ (ET AL.) AND THE PREFERENTIAL OPTION FOR THE POOR

One could construe four theological arguments that cumulatively provide a rationale for – and are at the same time expressions of – the notion of a preferential option for the poor.[1]

---

[1] There is a certain circularity involved here: the option for the poor historically precedes the development of Latin American liberation theologies (see below). Therefore these theologies are expressions in different ways of the underlying option; but in turn these "expressions" become arguments for a reinforcement of the option.

1.1 The methodological argument

The advent of a cluster of liberation theologies – Latin American, black, African, feminist/womanist, gay/lesbian and ecological – was accompanied by a specific understanding that what is at stake is not just new theological themes on liberation, but the very way of constructing theology as such. Despite the inner complexities of, and differences between, this pluralistic array of liberation theologies, there is a specific methodological convergence: **Liberation theologies generally take as their methodological point of departure the oppressive experience of those who fall within the focus of that particular theology.** These focal points explain in each case who would be seen as "poor, marginalised and oppressed". This includes economically or materially poor people, racially oppressed black people, culturally marginalised or colonised people, middle-class women and poor black women, gay and lesbian people, people suffering from HIV/AIDS, as well as the oppression of animals and the non-human world as a consequence of a narrow anthropocentric construction of reality.[2]

For the purposes of this essay a very general description of Latin American liberation theology is undertaken.[3] There is a twofold motivation of this particular choice. First: the historical origin of the specific term "the preferential option for the poor" lies in Latin American Catholicism. What later became Latin American liberation theology has the closest ties to these historical roots. The first indications of the term are already present in *Gaudium et Spes,* emanating from Vatican II (1965). It found its way in more explicit forms into the second general conference of Latin American bishops at Medellin (1968), and was taken up explicitly as a chapter entitled "The preferential option for the poor" in the final document of the third bishops' conference in Puebla, Mexico (1979).[4]

Second: although "the option for the poor" has been adopted by other liberation theologies, and later by the ecumenical movement,[5] Latin American liberation theology is, in my view, the best example of a theology constructed specifically around this option as lens through which all theological loci are viewed.

In a short illuminating passage Gutierrez explains the **preferential option for the poor**: "The very term *preference* obviously precludes any exclusivity; it simply points to who ought to be the first – not the only – objects of our solidarity". He points out that liberation theology "has insisted on the importance of maintaining

---

2   The literature in each case is too vast to cite here. For a very useful overview of some of these theologies from a South African perspective, see the first part of *Initiation into theology*, edited by Maimela and König (2001).

3   It must be made clear: one cannot write a few paragraphs on such a vast theology (or theologies) without making some fairly sweeping generalisations and a loss of specifics. It is also impossible to refer to all the relevant literature at each point. The value, though, of the "generalist" approach adopted here is that it serves a heuristic function in the elucidation of a specific focal point. It is for the reader to judge whether the exposition below contradicts the general thrust of liberation theologies from Latin America.

4   See the discussion of original documents by Gutierrez (1993:239-240) and the more detailed overview and analysis by Bedford-Strohm (1993:151-166).

5   This theological view is, for example, echoed by the ecumenical church in an exposition of the Nicene Creed: "In the particular case of human oppression, the victim is assured that God is never on the side of the oppressor, the bringer of death, but will, in justice, protect the rights and lives of the victims" (WCC 1991:63).

both the universality of God's love and the divine predilection for 'history's last'" (1993:239). What the word **option** seeks to emphasise "is the free commitment of a decision. The option for the poor is not optional in the sense that a Christian need not necessarily make it, any more than the love we owe every human being, without exception, is not optional. It is a matter of a deep, on-going solidarity, a voluntary daily involvement with the world of the poor" (1993:240). The reference to **the poor** denotes at least three forms of poverty: material poverty (physically poor), social poverty (being marginalised as a result of racial, cultural or gender oppression), and spiritual poverty (lack of openness to God's will and solidarity with the poor) (1993:235-7).[6]

The methodological renewal brought by liberation theology was formulated by Gustavo Gutierrez in a classical exposition back in 1971. According to him, liberation theology "offers us not so much a new theme for reflection as a *new way to do theology*" (Gutierrez 1973:15, original emphasis). He thus states: "Theology is a critical reflection on Christian praxis in the light of the Word" (Gutierrez 1973:13). The starting point of theological reflection is not revelation or tradition, but "purely and simply, the daily experience of the unjust poverty in which millions of our fellow Latin Americans are obliged to live" (Oliveros 1993: 4). What informs theological reflection at the beginning are the facts and questions derived from the world. And this world is the world of the poor and the marginalised, a reality of social misery. It is the experience of these poor and marginalised people from "the underside of history" that informs theology as liberating process.

There are actually three forms of theological expression inherent in "liberation theology" as such. Clodovis Boff calls them metaphorically the roots, the trunk and the branches of the tree of liberation theology. The "roots" are popular liberation theology done by ordinary Christians in base communities in a diffuse and less organised way with the basic method of confronting life conditions with the message of the gospel. The "trunk" refers to pastoral liberation theology done by church assemblies, (lay) pastors and religious orders with a basic three-step method of seeing, judging and acting. The branches – best known outside Latin America – are professional theologians who follow developed and rigorous academic arguments in a threefold mediation of theology, namely socio-analytical, hermeneutical and practical.

The socio-analytical mediation constitutes the material object of theology in its relation to the social sciences ('see"). The hermeneutical mediation constitutes the formal object of theology in its relation to Scripture and tradition ("judge"). The practical mediation constitutes the concrete object of theology in its relation to pastoral and historical action ("act").[7]

---

6   See the discussion below where the first two forms of poverty are linked to two different forms of justice: distributive and cultural.

7   See Boff and Boff (1984: 5-11); 49-55; Boff and Boff (1987: 24ff) as well as the very structure of Clodovis Boff's *Theology and praxis: epistemological foundations* (1987). This latter book is for me the most illuminating and penetrating discussion of the concept of a praxis-oriented theology. Perceptive liberation theologians are obviously aware of the fact that the very "starting point" in the socio-political realities or "experience" presupposes some **interpretation** of those realities. "Hermeneutics" in the sense of "reflective

The metaphor of the tree already points to the idea that the very methodological structure of liberation theology reflects and supports the preferential option for the poor. It is their experiences that inform liberation theology and provide pastoral and academic theologians with the core material for reflection in the light of Scripture and tradition. Liberation theology is therefore much more dialectical[8] than analogical, and more historical-practical than merely analytical. This in turn implies both an epistemological and a methodological break with mainline, traditional (Western) theology.[9]

We can thus attempt a first reply to the question: Why this priority option for the poor? The methodological answer is: Because the lived realities of the poor present themselves as the starting point of reflection on faith and constitute the "hinge" of the praxis[10] process toward the liberation of the oppressed (see Sobrino 1984:27).

1.2 The hermeneutic-exegetical argument

If the methodological starting point is the experiences of the poor, a hermeneutical discussion of liberation theology must commence with the poor, ordinary people as primary readers of the Bible. The methodological option for the poor here turns into an epistemological and hermeneutical privilege: we learn the truth of the Bible through the eyes and life histories of the poor. "No theoretical reading or quest for ideas is involved. The reading of the Bible as done by the poor is a matter of life and death, freedom and domination" (Gorgulho 1993: 124). The primary context is the base communities and not the seminary or the university, and the "source" of biblical and exegetical reflection should be the readings accomplished by the poor.

The implications are that the Bible is not read as past history, but as a mirror of history occurring today. The chief aim is not an isolated interpretation of the Bible for the sake of increased erudition, but an interpretation of life with the aid of the Bible, which itself becomes a source of life. There is no search here for a "neutral" reading – the poor engage in a committed reading as they search for way out of their oppression toward liberation (see Gorgulho 1993: 124-125).

One of the most significant shifts in 20th-century hermeneutical studies occurred with the shift from the text to the reader as locus of meaning (see Lategan and Vorster 1985). Meaning, it is argued, does not reside somewhere "in the autotelic text" where it is merely "retrieved" through historical, grammatical and structural analysis. Meaning is constructed by an interaction between text and reader. Without the reader the text is voiceless. In some extreme reader-oriented views, the text is

---

interpretation" indeed underlies the whole liberation theological enterprise. See the discussion under 1.2 that follows below.

8   This term should not be interpreted in the Barthian sense of the word. Its origin lies in left-Hegelian and Marxist thought and refers to the development of history through dialectical movements of thesis, antithesis and synthesis.

9   See how Gutierrez (1973: 3-15) attempts to link classical theologies to a liberation theology. For more details, read Sobrino (1984:7-38) for an interesting and illuminating juxtapositioning of liberation and Western theologies.

10 The word "praxis" refers to the continuous movement from practice ("experience") to theory ("reflection") and back ("action'). For a detailed philosophical discussion, see Chapter 1 of the unpublished thesis by Naudé (1987).

in fact constructed by the reader.[11] Thus the important question is no longer "What is read?", but rather "Who reads?" And the answer from liberation theology is straightforward: the poor and the marginalised are the preferred readers.

Where a reader-oriented approach is coupled with a hermeneutics of suspicion[12] – specifically those from a Marxist or neo-Marxist origin – two crucial insights come to the fore.

First: in what has become known as materialist readings, the production of the Biblical text is itself viewed with a "suspicion" based on who owns the means of production in the text-producing communities. Where a text originates or is edited over time by people in position of political and economic power, it tends to show features of "status quo" texts. The opposite is naturally also true, so that the reader should seek out and rather follow the guidance of texts reflecting the views "from the underside" of society.

Second: in what has become known as social constructivist readings, the socio-economic position of the reader is itself of crucial importance. If the reader is the primary locus of meaning, such meaning will tend to reflect her/his social position. In short, rich and powerful people construct different meanings from those constructed by the poor and the marginalised.[13] And as many texts seem to address the needs of the latter, the epistemologically privileged position now becomes one of hermeneutical privilege.

Based on these hermeneutical arguments, the exegetical key consequently shifts from notions such as "justification by faith alone" (dominant in Reformed exegesis), the two kingdoms or the creative tension between law and gospel (arising from Lutheran work) towards the "liberation of the poor and the marginalised".

"From its point of departure in the anguish of the poor of this world, the whole biblical message emerges as a proclamation of liberation" (Boff and Boff 1984:26). Themes from the Old Testament are liberation from Egypt; the special care for foreigners, widows and orphans in the law; social criticism against oppressing the poor in the prophets; and the admonitions against riches and calls for caring for the poor in the wisdom literature. In the New Testament much is made of Jesus' relation and ministry to sinners and marginalised people, and of the Lukan emphasis in Luke-Acts on the physically poor, the sharing of goods, and care for the widows in the earliest Christian communities. There is an emphasis on the egalitarian elements in the Pauline corpus (such as Galatians 3 and Ephesians 2), and the obvious option for the poor in the book of James.[14]

---

11 For a concise discussion of hermeneutical approaches that emphasise the role of the reader, see Jonker and Lawrie (2005: 112-128).
12 See Jonker and Lawrie (2005:167-228) for a general overview of "the hermeneutics of suspicion" with a specific discussion by Lawrie of Marxist approaches on pages 189-199.
13 See the many fruitful analyses of the insights of "ordinary readers" as set out by the South African Old Testament scholar Gerald West, for example, West (1995, 1999).
14 As indicated above, the primary literature here is once again overwhelming. For an excellent summary and overview, read Pixley and Boff, *The option for the poor in the Old Testament* (1989: especially pp. 17-52) and *The option for the poor in the New Testament* (1989: 53-67).

Why this priority option for the poor? A second answer, highly simplified, is: Because the Bible tells us so.

1.3 The Trinitarian argument

This group of arguments is in many ways an extension of the hermeneutical views, though they represent the "doctrinal" dimension of the option for the poor.

God

If you live under wretched socio-economic or marginalised or oppressive conditions, and if you then read the Bible from the perspective of the poor, the very image of God that appears is "the God of the oppressed". Gustavo Gutierrez calls this the theocentric basis of the option for the poor (1993:239). And Jon Sobrino writes: "In my opinion, God's manifestation, at least in Latin-America, is his scandalous and partisan love for the poor and his intention that the poor should receive life... The mediation of the absolutely Other takes the form of those who are really 'other': the oppressed" (Sobrino 1984: 2, 33).

Here hermeneutics becomes theo-logy. In situations of entrenched economic injustice, God is on the side of the poor and is a different God from those who proclaim a prosperity gospel, perceiving God as guarantor of privileges and power. A theo-logy that defends oppressive conditions is a false theo-logy. "God" turns into idolatry; religion turns – as Marx rightly observed – into the opium of the people.

Jesus Christ

Liberation theologians have made rich contributions to our understanding of Christ.[15] One could point to a number of shared emphases[16] that reinforce the option for the poor.

There is a definite return to the historical Jesus, although not in the "archaeological" or "historicist" sense of the word. Jesus is seen first and foremost as materially poor himself. His seeking out and healing of marginalised people demonstrates his own commitment to the poor. As "Word made flesh" he is the incarnation and revelation of God as the God of the poor. His ministry and preaching point to the coming kingdom of God with its radically inverted value system where the first will be last, and the last first.

Latin American liberation theology moves away from explaining the cross in terms of expiatory theories of reconciliation to a historical recovery of the cross as the world's condemnation of the poor and at the same time judgment against the sin of marginalisation. There is an intrinsic link between cross and resurrection. The latter stands as the triumph of justice over injustice and as sign of hope for the crucified of history. Christology is not merely constructed by way of theories about Jesus or the post-Easter Lord, but by following Jesus in his solidarity with the poor. The

---

15   One immediately thinks of the seminal works by Jon Sobrino as published in English: *Christology at the crossroads* (1978), *Jesus the liberator* (1993) and *Christ the liberator* (2001).
16   I roughly follow the exposition by Julio Lois (1993), but add interpretations based on my reading of the primary literature.

only way to Christology, i.e. knowledge about Christ, is through discipleship, the following of Christ.

Holy Spirit

The Holy Spirit[17] is the One who fills the prophets that speak against oppression, who prompts the songs of liberation sung by Miriam, Simeon and Mary, who creates the church as egalitarian prophet community (Acts 2), who groans with the whole creation, crying for justice and truth (Rom 8). Based on these biblical insights, the Spirit is the Divine force that works in history toward the radical transformation of society. The poor experience this Spirit as the Spirit that spurs them on to action, that delivers them from slavery and lets them experience freedom, that leads them from oppressed silence to the freedom of the word, crying out "Abba Father", that makes possible the experience of a new community, that brings – amidst death – living waters of life (see Comblin 1993:464-471).

Trinity

Not only as separate Persons, but in community, the Trinity[18] serves as example of self-donating love, non-hierarchical communion and as the basis for our critique of society. To create social embodiments of the Trinitarian communion would require a new society that avoids the aberrations of both the excessive individualism underlying capitalism and the collectivism of socialism. "The sort of society that would emerge from inspiration by the Trinitarian model would be one of fellowship, equality of opportunity, generosity in the space available for personal and group expression" (Boff 1998:151).

Why this preferential option for the poor? A third reply that would come from Liberation Theology is: Because this is how God as Trinitarian God has revealed God-self. As Boff puts it: "Oppressed Christians find an incomparable inspiration for the liberation struggle **in the God of their faith**" (1998:152, my emphasis).

1.4 The ecclesiological argument

The church is not so much a church for the poor as a poor church (see Sobrino 1985:84-124).[19] "Poverty is not a virtue unless it leads to the fellowship of the really poor. The poor church will therefore have to be understood as the church of the poor…" (Moltmann 1981:336).[20]

---

17 Comblin refers to the fact that pneumatology is quite under-developed in Latin American theologies. The recent rise of popular Pentecostal movements in both the Protestant and Catholic churches serves as impulse to move beyond the patristic tradition of Latin theology (1993:462-463).
18 Perhaps one could say that Leonardo Boff has done the most interesting work on Trinitarian theology among the liberation theologians. See his *Trinity and society* (1988) and *Holy Trinity, perfect community* (2000) as examples of what has become known as "social trinitarianism".
19 Sobrino develops his ecclesiological views in this regard with a strong reliance on Western theologians such as Moltmann (see next quotation) and Hans Küng, but obviously adds his own perspectives from the Latin American situation.
20 This is a quotation from Moltmann's exposition of the marks of the church that, according to him, is holy in poverty. He argues that because Christ has been made poor "so that

Sobrino attempts to overcome three obstacles in understanding the church as a church of the poor: an idealist universalism, an ethical approach to the poor, and a segmental approach to view the poor in the church as part of a wider sociological group.

First: the Second Vatican Council reintroduced the metaphor "people of God" for the church, and although this is clearly a move away from the strict hierarchical and mystical understandings of the church towards a more democratic or participative notion, Sobrino maintains that a universalistic understanding of the people of God is still too vague. He argues that – as in the times of Isaiah and Jesus – the good news is that the poor are the locus where God is to be found (Matthew 25). The poor therefore have the sacramental value of being "a structural channel for the coming into being of the true Church" (1985:93). The church was historically born of the poor and they remain the theological locus of being the church.

Second, a "church of the poor" is not an expression of the idea that the church has an ethical obligation to assist the poor whilst ignoring the phenomenon of poverty itself. Yes, one can build a church **for** the poor, but that is not synonymous with a church **of** the poor, because the first assumes that "the Church is constituted in logical independence of the poor, and then goes on to ask what this Church must do for the poor. A Church **of** the poor, however, poses a strictly ecclesiological problem; it concerns the very being of the Church" (Sobrino 1985:92).

Third: "church of the poor" does not simply imply that the poor are part of the church alongside others who are non-poor and who remain unaffected by the plight of the poor segment of the church. The Spirit of Jesus, which is in the poor, recreates the entire church to become a church of the poor. The poor are the theological source of the entire church and being a church of the poor is the only way to seek and find God. Solidarity with the poor by being poor is an expression of the church's own kenosis (Sobrino 1985:95).

A fourth reply to the question as to why there is a preferential option for the poor would be: The poor church expresses the essence of being church in the world today.

Theological conclusion and implications for understanding justice

Much more could be said on this topic. But the profile drawn above is adequate for our purposes here: the preferential option for the poor is supported by and expressed in at least a four-dimensional theological construction:

1. A methodological starting point in the experience of the poor, which is then mediated through a praxis-oriented process;
2. A hermeneutical choice to take the reading of ordinary people as point of departure; a "reading with suspicion" which particularly focuses on the social construction of both the text itself and the social location of the reader;
3. A doctrinal image of God, Jesus Christ and the Spirit as separate persons opting for the poor, and as a triune community manifesting justice and charity;

---

you might become rich" (2 Cor 8:9), the church is sanctified "wherever it participates in the lowliness, helplessness, poverty and suffering of Christ" (1981:355).

4. A vision of the church as a poor church whose sanctification is bound up with solidarity with the poor.

The implications of this theological construct for our understanding of justice are profound. For the sake of focus, let us look at the views expressed by Jon Sobrino in his discussion of the integral relationship between faith and justice.

He takes the kingdom of God as point of departure: because God's reign embraces the totality of human relations and includes all of history, justice – as the concrete embodiment of love – must be understood in equally holistic terms. Justice concerns itself therefore not merely with interpersonal relations but with structural relations as well. As humans are divided into "oppressor and oppressed", justice must concretely address the sin of structural economic disparity.

The **partisan** nature of this justice is expressed unreservedly: "Love in the form of justice has meant historically doing justice to the vast majority of the human race, namely, the poor... Historically, therefore, the concretisation of love as justice is a necessary and effective way of giving flesh to the great Christian truth that **God is partial to the poor majority**" (Sobrino 1984:77, my emphasis).

A more specific question is: What forms of justice are at stake in the preferential option for the poor? The answer lies in a connection between two of the "poverty notions" referred to above: to address material poverty, distributive justice is necessary; to address socio-political poverty (marginalisation), cultural justice is necessary.

Distributive justice[21] is a form of socio-economic justice that regulates the distribution of goods and services amongst the people of a specific society or amongst societies in a regional or global arrangement. The result of such a distribution will obviously depend on the meta-ethical notion of justice and the specific theory of justice adopted. Egalitarian understandings of justice will, for example, seek to spread benefits more equally than an entitlement notion of justice.[22]

In the language of Latin American liberation theology, this is justice for the poor.

Cultural justice[23] is a form of social justice that regulates the relationships amongst individuals from different cultural backgrounds, or amongst whole cultural groups themselves. This may happen within or beyond the boundaries of nation-states and/or on a global scale. Cultural justice aims to respect and protect distinct features of cultures, works against forms of marginalisation based on factors such as race or gender, and actively promotes the celebration of the wide range of cultural and human diversity in a particular society or in the world as such.

---

21 For a definition and wide-ranging discussion of different theories of distributive justice, see Roemer (1998).
22 This difference is, for example, illustrated in the debate between John Rawls (egalitarian view) and Robert Nozick (entitlement view).
23 This is a form of justice not widely discussed in the literature yet. I found the essay by Kwenda (2003) very helpful in this regard. He argues that cultural justice is established when people are allowed unselfconscious living, i.e. they live in acceptance and appreciation of their own identity. For an analysis of the link between cultural justice, identity and globalisation, read Naudé (2005) and the first chapter in this book.

In the language of Latin American liberation theology, this is justice for the marginalised.

The second part of this essay aims to establish whether and in what way the same kind of preference emanates on completely different grounds from the philosophical theory of justice as presented by the eminent political philosopher, John Rawls. In other words, what are the philosophical grounds – if any – for partisan justice?

2. PARTISAN JUSTICE FROM A PHILOSOPHICAL PERSPECTIVE: JOHN RAWLS ON "THE LEAST ADVANTAGED REPRESENTATIVE MAN" AND "BURDENED SOCIETIES"

2.1 Prioritarian distributive justice

In his well-known *A theory of justice* Rawls develops a difference principle (1971:60-90) in which re-distributive policies allow for social and economic inequalities, but only if they result in compensating benefits for everyone, "and in particular for the least advantaged members of society" (1971:14-15). The protection or improvement of the least advantaged therefore receives absolute priority in determining justice.

Rawls's defence of this priority is philosophically based on his choice against sum-utilitarianism and his preference for the contract tradition stemming from Hobbes, Locke, Rousseau and Kant. His methodological defence is based on his strategy to show that the difference principle (or maximum criterion) would be the rational choice for members of a future society who find themselves behind a veil of ignorance (1971:136-142) in an original contract position (1971:17-22). The (re)distribution of primary goods, identified by Rawls as "rights and liberties, opportunities and powers, income and wealth" (1971:62, 92), must always satisfy the criterion of improving the worst-off person's situation.

The measurement of this "worst-off" person, or what Rawls calls the identification of "the least advantaged representative man" (1971:91), may be determined by economists in terms of the Gini index coupled to social welfare functions, or by the Lorenz curve, which depicts the percentage of the total amount of income possessed by any given percentage of the poorest amongst the population (e.g. the poorest 20% of people share in 4% of total income).[24]

In his later book, *The law of peoples* (1999), Rawls extends his notion of "justice as fairness" to an international society composed of different peoples who have "distinctive institutions and languages, religions and cultures, as well as different histories" (1999:54-55). In an initial compact (the second original position), where representatives of the peoples meet behind a thick veil of ignorance (1999:32-33), eight principles of the "Law of Peoples" would hypothetically be agreed to (1999:37). This is not an agreement between free and equal individuals as in Rawls's "domestic version", but an agreement reached by distinct peoples via their rationally inclined representatives.

---

24 Frankfurt (1987) argues that this "priority" of those "worst off" should be given only to those below a certain threshold. One could apply his view to the current distinction between people living in poverty and those living in absolute poverty.

In what way could Rawls's "international" version of justice as fairness be interpreted as prioritarian as described above? Let us look at the principles of justice among free and democratic peoples as formulated by Rawls (1999:37).

1. Peoples are free and independent, and their freedom and independence are to be respected by other peoples.
2. Peoples are to observe treaties and undertakings.
3. Peoples are equal and are parties to the agreements that bind them.
4. Peoples are to observe a duty of non-intervention.
5. Peoples have the right of self-defence but no right to instigate war for reasons other than self-defence.
6. Peoples are to honour human rights.
7. Peoples are to observe certain specified restrictions in the conduct of war.

Whereas the first seven principles all presume equality and non-partisanship, the addition of the last principle[25] is significant:

8. Peoples have a duty to assist other peoples living under unfavourable conditions that prevent their having a just or decent political and social regime.

This is, according to my interpretation, the only law that moves Rawls's egalitarianism toward its special version of prioritarianism, namely "a duty" toward those "living under unfavourable conditions". Rawls refer to these as "burdened societies"[26] because they "lack the political and cultural traditions, the human capital and know-how, and often, the material and technological resources needed to be well-ordered" (1999:106).

Buchanan argues that Rawls does not adequately address the inequities built into the "global basic structure". The latter is seen as "a set of economic and political institutions that has profound and enduring effects on the distribution of burdens and benefits among peoples and individuals around the world" (Buchanan 2000: 705). Rawls's laws therefore inadequately address issues of distributive justice in the current global order. Buchanan subsequently adds three further laws pertaining to global equality of opportunity, democratic participation in global institutions and a principle designed to limit inequalities of wealth among nations.

It may be argued, however, that a strong interpretation of the eighth principle does indeed imply re-distributive action: the "duty to assist" can hardly be practically conceived without some "transfer" or "sacrifice" from decent peoples living under more favourable conditions than those in the opposite situation.[27] Anton van Niekerk has convincingly argued that this duty is not merely a duty of charity, but indeed of justice. And that this law – even if construed as duty of charity – has no diminished moral force (Van Niekerk 2004:183).

---

25 Rawls himself remarks: "This principle is especially controversial" (1999:37, note 43).
26 A well-ordered and even rich society may become a burdened society through a natural disaster. Irrespective of the cause, Rawls argues that a rational view of reciprocity would agree to the principle that peoples have a duty to assist burdened societies.
27 The G8 debt relief programme or South Africa's contributions to the SADC countries are cases in point.

The difference principle returns with the special and exclusive focus on "peoples living under unfavourable conditions". Here the earlier **individuals** who are worst off in a specific society are matched by **peoples** who are comparably worst off in the global system.

Some qualification is required, however: Rawls does not accept a blanket global difference principle.[28] "Well-ordered peoples have a **duty** to assist burdened societies. It does not follow, however, that the only way, or the best way to carry out this duty of assistance is by following a principle of distributive justice to regulate economic and social inequalities among societies" (1999:106, original emphasis).

The three guidelines[29] for the duty to assist (1999:106-113) clarifies this. The aim of assistance is not primarily to reach greater equality in economic wealth, for example, but to ensure that burdened societies are able "to establish reasonably just basic institutions for a free constitutional democratic society and to secure a social world that makes possible a worthwhile life for all its citizens" (1999:107; see also page 5). The duty to assist is therefore a transitional duty linked to a specific target, after which the duty is no longer in force as the former burdened society is now able or has become a member of the Society of Well-ordered Peoples (see 1999:117-119).

This does not imply that no re-distributive justice or reducing of inequalities is required. It also does not exclude direct financial assistance (though Rawls is at pains to focus on political culture rather than economic aid).[30] The Society of Well-ordered Peoples may and will probably have members that are rich and poor in relative terms, but the latter will not be so poor (burdened) as to make the establishment and maintenance of a well-ordered society impossible.

Rawls explains that one of the preconditions for establishing just basic institutions is meeting peoples' basic needs. "By basic needs I mean roughly those that must be met if citizens are to be in a position to take advantage of the rights, liberties, and opportunities of their society. These needs include economic means as well as institutional rights and freedoms" (1999:38, note 47), and may (in my interpretation) be linked to the presence of adequate "primary goods" to secure a social world in which just political institutions can be built.

The duty to assist in the context of relations amongst peoples therefore carries – despite qualifications and restrictions – the same egalitarian consequences as the difference principle in domestic societies.[31]

---

28 Here Rawls differs from Charles Beitz, whom he discusses on pp. 115-119.
29 Simply put, these guidelines are: assistance is not aimed at reduction in wealth inequalities per se, but in establishing just institutions; the establishment of a political culture and political virtues are crucial; and, despite being relatively poor, the inclusion of the burdened society in the Society of Peoples is the ultimate aim.
30 "What must be realized is that merely dispensing funds will not rectify basic political and social injustices (though money is often essential)." A focus on human rights and the establishment of a democratic political culture are more important (1999:108-109). Rawls takes his cue from inter alia Sen's case studies of famine that show the political and economic factors are mostly more important than "natural" factors such as droughts. This reinforces Rawls's view that assistance of peoples must carry political consequences, i.e. the creation of just institutions.
31 Rawls remarks that among various interpretations of liberalism, "justice as fairness is the most egalitarian" (1999:14, note 5)

The principle, if applied to asymmetrical power relations has the following implications.

In situations where, for example, indigenous people share membership of a domestic society with better-off persons, and they happen to be in the worst-off position (which is mostly the case), the difference principle would require that such people receive absolute priority in any re-distributive policy decision.

And in situations of global distributive decision making, Rawls's principle of assistance would require that, whatever the outcome of such a decision, it should not diminish the fulfilment of basic needs of the poorest people to the margin where citizens are unable to build just institutions or take advantage of available rights and opportunities. The rational and just thing to do in the (second) original position is to maximise the minimum, where the latter is linked to the potential to build a well-ordered Society of Peoples, because the people you represent in the second original position might find themselves to be a burdened society.

2.2 Prioritarian cultural justice

The link between justice as fairness and culture is addressed by Rawls in a number of ways in *A theory of justice* (see 1971:101, 325, 331, 525). The most important aspect for our argument here is Rawls's insistence that "perhaps the most important primary good is that of self-respect". It is worth quoting him in full:

> We may define self-respect as having two aspects. First of all ... it includes a person's sense of his own value, his secure conviction that his conception of the good, his plan of life, is worth carrying out. And second, self-respect implies a confidence in one's ability, as far as it is within one's power, to fulfil one's intentions. When we feel that our plans are of little value, we cannot pursue them with pleasure... Nor plagued by failure and self-doubt can we continue our endeavours. It is clear then why self-respect is a primary good... **Therefore the parties in the original position would wish to avoid at almost any cost the social conditions that undermine self-respect** (1971:440, my emphasis).

That Rawls is – even in this domestic version – not merely speaking in individualist terms is apparent from his discussion of historical identity and social unions as the mark of just and well-ordered societies (1971: 525ff). It takes very little insight to see in Rawls's quotation the intrinsic link between justice and what was referred to as "culture". Being self-consciousness in a negative sense, always being one step or sentence or technological innovation behind, undermines self-respect and leads to cultural diffidence. This is a disposition that causes indigenous people either to be ashamed of their culture or to simply ignore it as irrelevant in the world beyond their own confines. It is the internalised conviction that "one's own" (language, music, race, gender, art) is worse than that of "the dominant other" and of no significance in greater society.

One can therefore read Rawls as saying that cultural justice, the social condition that strengthens self-respect, would be promoted at all cost by the parties in the original position. You would do that because you could theoretically belong to an indigenous people or minority race/gender group, and so vulnerable to the homogenisation and assimilation forces of dominant national and Anglophone global cultures.

Rawls's *The Law of Peoples* is also specifically fruitful in promoting issues underlying cultural justice.

His choice of "peoples" instead of "nations" or "states" is significant as he argues that peoples and not states are the actors in the Society of Peoples. Liberal peoples have three basic features which are linked to institutions, culture and morality (1999:23-25). "The term 'peoples', then, is meant to emphasise these singular features of peoples as distinct from states…". He further places particular emphasis on the wide range of distinctive features amongst different peoples: they have "distinctive institutions and languages, religions and cultures, as well as their different histories" (1999: 54-55); they have distinct values, traditions and ideas of justice, and are united by "common sympathies" (Rawls 1999:24, 25).

Compared to states, peoples perceive their interests inter alia in terms of honour.[32] Echoing the notion of self-respect in domestic societies, Rawls explains: "This interest is a people's proper self-respect of themselves as a people, resting on their common awareness of their trials during their history and of their culture with its accomplishments." This interest "shows itself in a people's **insisting on receiving from other people a proper respect and recognition of their equality**" (1999:34, 35, my emphasis).

The priority view underlying the eighth principle is equally applicable to cultural issues. The "duty to assist" has a specific focus, namely to alleviate "unfavourable conditions". What are these conditions? Those that prevent "a just or decent political and social regime" in which this proper respect and recognition of cultural equality are absent. Cultural injustice arises precisely where legitimate differences are denied political-legal protection, and where social conditions prevent people from experiencing "unselfconscious living" (see Kwenda 2003:73).

Rawls's emphasis on the "distinctiveness" of peoples has drawn criticism from cultural relativists (see Cohen 2004:117). His views, however, are based on his strong conviction that tolerance is a basic principle underlying international cooperation. There must be respect for peoples' freedom and independence (first principle); duty of non-intervention (principle 4), and the honouring of human rights (principle 6), which would – in the context of this paper – include the freedom to live under conditions of cultural justice in both national and global contexts. For Rawls this even includes the freedom to choose against ordering society according to liberal principles, whilst remaining "decent societies" (1999:64-67).

Philosophical conclusion

It was argued in section one that the preferential option for the poor is the basis of Latin American liberation theologies and has serious implications for our understanding of both distributive and cultural justice. Section two undertook a reading of Rawls to establish whether these forms of justice are present in their

---

32　See Rawls's extension of what Rousseau calls *amour-propre* (1992: 34, footnote 38), as well as his reliance on Rousseau's notion of the contract throughout his work (see 1999:7, 13 as an example).

partisan form as is the case in liberation theologies. We have seen that a Rawlsian proposal for an egalitarian and prioritarian conception of justice requires the priority of both the least advantaged representative individual in a domestic society, and the meeting of the basic needs of those peoples living under the most unfavourable conditions in a global society.

We now look at the work of well-known economist Joseph Stiglitz to discern whether and in what way he expresses the idea of partisan justice.

2.3 Partisan justice from an economic perspective: Joseph Stiglitz and the differential treatment of poor nations

It has to be said up front: Joseph Stiglitz, winner of the 2001 Nobel Prize for Economics and until January 2001 the chief economist of the World Bank, does not assume an ideological anti-globalisation position. He would, I assume, not be comfortable with some of the Christian prophetic critiques of globalisation that are strong on rhetoric, but weak in discernment and policy. He is committed to a market position and understands that economic globalisation is a complex phenomenon with both positive and negative consequences (Stiglitz 2006:22-23). His critique of economic globalisation, eloquently detailed in his bestseller *Globalization and its discontents* (2002), is fierce, but his ultimate aim is "to make it work".

Stiglitz commences his book *Making globalization work* (2006) with his interpretation of the slogan "Another world is possible", which is the motto of the World Social Forum, a gathering of 100 000 people in Mumbai, January 2004. One could isolate a number of important convictions that underpin his argument for the differential economic treatment of poorer nations. In arguing for such a differential trade system, he challenges a number of traditional, conservative economic views on market fundamentalism.

He rejects the separation of efficiency and equity considerations in the context of a market economy. The belief that markets and the pursuit of self-interest would – through an invisible hand – lead to economic efficiency is only partially true. If markets by themselves lead to socially unacceptable income distributions, questions around equity arise. And to address equity, economic policy has to include appropriate government intervention and regulation (see his reference to Keynes on page xvii!). Stiglitz argues that economic efficiency should not be isolated as the sole criterion of economic performance, but that so-called non-economic values such as "social justice, the environment, cultural diversity, universal access to health care, and consumer protection" should be co-determinants of economic success (Stiglitz 2006:xvii; see also xiv, 17, 22).

Stiglitz further rejects two long-standing premises of trade liberalisation. The first is that liberalisation of trade automatically leads to more trade and higher economic growth, and the second is that such growth inevitably leads to a "trickle-down" benefit for all (Stiglitz 2006:23, 99). Apart from his own research in information economics, he argues that neither economic history nor current economic theory supports these two premises. There are consequently no grounds to believe that the best way to help the poor is simply to strive for more liberalisation of trade and higher growth. Opening up the markets **alone** will not solve the problem of poverty, but may even make it worse (Stiglitz 2006:14).

In his only reference to Rawls (p. 296, footnote 15) Stiglitz does intimate that a fairer and more equitable trade system would "entail putting ourselves in others' shoes: what would we think is fair or right if we were in their position?" (Stiglitz 2006:22). What type of international trade regime would we, in Rawlsian terms, choose behind the veil of ignorance? It is in this context that Stiglitz argues for his **differential option for the poor** and – reminiscent of Rawls – suggests that trade regimes be judged by whether they make the poorest countries actually worse off (Stiglitz 2006:58).

When trade agreements were established between advanced industrial nations under GATT, the principles of non-discrimination, equality and reciprocity were upheld. Such countries would not discriminate against other members of GATT and each country treated all others the same – all were considered to be "the most favoured." This system of multinational trade was founded on strict reciprocity. Each country agreed to lower tariffs and to open up markets if the others reciprocated (Stiglitz 2006:75). Coupled to these arrangements was the principle of national treatment: foreign producers were subject to the same regulations as domestic ones.

When GATT was replaced by the WTO in 1995, these principles were carried over into the new, much more expanded trade regime. There is much hard empirical evidence (listed by Stiglitz 2006:77-78; 85-97) to show that an asymmetrical system, with grossly uneven playing fields and uneven implementation, subsequently evolved and that actually made developing countries worse off (Stiglitz 2006:58). What is needed is a global trade regime "that promotes the well-being of the poorest countries and that is, at the same time, good for advanced industrial countries as a whole," although current special corporate interest groups might suffer and lose some of their unfair advantages.[33]

In what he calls "fair trade for the poor" Stiglitz suggests a reform of international trade. This reform would entail that the principle of "reciprocity for and among all countries – regardless of circumstances" be replaced by the principle of "**reciprocity among equals, but differentiation between those in markedly different circumstances**" (Stiglitz 2006:83, my emphasis).

In practice, Stiglitz proposes a three-tier system of rich, middle-income and poor countries – a classification based on agreed empirical norms.[34] The rich countries open up their markets to others in their own group, but also to the middle-income and poor countries, but without reciprocity or political conditionality expected from the latter two groups. The middle-income group opens trade to all in its own group and to the poor countries without conditionality, but is not required to extend such preferences to the rich countries. In such a system developing nations will receive "special and differential treatment", as has already happened in some bilateral trade agreements[35] (Stiglitz 2006:83). However, such preferential treatment should not be voluntary, but should become part and parcel of WTO negotiations and be enforced in fields such as agriculture, tariffs and non-tariff barriers.

On what grounds would this proposal be accepted? Stiglitz consistently argues for two grounds: conscience/morality and self-interest. Concerning self-interest, he notes that greater stability and security in poor and developing nations will

---

33 Stiglitz 2006:82; on "special interests" see also 13, 24.
34 See Charlton (2005) for a similar argument.
35 See examples of such agreements from the EU in 2001.

contribute towards stability and security in the developed world (Stiglitz 2006:59). The flood of immigrants from poor to rich countries might be slowed down if the circumstances compelling people to leave are improved. Obviously there are also responsibilities on poor countries with regard to governance (Stiglitz 2006:58). A fairer trade regime would in the long run diminish the need for development aid and debt write-offs – mainly sponsored by developed countries. In fact, rich countries have cost poor countries three times more in trade restrictions than what they give in total development aid (Stiglitz 2006:78). The growth attained under a differential system has a far greater chance of actually benefiting everyone (excluding special interest groups).

The emphasis on morality must be seen in the context of Stiglitz's introduction of "non-economic" values as well as the retention of equity with efficiency. He does not argue his case at length, but simply states that to create a trade regime with differential and special treatment is a moral issue and a matter of conscience (Stiglitz 2006:100-101, 59). The empirical and social realities of poverty amongst and within countries are socially unacceptable and constitute moral appeals in themselves. "It appears that is better to be a cow in Europe than a poor person in a developing country," he writes (Stiglitz 2006:85), referring to agricultural subsidies for cows in the EU that are equivalent to the poverty line of $2 a day per person in poor countries.

One might conclude(albeit with some hesitation) that Stiglitz adds economic flesh to the theological and philosophical bones of the preferential option for the poor and the priority of the least advantaged representative man, or special assistance to burdened societies argued for above.

This concludes the trilogy of views that contend that a particular form of prioritarian (distributive) justice is morally defensible. It is now opportune to draw out some of the implications of this concurrence between views from the fields of theology, philosophy and economics.

4. IMPLICATIONS OF PARTISAN JUSTICE FOR LOCAL AND GLOBAL ETHICS

Following some of Bedford-Strohm's points (1993:306-313), several implications are listed as the conclusion to this essay.

First. There are obviously differences of interpretation, content and motivation between the three positions outlined above. Some might even suggest that my exposition suffers from a strong antecedent bias! Whatever these differences are, it is possible to see a synergy between a global ecumenical consensus, one of the most plausible political philosophies of the 20th century, and the work of a leading economist. This (constructed) consensus gives **social and political credence** to the notion of a preferential option for the poor. This synergy is no small achievement as it bears witness to the influence of theological ethics (broadly speaking) on political theory, but in turn provides evidence of secular arguments for and confirmation of a primary theological notion. The option for the poor is obviously open to different interpretations and some may even speak up against it; but the fact of the matter is: this option can no longer be ignored. Not by Christians who read the Bible or take the voice of the church seriously, and who could reject the notion as mere "political talk". Nor can this option be ignored by rational secularists who would under normal circumstance be prone to reject the idea as merely "church talk". Partisan justice is firmly on the international political and economic agenda - and it has legitimacy.

Second. One of the strongest criticisms of the option for the poor has been that is strong prophetic talk, but unless given more precise content on principles of (re)distribution, it would serve only a narrow rhetorical function. Poverty is obviously a relative concept: the poor in one society (Belgium) may be rich when compared with another (Somalia). Liberation theologians in particular attempted to define "the poor" in material, socio-cultural and spiritual terms (see Pixley & Boff 1989:166). It is possible today to extend definitions of the poor to our global society and work with adjusted empirical data of the baseline (expressed in, for example, dollar terms) below which people will be considered poor. Theological and church literature did not put forward a practical measure to guide redistributive policies that would ensure the option for the poor and reduce inequalities. The value that Rawls adds is to develop a universal criterion which formally addresses any situation, no matter how and where this baseline is set: inequalities are allowed only insofar as they benefit the least advantaged representative person in a particular society or the least advantage peoples in a global setting. And the value that Stiglitz adds is that he is able to integrate differential treatment of poorer nations into the very procedures and agendas of current trade negotiations, suggesting practical ways of implementation.

Third. The option for the poor assists us to understand the crucial importance of another form of justice, namely **participative justice**. Bedford-Strohm makes the astute observation that both material and socio-cultural poverty find their origin in "fehlende Teilhabe" ("inadequate participation"; 1993:169). People are materially poor because of a lack of participation in the (in)formal economy – that is one of the most urgent issues in discussions of global economic justice today. And people are socio-culturally poor because they are excluded and marginalised from full participation in society on the basis of their race or culture or gender or something else. Participative justice breaks through the paternalism and ultimate failure of development aid, where "things are done for the poor", and establishes a crucial link – clearly demonstrated by Rawls and insisted upon by liberation theologians– between democracy and egalitarian, well-ordered societies. Distributive and cultural justice in their focused form as partisan justice can only be realised through extending participative justice.

Fourth. All three proponents of the option for the poor emphasise that – contrary to popular perception – this option is not exclusive, but precisely **inclusive**.

God's solidarity with the poor – so clear in the biblical trajectories – is a pastoral and not a salvation-historical notion. It requires a prioritising not exclusion. That Jesus sides with the poor and was poor himself in no way detracts from the universal significance of his cross and resurrection. Care for the poor, the widows and the orphans are a sign of a just, covenant community in which all are involved. James teaches that showing no preferential treatment to the rich serves the whole faith community and is the mark of a sincere religion before God.

Rawls has similar intentions. The choices made in the original position, where all participate equally behind the veil of ignorance according to the maximin principle, are designed precisely to contribute to a stable, well-ordered society, locally as well as globally.

Stiglitz acknowledges that the situation of a super-rich North and dismally poor South is not sustainable in the long run. Nor does an extreme gap between rich and poor within one nation contribute to social stability, because such stability is a basic requirement for all to achieve fulfilment in life. His proposal of a three-tier trade arrangement ensures the inclusion of the poor nations and participation under conditions of differential treatment. This links up with the inter-play between conscience and self-interest that he puts forward. A differential treatment of poor countries includes – and in the long run actually benefits – the rich. It is aimed at a global system in which trade is not a zero-sum, but a positive-sum game (Stiglitz 2006:99).

In short: whether you argue from a deontological or instrumental ethical perspective, the option for the poor is an **inclusive** strategy worthy of universal support.

Fifth. It is quite evident that the option for the poor is a **critical** notion. It is not just another interesting theory amongst other. It has the ability to allow us to assess and judge current socio-economic policies and outcomes. In terms of Gustafson's stratification of moral language, the option for the poor can make the transition from prophetic to policy statements. There is not room here to develop a detailed example, but it has been suggested[36] that the core indicator of public policy should not be economic GDP growth, but whether the past year has led to an improvement in the position of the least advantaged persons/groups in society. An annual "poverty report" should be the primary driving factor behind public policy as well as the basis for a policy or cabinet score-card at the end of each year. The same holds for international trade: the question is not simply whether trade has increased in volume or financial terms, but whether a trade regime has led to the improvement of the poor countries' relative position measured over time.

It does not take a lot of imagination to see the radical impact on public policies of the preferential option for the poor as expressed in the notion of partisan justice. Some empirical case studies are needed to test partisan justice as a form of applied ethics.

BIBLIOGRAPHY

Bedford-Strohm, Heinrich 1993. *Vorrang für die Armen. Auf dem Weg zu einer theologischen Theorie der Gerechtighkeit*. Gütersloh: Chr. Kaiser Verlag.

Boff, Clodovis 1983. *Theology and praxis: epistemological foundations*. New York: Orbis.

Boff, Leonardo 1988. *Trinity and society*. New York: Orbis.

Boff Leonardo & Boff, Clodovis 1984. *Salvation and liberation*. New York: Orbis.

Boff Leonardo & Boff, Clodovis 1987. *Introducing liberation theology*. New York: Orbis.

Buchanan, A 2000. Rawls's Law of Peoples: Rules for a vanished Westphalian world. *Ethics* 110 (4): 697-721.

Charlton, Andrew 2005 A proposal for special treatment in market access for developing countries in the Doha round. In *Trade policy research 2005*, edited by John M. Curtis and Dan Ciuriak. Ottawa: Department of International Trade.

---

36   See Bedford-Strohm 1993:317.

Cohen, Josua 2004. The importance of philosophy: Reflections on John Rawls. *South African Journal of Philosophy* 23/2, 113-119.

Ellacuria, Ignacio and Sobrino Jon (eds) 1993. *Mysterium Liberationis. Fundamental concepts of liberation theology*. New York: Orbis.

Frankfurt, HG 1987. Equality as a moral ideal. *Ethics* 98 (1): 21-43.

Gorgulho, da Silva Gilberto 1993. Biblical hermeneutics. In Ellacuria and Sobrino, 123-149.

Gutierrez, Gustavo 1973. *A theology of liberation*. London: SCM.

Gutierrez, Gustavo 1993. Option for the poor. In Ellacuria and Sobrino, 235-250.

Kwenda, Chirevo V 2003. Cultural justice: the pathway to reconciliation and social cohesion. In Chidester, David, Dexter, Philip and Wilmot, James. 2003. *What hold us together. Social cohesion in South Africa*. Cape Town: HSRC Press, 67-80.

Lategan, Bernard C and Vorster, Willem S 1985. *Text and reality. Aspects of reference in biblical texts*. Atlanta: Scholars Press.

Lois, Juan 1993. Christology in the Theology of Liberation. In Ellacuria and Sobrino, 168-193.

Maimela, Simon and König, Adrio 2001. *Initiation into theology*. Pretoria: Van Schaik.

Moltmann, Jürgen 1981. *The church in the power of the Spirit. A contribution to messianic ecclesiology*. London: SCM.

Naude, PJ 1987. *Ortopraksie as metodologiese prinsipe in die sistematiese teologie*. Ongepubliseeerde DTh-tesis. Stellenbosch: Universiteit van Stellenbosch.

Naude, Piet 2005. The ethical challenge of identity formation and cultural justice in a globalizing world. *Scriptura* 89, 536-549.

Oliveros, Roberto 1993. History of the Theology of Liberation. In Ellacuria and Sobrino, 3-32.

Pixley, George V and Boff, Clodovis 1989. *The Bible, the church and the poor*. New York: Orbis.

Rawls, John 1971. *A theory of justice*. Oxford: OUP.

Rawls, John 1999. *The law of peoples*. Cambridge, Massachusetts: Harvard University Press.

Roemer. John E 1998. *Theories of distributive justice*. Cambridge, Massachusetts: Harvard University Press.

Sobrino, Jon 1984. *The true church and the poor*. New York: Orbis.

Sen, Amartya 1988. *On ethics and economics*. Oxford: Blackwell.

Stiglitz, Joseph, E 2002. *Globalization and its discontents*. New York: WW Norton.

Stiglitz, Joseph, E 2006. *Making globalization work*. New York: WW Norton.

Van Niekerk, Anton A 2004. Principles of global distributive justice: moving beyond Rawls and Buchanan. *South African Journal of Philosophy* 23/2: 171-194.

West, Gerald 1995. *Biblical hermeneutics of liberation: Modes of reading the Bible in the South African context*. New York: Orbis.

West, Gerald. 1999. *Academy of the poor: towards a dialogical reading of the bible*. Sheffield: Sheffield Academic Press.

World Council of Churches 1991. *Confessing the one faith. An ecumenical explication of the Apostolic faith as it is confessed in the Nicene-Constantinopolitan Creed (381)*. Geneva: WCC.

1.3 BETWEEN HUMILITY AND BOLDNESS

Explicating human rights from a Christian perspective[1]

1. INTRODUCTION: A CAUTION TO REMAIN HUMBLE

A reflection on the link between Christian theology and human rights in their 20th-century manifestations should start with a note of humility. Although one may construct a historical and conceptual relation between Christian theology and the *Universal Declaration of Human Rights* (1948), there are a number of reasons why such a relation varies widely – from strong support to active opposition.

The notion of an inalienable human dignity that underpins human rights has been linked to the creation of humans in the image of God (Gen 1:26). To this we return below, but the strong influence of the doctrine of hereditary sin inhibited the development of rights based on universal dignity. It is precisely because of sin that humans are unworthy and therefore not in a position to claim rights.

The notion of a common humanity – crucial for the development of universal rights – was eroded by the sharp distinction at various stages of history between what was considered orthodox versus heterodox; true Christians versus heretics; cultured, civilised, Western Christianity versus uncivilised, inaccessible, indigenous peoples; Jews and anti-Semitic movements; and – in contemporary times – Christian culture and values versus those of Islam.

One can still discern some Judeo-Christian roots for the rights of all persons in the early sixteenth century: Luther's interpretation in 1521 of the *Magnificat* clearly refers to human beings' rights to life and property and the "higher goods" of faith and the gospel, as well as freedom of conscience before the state (Huber 1992: 580). Calvin's notion about religious freedom and the ethical responsibilities of the covenant fostered the idea of reciprocal rights and duties. And the papal bull *Sublimis Deus* of 1537 regarded non-European Indians as "true persons", able to participate in the Catholic faith and sacraments (Huber 1992: 579).

Once the humanist notion of an autonomous individual person developed, where worth and dignity are seen in secular terms, it was very difficult for Christian theology to regain lost ground.

Although the English and American revolutions were still shaped by a Christian creation theology and anthropology, the French revolution was in fact anti-clerical and fundamentally secularist. After Locke, who established pre-state rights based on the dignity of humans in their natural state, and after Kant who established an argument for the equal worth of all persons in the autonomy of reason, from the 18th century onwards the notion of human rights was built on an anthropocentric and sometimes atheistic foundations.

---

1   The German version of this paper was written by invitation for a special edition of *Ökumenische Rundschau* (2007/1) on human rights and the ecumenical church.

The paradox of theology in Enlightenment and post-Enlightenment times was that, although the roots of human rights could at least partially be claimed by the Christian tradition until the 16th century, mainline confessional traditions began to consider the humanist ideas underlying human rights as a body of thought that should be resisted. The motivations for such resistance obviously differed.

Catholics saw secular humanism and liberalist ideas of freedom as a threat to the ecclesial and political authority of the church; Protestants rejected the underlying optimistic anthropology that was steeped in a form of materialism, thereby negating justification through faith and self-knowledge through being known by God. The specific situation for Germany as summarised by Huber and Tödt may be typical of a wider trend: "In the nineteenth and in the first half of the twentieth century, German Protestantism encountered human rights mainly from a critical, if not hostile, distance" (1977:45, my translation).

Official theological endorsement and support for the 20th-century notion of human rights as expressed in the Universal Declaration are therefore rare before 1948. One could refer to Pope Leo XII's *Rerum Novarum* (1891) as a bold statement on the equal worth of all people, and we must not exclude Christian involvement through the *Commission of the Churches on International Affairs* (CCIA, established 1946) in the securing of religious rights in the Declaration itself.

It was only after 1948, however, that theological responses from all traditions began to emerge slowly but surely. Even then there was theological resistance in some cases. In South Africa the white Reformed churches adopted an explicitly negative stance toward human rights on the basis of two broad considerations: the idea that humans could claim inherent natural rights in an autonomous manner contradicts Scripture where God's grace is the source of rights; and individual rights cannot be claimed without rights for communities (see Du Toit 1984:7-9). Though both points have some validity in themselves, one should read them within an ideological-critical framework to understand what they actually meant in the historical context between 1948 and 1974, when this view was first published (NG Kerk 1974:72).

Yes, Christian theology today should approach the issue of human rights with a humility born of our paradoxical past. Our tradition has been both a source of support of, and of resistance against, human rights in their modern form. Historically, the religious wars in Europe had already pointed away from religion as the common foundation for society and an emerging world order. We know from modern and contemporary history that religion may be a source and the very focal point of conflict. This can be based on intra-confessional grounds, as in Northern Ireland and apartheid South Africa, or on inter-religious conflicts such as those in the Middle East and Sudan.

I am convinced, however, that humility need not lead to silence. The question is not whether Christian theology should speak, but rather how and what it should say. This immediately raises the methodological question: How shall we approach a discussion of human rights theologically?

2. A FEW METHODOLOGICAL CONSIDERATIONS

There are basically two opposing views on the grounding (*Begründung*) of human rights in the convictions of Christian theology.

2.1 There are those who claim that such grounding is indeed possible and that it is very important to show the Christian foundations of human rights as such. Prime examples of this view are the Catholic and Reformed approaches to human rights.

Typical of their theological approach, Catholics are able to ground human rights in both the natural law tradition (see Hughes 1998) and in the salvation-historical perspective of the special grace of God in Christ. The recently published *Compendium of the Social Doctrine of the Church* states clearly: "Faith and reason represent the two cognitive paths of the Church's social doctrine: revelation and human nature," establishing a complementary relation between the truth of revelation and the truth of human nature (2004: 41). The ultimate source of human rights is therefore found both "in man himself and in God his Creator" (2004: 83). Human rights are built on the dignity of the human person as primary principle of social doctrine, followed by the common good, subsidiarity and solidarity (2004:88).

The Reformed position is obviously theologically different, but structurally it shares the conviction of a grounding of human rights in theological doctrine. In the context of the World Alliance of Reformed Churches, Moltmann writes as follows:

> On the ground of the creation of man and woman in the image of God, on the ground of the incarnation of God for reconciliation of the world, and on the ground of the coming kingdom of God as consummation of history, the concern entrusted to Christian theology is one for the humanity of persons as well as for their ongoing rights and duties. The specific task of Christian theology in these matters is grounding fundamental human rights on God's right to – i.e., his claim on human beings, their human dignity, their fellowship, their rule over the earth, and their future (Moltmann 1977:130).

By grounding human rights in creation, incarnation and eschatology, Reformed theology shifts the basis of these rights away from the natural law tradition, from an idealist anthropology and from these rights' assumed origin in evolutionary historical processes (Lochman 1977:21). In this way the theo-logical contribution to human rights is underscored, claiming their universal regard by all.

2.2 The opposite view is that one should not attempt such a grounding of human rights in theology. Again the motivations for this view are greatly differentiated, although structurally the same.

2.2.1 Erich Weingärtner's article on Human Rights in *Dictionary of the Ecumenical Movement* takes a fairly negative view of the history alluded to above: "In the light of early official church opposition to human rights, that they viewed for much of their history as the product of humanistic philosophy, the claim of a 'theological basis of human rights' might be considered somewhat presumptuous". Where churches attempt to derive human rights from traditional theological concepts, it may be construed as an *a posteriori* attempt, functionalising theology to regain churches' credibility "or to justify Christian engagement in human rights activities" (Weingärtner 2002: 550).

2.2.2 The specific **Christian** grounding of human rights inevitably implies the particularising of rights to the view of one religion, whilst these rights should by their very nature be universal to have any global effect. "An exclusive Christian grounding contradicts the fact that the concept of human rights itself will only be taken seriously if the access of all people, irrespective of their religious or political convictions, are held open to them".[2] Where human rights are exclusively grounded in the specifics of the Christian tradition, a certain monopolising and imperialist tendency emerges, even against the intentions of theologians and churches who do this exactly to support human rights.

Let us turn to more specific theological arguments for opposition to the grounding of human rights in theology.

2.2.3 The traditional structure of Lutheran theology in terms of the two kingdoms is very useful in establishing a theological link with human rights in a different way. By assuming the two domains of the sacred/the church and the secular/the state, Lutherans are able to honour the secular nature of modern human rights without having to embrace secularism or its concomitant autonomous anthropology. The key lies in Luther's distinction between the gospel of grace that guides the church in love, and the universal significance of the law that precedes both Israel and the church, and establishes universal principles of justice accessible to all.

The Lutheran World Federation states clearly in its *Theological Perspectives on Human Rights* (1977) that "we need reason, illuminated by the law and the Gospel guided by love, in order as Christians to deal responsibly with human rights". This rational approach to the issues of earthly life stands in contrast to the biblical faith that is normative in the life of the church. It is consequently "not our task to deduce (human rights) theologically from specifically Christian premises" (quoted in RES 1983:41).

2.2.4 Latin American liberation theologies developed a theological method that seeks its point of departure in the experience of the suffering poor on the "underside" of history. "Theology is a critical reflection on Christian praxis in the light of the Word", says Gutierrez in his classical *A theology of liberation* (1973:13). This theology starts with an analysis of the historical situation of oppression with a view to discovering its meaning in the light of the gospel "with the purpose of making the Christians' commitment more radical and clear" (1973:13).

To be honest, liberation theologians from Korea, Africa and North America would argue that the question of grounding human rights in pre-existing theological categories is not their urgent concern. Seeing that theology is the theory of a definite practice based on the experience of oppression, the theoretical question of "grounding" is not their primary interest. The need for and the role of human rights as part of securing political and economic liberation are acknowledged, but the exact grounding of these rights in theology is not explicitly on the agenda.

In a situation of life and death one does not have the luxury of an articulated prior justification to struggle for liberation. One could say with HR Reuter that "Human

---

2 Huber (1992: 583, my translation). See the discussion of Martin Honecker by Huber/Tödt (1977:68).

rights demands are ... to be understood as a historic answer to **exemplary experiences of injustice**" (quoted by Link 2004:207; emphasis in the original; my translation).

2.2.5 From a completely opposite angle, evangelical and charismatic theologies could also be classified in groups who do not link the grounding of human rights with theology. The "evangelical" churches and "charismatic" groups are hugely diverse, and (as in most cases above) one is compelled to draw very broad outlines in which some representatives of these groups might not fully recognise themselves. (The construction of typologies and models always represents a paradoxical challenge: there is a gain in overall clarity and prospect, but a loss of particulars and detail).

The evangelical view is more coherent and has undergone a definite shift away from the traditional dualism between "socio-political issues", on the one hand, and "evangelical mission", on the other. In the first phase up to the *Lausanne Covenant* of 1974 the world is seen by evangelicals as a sinful place, and, although some good remains, the kingdom of God is primarily transcendent, and there is little hope of reforming the structures of society. Salvation is highly personal, the church is a haven and refuge, and its task in the world is personal witness through mission, and not to become involved in reforming social structures – or by implication – fighting for human rights.

In this regard, there is some agreement with charismatic groups/churches whose view on reality is constructed in terms of the struggle between the devil and Christ, darkness and light. We now live in the dispensation of the power of the Spirit, manifest in healing and exorcism. This is the motivation for reborn Christians to continue as soldiers of spiritual warfare in the expectation of Christ's imminent and triumphant return.

It is evident that this kind of theology is not open to the idea of grounding social reform and human rights in Christian categories. Although some of these groups are involved in social charity projects, their theological framework renders a theoretical justification for human rights unnecessary.

The developments in evangelical theology between 1974 and the Grand Rapids consultation of 1982 close the gap between "social activity" and "evangelism". The report *Evangelism and Social Responsibility – an Evangelical Commitment* attempts to see social activity as a consequence of evangelism, as a bridge to and a partner of evangelism (see Reformed Ecumenical Synod 1983:51-52). The tension remains, however, and the clear but uneasy distinction between social action and evangelism will probably inhibit evangelical theology from making a sustained contribution towards understanding the link between Christian faith and human rights. The evangelical understanding of a comprehensive salvation – personal, communal and societal – does hold some promise for the future.

2.3 The question now arises: Is there a third way possible between grounding human rights in theology and rejection of such a process? Here I wish to refer to the creative and well-known attempt by Huber and Tödt to construct a model of "Analogie und Differenz" (analogy and difference).

Huber and Tödt are critical of both Catholic and Reformed efforts as outlined above, but at the same time do not endorse a discussion of human rights without clear theological criteria (Honecker), or based only on limited theological parallels (Rendtorff).

They reject the notion of grounding (*Begründung*) if that implies deductive reasoning where human rights are derived and legitimised from selected antecedent theological premises. "These rights cannot be extrapolated from theological major premises" (Huber und Tödt 1977:158, my translation). They are also not willing to accept the emergence and further establishment of human rights as a purely secular process devoid of a theological contribution. "We therefore accept that there are aspects of human rights that stand in **analogy** to what faith as a gift of God unlocks for all human persons, but that, simultaneously, there is a **difference** between each human-historical community if compared to what we clearly discern in our participation in the reign of God expressed in the body of Christ" (Huber und Tödt 1977:162, my emphases and translation).

What is the task of theology then? It can be expressed as a threefold task, namely to **provide access** (*Zugang*) to the historical development of human rights, to **foster a deeper understanding** of human rights from a Christian perspective, and to **contribute to the struggle for the realisation** (*Verwirklichung*) of these rights (158).

How is this task accomplished? The answer lies in two dialectical movements: the one starts off with "the basic outline of human rights" that are explained "in their analogy and difference to the basic tenets of the Christian faith" (see pp. 162-175, my translation). The other moves in the opposite direction and allows us to interpret "specific theological dimensions... in their significance for our thoughts on human rights" (Huber und Tödt 1977:160, my translation; see pp. 175-193).

I personally prefer the first movement as it accepts the achievement and development of human rights in their paradoxical relation to theology, and places theology in the more humble but very important role of explication, and not grounding. This explication is now explored in section 3 below.

3. THE EXPLICATION OF HUMAN RIGHTS FROM A THEO-LOGICAL PERSPECTIVE

3.1 There is little doubt that the core question facing us in a discussion of human rights is: Wherein lies the dignity of the human person?

Is it derived from the nature of things or natural law? Is it embedded in the self-reflecting being (Descartes)? Does it lie in the *Vernunft* of the autonomous individual (Kant), or the self-realising, subjective spirit (Hegel)? Should we look to Africa and derive dignity from *ubuntu*, the energy that exudes from every human being?

Christian theology (with Judaism and Islam) interprets human dignity theo-logically: Human beings are created in the image of God and this is the foundation of human dignity (see Moltmann 1999:119, 122; Link 2004:211-212).

In this way both the analogy and difference between human rights and Christian theology are evident. This inalienable dignity is endorsed by both (*Analogie*), but the reference point is not the same (*Differenz*). The EKD report *Die Menschenrechte im ökumenischen Gespräch* states unambiguously: "The Enlightenment's concept of man is not identical with the Christian one... he is entitled to these rights because of his rational nature. Christian faith disputes this rational understanding of man if and when it sees him on his own and understands and explains him from within" (EKD 1979:13, my translation). This self-referentiality is exchanged for a theological reference point: each human person is created *imago dei*.

3.2 The next logical question is: In what way can *imago dei* concretely elucidate human rights? The answer may be sought in an exploration of the question: **Who is God** in whose image we are created?

The "image of God" is a fundamentally relational concept that moves as it were in two directions. It firstly relates human beings' dignity to their being created in the image of the triune God, and an exploration of this God yields fruitful results for our understanding and realisation of human rights. But God's immanence, Karl Rahner has taught us, is only known through God's economy. Therefore the historical revelation of God in creation and history is just as important for a Christian interpretation of human rights.

Let us briefly explore these two viewpoints on God's immanence and economy.

The Christian tradition concurs that this creator God is a unity of three distinct Persons, described (in somewhat patriarchal language) as Father, Son and Holy Spirit. We know from Scripture that the Father created us in the image of the Son, the archetype of God's image (Col 1), and that the Holy Spirit is the One who continually renews us into conformity with the Son. "The image of God is then that being which takes shape by virtue of the creating and redeeming agency of the triune God" (Gunton 1993: 117; see Koopman 2003:197).

Without exploring the detail of dogmatic history here, one could say that the creative tension between distinct personhood and reciprocal indwelling (*perichoresis*) in the Trinity provides important clues for our understanding of human rights.

Individual human rights, requiring freedom and equality, reflect the unique and distinct Personhood of the triune God. The three Persons each have their own identity and are ascribed specific deeds in salvation history in which the other Persons are always also present, but which never violate each Person's distinctiveness.

Social rights, requiring participation, reflect the plurality and participative community of divine Persons, where the Father creates through the Son and the Spirit; where the Son is resurrected by the Father through the power of the Spirit; and where the Spirit proceeds from the Father and teaches the truth that the Son reveals.

If God created us in God's image of man-and-wife, the right of marriage and family, **gender equality and procreative rights** are indeed embedded in the aeteological creation accounts. So is our duty toward the **rights of future generations** that come about because of the blessing of procreation, to multiply and fill the earth (Gen 2). It makes no sense to have children whose very safety and livelihood are threatened by our overstepping the ecological capacity of the earth, or misusing technology to develop weapons of mass destruction.

If God declares his creation good and asks us to be its guardian, this clearly supersedes any anthropocentric notion of human uniqueness and provides an explanation of **ecological rights**, including the rights of animals and other living species (Ps 8; Ps

104). "As the image of the Creator, human beings will love all their fellow creatures with the Creator's love." The image of the Creator requires from us to be a "lover of all the living" (Moltmann 1999:132; see Conradie 2003:313-314)

If God reveals Godself as One who cares especially for widows, orphans, foreigners, refugees, the marginalised and the poor, **socio-economic rights** in the context of a global economy must be pursued within the perspective of the "Vorrang für die Armen" ("preference for the poor"; Bedford-Strohm 1993). The realisation of this "Vorrang" is indeed constitutive of our living out the image of God by standing where the righteous God stands, namely with the poor and against the mighty (Belhar Confession, article 4; see the text in Cloete and Smit 1984).

This is just a glimpse of what the systematic theological task in relation to human rights might entail. If space would allow this, the development of freedom, equality and participation as core principles of human rights could be reconstructed from a Trinitarian perspective. But this is a task for another occasion.

3.3 The important question in our contemporary situation is not only what contribution "internal" Christian theological resources could make, but whether we do not urgently require a "theology of the religions" that could underpin inter-religious dialogue. The controversial but important contributions of Hans Küng need to be mentioned here. He was instrumental in the drafting of the *Declaration toward a Global Ethic* accepted by the Parliament of World Religions in 1993, followed by a *Universal Declaration of Human Responsibilities* in 1997. There can be no world peace without peace between the religions, he argued prophetically in 1991.

In terms of this essay, one must reiterate the need for interpretation of human rights from the unique perspective of different religions. This plurality is important, because the support for human rights (if indeed that is the outcome) will only gain credibility in non-Western contexts if religious leaders in the Middle East, Latin America, Africa, India, Japan and China make the case from their specific religious points of view. Let us not fear analogies and differences here!

Despite ecological depravation and weapons of mass destruction, all religions face and share the same planet. Indeed, as Paul Knitter wrote, "no peace with the earth without peace between the religions." There are, writes Sean McDonagh, "no Catholic lakes, Protestant rivers or Muslim forests" (see Conradie 2003:329, 330 for references).

The development of criteria and guidelines for fruitful inter-faith dialogue is one of the most urgent items on the ecumenical agenda in the first half of the 21st century.

4. THE RELATIVITY OF HUMAN RIGHTS

This essay started off on a plea for humility from theology. It now concludes with a call for humility from the proponents of human rights. This latter call is based on the relativity of human rights discourse and practices.

4.1 As long as the discourse on rights takes its presuppositions from **human** rights, "does this not imply that a certain anthropocentrism is hermeneutically inevitable?" (Conradie 2003:314-5). In other words: can we use rights language to describe the rights of other living species without an unintended, implied reference to their "usefulness" for homo sapiens? Can a human rights language be really universal if it by implication excludes the huge reality of non-human species and non-living creation as such? Should we not replace universal rights with **cosmic** rights? If so, what does this mean for theology and the use of theological metaphors, or should we accept the anthropocentric bias of the linguistic turn?

4.2 Human rights are **relative to their own historical development** in Western Europe and North America. We know that the philosophical anthropology and specific historical events that underlie the development of human rights in their 20th-century form are different from their manifestations in Africa, the Middle East and the Far East. The difficult question is whether the assumed universality of human rights is not the merely a reflection of specific Western developments (see Lindholt 1997). Or is there, despite the particular histories and philosophies, a certain supra-cultural truth implied by the declaration of human rights? Or even if we acknowledge their relativity, does it matter now that the original rights to personal freedom were extended to include second- and third-generation rights, precisely to respond to situations outside the West? Must all people now accept human rights as a common legacy, because we need a certain "modernist" centre, an agreed moral charter, to live harmoniously in a pluralist, global world? If one rejects human rights as "Western", what is the alternative?

4.3 The power or otherwise of human rights is also **relative to the historical and geographical particularities of their application.** Let me use South Africa, my home country, again as an example in a very sketchy way.

The declaration of human rights was accepted in the same year that the National Party came into power in South Africa (1948). This party systematically introduced race-based policies on a comprehensive personal and all-encompassing spatial scale. Later, when the resistance to apartheid increased, gross human rights violations were committed by the security forces. The system was underpinned by a moral legitimacy derived from neo-Calvinist, Kuyperian Christian theology that *inter alia* led to the formation of race-based churches in the same Reformed family (see Naudé 2005).

In a situation that was shielded from the impact of modernity and secularism, the struggle against apartheid was not fought through a recourse to human rights, but through exposing the false Gospel on which a so-called "Christian society" was built. Both proponents and opponents of apartheid theology knew that the battle was indeed one of ecclesiology (the unity of church), Christology (reconciliation in Christ) and justice before God.

Yes, after 1994 and the adoption of a bill of human rights in our Constitution, as well as the country rejoining the global world, a theology without recourse to a human rights discourse is unthinkable (see Villa-Vicencio 1995). But to claim that no political liberation is possible without human rights is to overestimate their power and to underestimate other social forces in the absence of modernity, materialism and secularism.

4.4 Human rights are clearly also **relative to their limited application in the Christian church**. The church may support freedom of expression in society but, for the sake of her identity, she limits freedom of speech to the orthodox boundaries of the faith community. The church may support freedom of religion in society, but cannot match such freedom with membership of the faith community that confesses Christ and not Mohammed or Buddha or atheism. In some churches full equality between men and women, or between officials and laity, has not yet been realised, or is even resisted. In the ethical realm it is possible in a situation of state-church separation to acknowledge the equal marriage rights of gay persons under the Constitution, but still maintain that for the church such marriages fall outside her notion of holy matrimony.

4.5 The pursuit of human rights is **relative to the uncomfortable truth of the gospel of love**. Over against an attitude of entitlement to human rights (on whatever grounds) stands the utterly foolish message: Greater love has nobody than to give up his/her right to life for the sake of a brother and sister. Follow the Son of Man, who did not come to establish his right to be served (Mark 10:45), but – though rabbi and master – washed the feet of his disciples. The same attitude should be in us that was in Christ, who did not cling to his right to the Godhead, but humiliated himself until a God-forsaken and unprotected death on the cross (Philippians 2).

The intention of this section on relativity is not at all to diminish the importance of human rights. It aims to warn against an imperialist human rights propaganda, or an idolatrous faith in human rights as our deepest source of hope for the future.

5. A SHORT CONCLUDING WORD

From where I write in Africa, amidst glaring poverty and the Aids pandemic, the most important matter is not new declarations of intent regarding human rights, but their actual implementation so that people can regain their God-given dignity. The task of this systematic reflection was to illuminate, interpret and support the realisation of human rights from a Christian perspective on a global scale. For this we need the commitment of the ecumenical church.

BIBLIOGRAPHY

Bedford-Strohm, Heinrich 1993. *Vorrang für die Armen. Auf dem Weg zu einer theologischen Theorie der Gerechtigkeit*. Gütershloh: Chr Kaiser/Gütershloher Verlaghaus.

Cloete, GD and Smit DJ (eds) 1984. *A moment of truth*. Grand Rapids: Eerdmans.

Conradie, Ernst M 2003. On a human rights culture in a global era. Some ecological perspectives. In: Karin Sporre and Russel Botman (eds) *Building a human rights culture. South African and Swedish perspectives*. Falun: Hogskolan Dalarna, 311- 333.

Du Toit, DA 1984. *Menseregte. 'n Empiriese en teoretiese ondersoek vanuit teologies-etiese perspektief*. Pretoria: RGN.

EKD 1979. *Die Menschenrechte im ökumenischen Gespräch*. Gütershloh: Gütersloher Verlaghaus Gerd Mohn.

Gunton, Colin 1993. *The One, the Three and the Many. God, creation and the culture of modernity.* Cambridge: Cambridge University Press.

Gutierrez, Gustavo, 1973. *A theology of liberation.* New York: Orbis.

Huber, Wolfgang 1992. Menschenrechte/Menschenwürde. *TRE,* Band XXII, 577-595.

Huber, Wolfgang und Tödt, Heinz Eduard 1977. *Menschenrechte. Perspektiven einer menschlichen Welt.* Stuttgart: Kreuz Verlag.

Hughes, Gerard J 1998. Natural law. In Bernard Hoose (ed.) *Christian ethics. An introduction.* London: Continuum, 47-56.

Koopman, Nico 2003. Trinitarian anthropology, ubuntu and human rights. In: Karin Sporre and Russel Botman (eds) *Building a human rights culture. South African and Swedish perspectives.* Falun: Hogskolan Dalarna, 194-207.

Kűng, Hans 1991. *Global responsibility: In search of a new world ethic.* New York: Crossroad.

Lindholt, Lone 1997. *Questioning the universality of human rights: the African Charter on Human and People's Rights in Botswana, Malawi and Mozambique.* Aldershot: Ashgate

Link, Christian 2004. Menschenrechte. Eine ökumensiche Herausforderung. In: Lena Lybaek, Konrad Raiser, Stefanie Schardien (Hrsg.) *Gemeinschaft der Kirchen und gesellschaftliche Verantwortung.* (Festschrift für Professor Dr. Erich Geldbach), Münster: Lit Verlag, 201-212.

Lochman, Jan Milic 1977. Human rights from a Christian perspective. In: Allen O. Miller (ed.) *A Christian declaration on human rights. Theological Studies of the World Alliance of Reformed Churches,* Grand Rapids: Eerdmans, 13-24.

Moltmann, Jürgen 1977. A definitive study paper: A Christian declaration on human rights. In: Allen O. Miller (ed.) *A Christian declaration on human rights. Theological Studies of the World Alliance of Reformed Churches,* Grand Rapids: Eerdmans, 129-143.

Moltmann, Jürgen 1999. *God for a secular society. The public relevance of theology.* Minneapolis: Fortress Press.

Naudé, Piet 2005. From pluralism to ideology: The roots of apartheid theology in Gustav Warneck, Abraham Kuyper, and theological Pietism. *Scriptura* 88:161-173.

Nederduits Gereformeerde Kerk 1974. *Ras, volk en nasie en volkereverhoudings in die lig van die Skrif.* Kaapstad: NG Kerk Uitgewers.

Pontifical Council for Justice and Peace 2004. *Compendium of the social doctrine of the church.* Nairobi: Paulines Publications Africa.

Reformed Ecumenical Synod 1983. *RES testimony on human rights.* Grand Rapids: Reformed Ecumenical Synod.

Villa-Vicencio, Charles 1992. *A theology of reconstruction: nation-building and human rights.* Cape Town: David Philip.

Weingärtner, Erich 2002. Human rights. *Dictionary of the ecumenical movement.* Geneva: WCC, 549-552.

1.4 "AM I MY BROTHER'S KEEPER?"

An African reflection on humanisation

This essay[1] is a substantial reworking of an address given by invitation at the annual Ugandan parliamentary breakfast on 8 October 2010 in Kampala. It is therefore a deeply contextual text – presented by an African in Africa and for Africans. By its very nature it can be seen as public theology and ethics in action, as the address focuses on topical (public) issues in Africa and was given "in the open" with President Museveni, cabinet ministers, judges, generals and members of parliament in attendance, including dignitaries from other nations in Africa and around the world.

"Am I my brother's keeper?" was chosen as theme for the 2010 event and it was left to the speaker to address the topic with his own interpretation.

1. STRATEGIES OF DEHUMANISATION

Africa is marked by deep ambiguities. It is a continent of immense natural beauty and bountiful resources. It is home to just under a billion people with a rich diversity of cultures, languages and religions. According to paleontological research, this continent is the motherland of *human sapiens*, the origin of all people on earth. Its benign weather conditions in most parts and fertile lands make this a wonderful continent on which to live and work.

Yet the dominant self- and other perception of Africa is pessimistic. On many international indexes Africa – and specifically sub-Saharan Africa – fares proportionally the worst.[2] The continent was subjected to intense dehumanisation over the last 450 years: slavery, colonialism, post-colonial misrule, exploitative immersion into the global financial system (Naudé 2010: 170-174), and now also vulnerability to climate change. The WARC declaration at Kitwe, Zambia (Oct 1995)[3] speaks of "the irony of this painful situation" and concludes that "instead of rivers of economic prosperity and justice flowing season after season in Africa, poverty, misery, hunger and chronic unemployment have become endemic in Africa" (Smit 2007:403).

Africa has become a continent of suffering from dehumanisation. Some of the factors responsible are historical. Their impact and effect are still evident, but the fact of their existence cannot be denied or altered. Other factors contributing to dehumanisation are contemporary and fall into two categories. There are indeed global forces over which Africa has little or limited control; and then there are factors such as regional

---

1 An extended form of this essay was published in the FS for Dirk Smit. It originally contained a brief summary of Smit's own theology, followed by this text on dehumanisation. This explains why most references in the essay are to Smit's work.
2 See the annual United Nations Human Development Index, which combines three measures – life expectancy at birth, educational levels (including literacy) and GNI – into one index, and how the lowest-ranking 30 countries are dominated by African states.
3 See Smit 2007:402-406.

and national policies and actions that are more within the reach of African leaders to determine.

One of the problems with us in Africa is that we fall into a "victim-and-blame mentality", implicitly giving up on the possibility of engineering our own destinies. Recent church documents such as the Kitwe Declaration and Accra Document are helpful in putting economic and ecological justice on the agenda, but unhelpful in two ways: they almost completely deny our complicity as Africans in our own misery,[4] and they analyse the situation from a supra-personal and global "systems" perspective only, with the unintended result that ordinary Christians and local churches are disempowered from acting, therewith reinforcing a victim mentality and even an entitlement attitude.[5]

Let us look a little closer at the strategies of dehumanisation in Africa.

1.1 The misuse of language

It was the existentialist philosophers who helped us understand that language does not only have a descriptive function, i.e. assisting us to make sense of reality and communicate information about that reality to third parties. Martin Heidegger, to name but one example, saw language in its ontological function, i.e. words do not only passively describe reality; they actually constitute and shape reality. "*Die Sprache ist das Haus des Seins*"[6] became a famous adage, and was one of the bases on which Heidegger and others distinguished between authentic and inauthentic existence. If one is able to use language creatively – opening up new realities – one lives authentically, in contrast to the mere repetitive language of "das man".[7]

People who start out on the road of inhumanity know this intuitively. Inhumanity starts with name calling. Name calling is a vicious strategy to categorise people in a derogatory manner. It creates the sharp boundary between "us" and "them": "we" the conquerors and "they" the lesser, indigenous ones; "we" the Arian race and "they" the Jews; "we" the Europeans and "they" the Africans; "we" the whites and "they" the blacks; "we" the mighty South Africans and "they" the lowly and unwelcome *makwerekere*.[8]

Derogatory language further serves the strategy of making sure that the "other" is seen as "less-than-human". It is difficult at first to socially isolate or physically remove or attack other human beings that are equal to or just like you. "They" must be made to appear inferior or even not-human. That is when language moves to call

---

4   The confession in Kitwe of "our sins of omission" is not an acceptance of co-responsibility, as it refers to a confession that "we did not resist enough" (Smit 2007:405).
5   For Dirkie Smit's wider critical analysis of the Accra document specifically, see Smit 2009b:177-184.
6   Literally: "Language is the house of reality."
7   This is a very free interpretation of the complex argument made by (for example) Heidegger on the constitutive role of discourse and understanding in the disclosed-ness of *Da-Sein*. See Heidgger 1996:150-156, and 180.
8   A reference by South Africans to the strange-sounding languages of foreigners (frequently attacked since 2008) in this country.

other people "cockroaches"[9] or "dogs" or "hyenas". It is easier to kill animals or crush cockroaches beneath your feet than actual human beings.

The gradual process of dehumanisation can end in actual killing and displacement of millions of people. The histories of many post-colonial countries tell the same sad story: to ensure power, ethnic cleansing takes place; warlords control parts of geographical areas so that chaos rules and those out of favour are forced to move (mostly on foot) to a place where they might or might not find temporary shelter. The worst cases remain genocide or religious wars. Once you fight with God on your side, it is a holy war you dare not (cannot?) loose – peace is a slap in the face of God (god) him- or herself.

It all starts with what we say to and about one another. Whether in Africa or elsewhere on the globe, we need to attend to the ethics of language. Words in fact do kill – socially at first, and then physically.

1.2 The loss of ubuntu and marginalisation of the "poor"

Since John Mbiti's famous book on African philosophy and religions (Mbiti 1969), we as Africans have proudly claimed *ubuntu* as our original contribution to theology, anthropology and sociology. The Cartesian *cogito ergo sum*, we said, fosters not only individuality, but a self-referential attitude or even "narcissistic individualism" (Smit 2007:84) and loss of community. Rationality ("I think") heralded the Enlightenment with its benefits of science and technology, and – in the famous Kantian formulation of an enlightened person – the questioning of traditional authority, as I make the truth out for and by myself.[10] We said this also led to rationalism and scientism which reduced truth to the empirical only, and the freedom of secularity turns into a closed secularism and even anti-religious sentiments in some European countries.

Ubuntu – "I am because we are, and since we are, therefore I am"[11] – makes the ontological point that we constitute each other's personhood. "Human beings are only human in their interdependency on other human beings. Sociality, belonging, mutual responsibility and service, connectedness, solidarity, caring and sharing are all important values, constituting our very being", writes Dirkie Smit in his interpretation of *ubuntu* (Smit 2007: 119). Progress and success are not something for self-enrichment, but for the enhancement of community. The vulnerable (children, the sick, the dying, the aged) will never be alone because *ubuntu* is the unwritten social security of societies without advanced systems of government care. A deep culture of sharing marks Africa, we say, and even if I have very little myself, I will still show compassion to the one who crosses my path.

It is today sad to see the corruption – and even complete loss – of *ubuntu*.

---

9 This word was used during the Rwandan massacres, and has now appeared again in South African political discourse (introduced by Julius Malema, EFF Leader, describing the leader of the opposition).
10 "Unmundigkeit ist das Unvermögen, sich seines Verstandes ohne Leitung eines anderen zu bedienen" ("Immaturity is the inability to use one's understanding without guidance from another" Kant 1999: 20; original 1784).
11 See Mbiti's discussion of this in the context of kinship, Mbiti 1969:108-109.

Ubuntu is corrupted when it loses its universal sense and is interpreted in a narrow nationalistic, ethnic or familial fashion. The question is how inclusive the "we" really is (Smit 2007:119). *Ubuntu* consequently means that I use my power in society to benefit those who are "of my own". I am a person through the ones close to me and they benefit from my patronage to the exclusion of others who are not from my nation, tribe, family or political party. This tribalisation of *ubuntu* lies at the heart of factionalism in Africa. It knows no conflict of interests and is blinded by the pursuit of power, money and position.

There are also signs that *ubuntu* has disappeared completely. The annihilation of *ubuntu* has its roots in the combined effect of Africans being swept off their feet by an "accelerated modernity" (Smit 2007:83) and cultural globalisation (see Naudé 2007) together with the interiorisation of the colonial master's image of us. The former implies an attitude of cultural diffidence ("global is always better than local"); the latter a deep sense of inferiority – if I do not look, act and talk like my former master (now the centre of the global village), then "I have not made it" yet.

The sad and ironic twist is thus that we embrace the corrupted Enlightenment values – individualism, materialism, rationalism, secularism – against which we protested at first.[12] But the more we adopt this new (so-called global) life style, the more we make ourselves believe we are good and successful people. In the meantime the weak and the vulnerable fall by the wayside; the old sit alone; the ones dying of AIDS are socially shunned; foreigners – many of them desperate – are attacked; and tax money (the small proportion that reaches the state's coffers in many African countries) is spent on stadiums and airports for the rich, and on benefits for the ruling elite, instead of invested in education and basic health care for the poor.

The result is that the contract between the state and the people (in African countries where there are forms of democratic rule) are barely upheld or executed. Many African countries cannot be seen as "well-ordered societies" (as described by Rawls) and find themselves mostly in the opposite position of "burdened societies", where many of the burdens are self-inflicted (Rawls 1999). Even in resource-rich countries such as Nigeria, Angola, the DRC, Sudan, South Africa (and with the newly found oil also here in Uganda), the question remains whether the benefits flow to ordinary people in the form of improved infrastructure and living conditions.

Why must we speak of the African "curse" of resources instead of "blessings?"

One of the reasons for this lack of service delivery is corruption in its many forms. The Corruption Perception Index published annually by *Transparency International* may be criticised on academic grounds and might show a degree of geographical bias. It has nevertheless become an international benchmark of progress or otherwise if one takes into account the millions of dollars lost to Africa (and others) on an annual basis. Of the 20 lowest countries' scores on this index, we must be ashamed that the majority are from Africa.

---

12 Read Smit's account of the moving Mandela Lecture by former South African president, Thabo Mbeki, who laments the loss of communality: "With every passing second, they (the demons embedded in our society) advise, with rhythmic and hypnotic regularity – get rich! get rich! get rich!" (Smit 2007: 116).

If we in Africa could translate the philosophy of *ubuntu* into political and governance terms, this continent would have a prosperous future in the comprehensive sense of the word. The philosophy is right. It is the policies and action that are missing.

2. THE CONSEQUENCES OF DEHUMANISATION

Let us look at the biblical passage (Gen 4)[13] from which our theme was selected. I assume this narrative is known to most people reading this piece. Cain, driven by jealousy, could – from his own perspective – claim victory over his brother Abel. This was in fact an ultimate victory, as Abel was no longer there to taunt him or seek favours ahead of him. When confronted by God (who had called him to restraint in advance)[14] with the simple question "Where is your brother?", Cain follows the well-known strategy of denial: "I do not know." He quickly attempts to turn possible exposure of his misdeed into a relinquishing of responsibility for his brother. His rhetorical question "Am I my brother's keeper?" is a hollow one, because Cain knows what the answer is (and he knows that God knows).

Inhumanity may seem like a victory over "the other", but it normally has destructive relational consequences.

As we learn from the Psalmist, acts of inhumanity against others are at the deepest level acts against the will of God. "Against you alone I have sinned", says David to God ("vertically" speaking) in Psalm 51, though he has ("horizontally" speaking) sinned against Uria, Batsheba and against Nathan (by lying about his act). Cain's troubled relation with God reaches a low point as God calls him to account and pronounces judgement on him to the point of cursing him in his personal capacity (4:11). An act of dehumanisation first and foremost strains the relationship with God.

The effects of this one act of inhumanity are then vividly portrayed in other relations.

- The familial bond between Cain and his parents is severed. The unity of the first family is destroyed. The joy of Eve's first-born ("I acquired a man with the help of the Lord", Gen. 4:1) turns into sorrow as the first parents in fact lose both their sons.

- There are also ecological consequences. The relationship with the earth, from which Cain and others in an agricultural economy lived, turns non-productive in the real sense of the word: if Cain works the fields, the land will no longer yield its potential (Gen. 4:12).

- The "political" consequence is that Cain's bond with his homeland is in jeopardy as he is sent into exile with no fixed future address (Gen. 4:12). He is to wander aimlessly – always on the run – with no opportunity to build a stable future home and family.

- His relationship with all other people is affected: they turn against him as his reputation as first killer would haunt him and make him the object of other

---

13 Quotations from this and other biblical passages are not from a specific translation and are free translations/interpretations by the author.
14 See Gen. 4:4-6, where the Lord addressed Cain's anger and warns him not give in to his sinful desires.

people's revenge. He himself knows that violence begets violence, and that it is very difficult to escape the cycle of attack and counter-attack. Hence his own admission that "each one who gets me, will kill me" (Gen 4:14).

It is clear: one act of so-called victory spins out of control and affects the network of relations at stake. One cannot dehumanise the other and then retain one's own humanity. The "victor" is – mostly unbeknown to him/her at first – always simultaneously "victim".

3. THE RESTORATION OF HUMANITY: A JUDEO-CHRISTIAN VIEW

We need not accept inhumanity as normal pattern of interaction on the African continent. In fact, our expectations for a different continent can be shaped significantly by the Judeo-Christian tradition. In situations of inhumanity the question is not only "What is the state of affairs?", but also and definitively: "Who is God?". "Whenever we speak about compassionate justice," writes Dirkie Smit, "we should begin by speaking about *God*" (2009a:377, original emphasis). This should then be followed by a call to return to God, or convert from our ways to this God. The Genesis narrative tells us who God is.

3.1 A return to God as Creator

The Bible commences with the simple but startling confession: "In the beginning God created the heaven and the earth." By God's creative word everything that is is called into existence. As part of this (first) creation narrative stands the creation of humans as pinnacle of God's work, as created in God's image (Gen. 1:26, 27).

The ethical implications of these confessions are now clear to us: we are stewards of this creation, given to us as gift by God to use responsibly. In theology the development of ecological ethics and environmental justice has strongly built on this creation tradition. And secondly, creation of people in the image of God has been seen as powerful support for the notion of human rights, particularly the first-generation and non-alienable right to life. You shall not kill another person (either by word, attitude or by physical means), because all people – no matter their race, class, gender, HIV status, sexual orientation or level of education – are image-bearers of God.

A return to the Creator-God will serve Africa well. We will act responsibly to protect and enhance the numerous natural gifts God freely gave us on this continent. We will understand that we are but stewards of the natural resources at our disposal to use for the good of all people and future generations. And we will see all other people – on this continent and elsewhere – as image-bearers of God, and therefore as brothers and sisters whose keepers we are. This is the religious ground of our indigenous philosophy of *ubuntu*.

3.2 A return to God as judge

In civil life we have created the law as judge of our actions. No ordered and just society is possible without a sound and independent legal system. Healthy democracies are, *inter alia*, known for their efficient and fair systems of jurisprudence. The law is important and is usually seen as representing the ethical minimum below which we should not fall.

But for a variety of reasons the law is not a perfect guide to action. Laws my have legal force, but may be unjust in principle and in effect; laws are slow to capture and regulate new realities, so that for a while there is a vacuum where no clear guidelines exist and where we have to wait for new cases to be heard to create paradigms for future cases; and laws may be uneven across the nations of the globe – creating loopholes for many who seek to flee from justice in one country to the next.

At a global level we have created the International Court of Justice in The Hague, but even this institution is not recognised by all or its injunctions respected by all – a fact that limits its possibilities to act as a court of appeal.

From a Judeo-Christian perspective God is seen as the ultimate Judge. The values and requirements of God's law should be our guide, as this law in many cases asks more from us than the law of the land. Because in God there is no darkness or inhumanity, God cannot accept our actions of inhumanity, either toward nature or toward other human beings. Like Cain, we are first and foremost not only accountable to other people (or the electorate), but to God. When – for whatever reasons – no court of law is able or willing to ask piercing questions of us, God does so indeed.

God's question to African leaders is straightforward and simple: "Where is your brother Abel?" This question is a metaphor for the question of millions of killed, maimed, displaced and marginalised people, who suffer not because of natural disasters, but because of inhumane wilful actions by those in power or seeking power.

We must not minimise the seriousness of God's judgement. This judgement must, however, not primarily be seen as "active revenge" on God's part. No, God's "judgement" mostly consists of leaving us to face the consequences of our own ill deeds. The judgement is realised first and foremost through the self-inflicted disastrous consequences of our inhuman actions. As in the case of Cain, the destructive consequences spread fast like a concentric circle from inner relations to the furthest corners of the earth on which we live.

But the Old Testament teaches us that God's fury and sorrow over sin do also cause him to act. God does – according to some biblical traditions – curse people and cities and countries and the earth. We therefore need to live in "the fear of the Lord" – a fear characterised by deep respect for God's holiness, mixed with a fear characterised by love for God's justice.

As African leaders, we do not only stand before earthly justices (or vigorously attempt to avoid even this justice). We are confronted by the living God in whom there is no injustice. To this God we are accountable; and by this God we are judged.

3.3. A return to God as graceful God

God the Creator-Judge is also a God of grace and restoration. "God's justice is a saving justice, a caring justice, a merciful justice…" (Smit 2009a:377). It is to the same God who cursed him and the earth (Gen.4:10-12) that Cain turns for alleviation: "My guilt is too big to carry", he says, explaining to God that he will be an ever-fleeing fugitive on the earth, and that each one that will meet him will want to kill him (Gen. 4:13-14).

God does not reject a humble and contrite heart. Confessing guilt and debt is the first step toward restoration. God's successive acts of grace are amazing in the context of this narrative. He precisely makes good on the consequences of Cain's inhumane act.

Cain would not be murdered, but rather protected by a sign so that others would know that whoever kills him will be repaid sevenfold (v.15). Instead of being an ever-fleeing fugitive, Cain finds a fixed abode in the land Nod, on the Eastern side of Eden (v. 16). Instead of being alone and cut off from community, Cain marries and receives a first-born son, Henoch, after whom a city is named. Verses 17-23 enumerate Cain's family tree and tell of the agricultural and economic achievements of his generations.

In theology we rightly focus on God as the God of the oppressed and the marginalised. We must not forget that God also extends undeserved care to the oppressor, to the one who causes suffering and inhumanity. When oppressors turn to God to seek grace, forgiveness and restoration, God is truthful and makes new beginnings possible.[15]

Not only to Cain, but also to the first parents, did God extend God's grace. Eve gives birth to another child, called Set, "as God gifted me another child in the place of Abel, because Cain killed him" (v. 25). The long genealogy starting in Gen 4:26 and extending to the whole of chapter 5 is an enumeration of God's faithfulness to Adam and Eve and their descendants.

The best place for an African leader is on his/her knees before God. The enormous burdens and ambiguities of this continent, and our own irresponsibility and misdeeds, must be brought openly before God. Some of us might say with Cain: "My guilt of neglect and burden of responsibility are too big to carry." Be sure of God's restorative response – our only hope for a new African future.

4. THE FUTURE OF HUMANISATION IN AFRICA

Genesis chapter 4 tellingly ends with a simple but important observation: "Then they (Adam's descendants) began to call on the Name of the Lord" (v. 26).[16]

This is the ultimate act of a restored humanity: to give honour and praise to God; to acknowledge God as creator, judge and the source of grace; to elevate God's Name above all other names available to us; to call not on our own power and ingenuity, but on God to create and co-create with us a blessed future in which culture, technology, and economy work together to make Africa a continent of humanity.

---

15 See Smit's essays on reconciliation, confession, guilt, truth, and seeking of forgiveness in the Christian tradition (Smit 2007: 287-342).
16 I interpret this verse in a doxological sense. The ecclesiological theme of worship is a key feature of Smit's theology. He maintains the public and political significance of prayer and liturgy, drawing on the insights of diverse authors such as John de Gruchy, Douglas Hall, Dietrich Ritschl, Nicholas Wolterstorff and Geoffrey Wainwright. See Smit 2007:425-453. See also his short statement: "Justice, compassion and worship – these three together. The one cannot do without the other" (2009a:378).

We need to dream a new dream and build a "transformative vision" for this continent in the good faith that God makes possible the impossible.[17] The dissonance and distance between Cain – guilty before God – and his subsequent history demonstrate how far God's restoration can lead. Cain has been received in tradition mostly in a negative way as representing the power of sin from the very beginning of humankind.[18] This view is only partially correct and not in line with the witness or structure[19] of the Genesis narrative.

Cain, the condemned, receives protection from God. Cain, the lone fugitive, receives a land to live in. Cain the murderer of his brother, receives his own children and is rich in descendants. Cain, the simple farmer whose sacrifice was rejected, turns into an architect and city builder (4:17). Cain, remembered in tradition mainly for his murderous act, brings forth generations of achievers in the field of agriculture (Gen. 4:20); music (4:21) and technology (4: 22).[20]

In many political and economic circles Africa is the continent of negativity; the land that disappeared off the global radar screen. There are even Africans who themselves share in a general Afro-pessimism and will do all in their power to leave this continent, as they have lost the will to expect a new and different future. That is the normal result if the concept of "future" is nothing more than the prolongation of existing potential. This type of future orientation will always sway between optimism and pessimism, depending on the perceptions of the situation at hand.

But what we call hope in the Judeo-Christian tradition is different. It does not look at the potential or constraints of the current situation and then make up a balanced score-card of what the future might look like. No, the Christian faith is directed at the promises of God and his ability to make all things new far beyond our calculations, efforts and best expectations.

Only God can turn a Cain into a blessing for himself, for others and for the world of his time.

Why not Africa also?

Nkosi Sikelel' iAfrika. God bless Africa ... and her leaders.

---

17 Dirkie Smit refers to Niebuhr's idea of a transformative vision as having both an affirming and critical function: affirming the important potential of politics, culture and economics, and "at the same time criticising the sinful aspects of a particular situation" (Smit 2007: 414, note 9).
18 Even the intra-canonical reception of the Cain narrative demonstrates this negative interpretation: Heb.11:4 mentions that Abel brought a better sacrifice than Cain; Mt. 23:35 talks about Abel in the context of the shedding of innocent blood; 1 John 3:12 calls for brotherly love in contrast to Cain, who killed his brother because he was filled with the Evil One; and Jude verse 11 is a call not to wander in the ways of Cain.
19 There is fair consensus amongst exegetes that Gen 2:4b-11:26 is structured around the sequential themes of God as creator; the problem of sin; God's judgement; and God's sustaining grace. For a discussion see William Lasor (et al.) 1994: 75-87; and for a more technical analysis, read the standard reference work on Genesis by Westermann (1974:24-88).
20 Westermann interprets the enumeration of different occupations here and elsewhere in Gen.1-11 as references to "die Kulturerrungenschaften der Menscheit", ("humanity's cultural accomplishments") each implying a new "Fähigkeit" ("competency/skill") (1974:15).

BIBLIOGRAPHY

Heidegger, Martin 1996. *Being and time*. (Translated by Joan Stambaugh). New York: State University of New York.

Kant, Immanuel 1999 [1784]. Beantwortung der Frage: Was ist Aufklärung? *Ausgewahlte kleine Schriften*. Hamburg: Felix Meiner, pp. 20-27.

Lasor, Willian Sanford; Hubbard, David Allan and Bush, Frederic WM 1994. *Old Testament survey. The message, form, and background of the Old Testament*. Grand Rapids: Eerdmans.

Mbiti, John 1969. *African religions and philosophy*. London: Heinemann.

Naudé, Piet 2007. The challenge of cultural justice under conditions of globalization: Is the New Testament of any use? In Breytenbach, Cilliers, Thom, Johan and Punt, Jeremy (eds): *The New Testament interpreted: essays in honour of Bernard C Lategan*. Leiden: Brill, pp. 267-287.

Naudé, Piet 2010. *Neither calendar nor clock. Perspectives on the Belhar confession*. Grand Rapids: Eerdmans.

Rawls, John 1999. *The law of peoples*. Cambridge, Mass.: Harvard University Press.

Smit, Dirk J 2007. *Essays in public theology. Collected essays I*. Stellenbosch: Sun Press.

Smit, Dirk J 2009a. *Essays on being Reformed. Collected essays 3*. Stellenbosch: Sun Press.

Smit, Dirkie 2009b. Theological assessment and ecclesiological implications of the Accra document 'Covenanting for justice in the economy and the earth'. Tentative comments for discussion. In Boesak, Alan and Hansen, Len (eds): *Globalization. The politics of empire, justice and the life of faith*. Stellenbosch: Sun Press, pp. 173-184.

Westermann, Claus. 1974. *Genesis. Band I/1*. Neukirchen-Vluyn: Neukirchener Verlag.

PART 2 –
ETHICS AND INTERPRETATION

2.1 TOWARD A POST-DISCIPLINARY INTERPRETATION OF THEOLOGY, ETHICS AND THE SCIENCES[1]

It is precisely the positive rigour of natural sciences, the intimate relation between science and technology, and, perhaps most importantly, the indispensable contribution of natural sciences in ethical debates – for example, ecology, political ethics and the diverse questions in medical ethics – that lie behind the imperative for a coalition of the sciences.

This essay attempts to develop arguments for inter- and trans-disciplinary cooperation between theology/religion and other knowledge fields in the university. The implications for ethics specifically are not developed in full, albeit the rise of applied ethics[2] over the last four decades makes it evident that it is especially in ethics that the spirit and practice of inter- and post-disciplinary work is an intellectual requirement if we are to find some consensus on moral questions raised, for example, in ecology, business, and information technology.

We know that applied ethics in its simplest form requires fluency in more than one disciplinary language. For example, the moral language of philosophy or theology, the technical language of the application field (sometimes more than one!), and a language that can bring the two together a in convincing argument for a chosen ethical stance, and, where appropriate, the language of policy implementation.

For the sake of the argument in this chapter, **inter-disciplinary** work is done between two disciplines whilst each discipline retains its own tradition, boundary and epistemic hallmarks. **Trans-disciplinary** work refers to cooperation amongst more than two disciplines, superseding the initial disciplinary boundaries. **Post-disciplinary** work refers to the generation of regional knowledge forms (e.g. gender studies, cultural studies, media studies, ecological studies) in which the original contributing disciplines and the boundaries amongst them are not overtly recognisable and the epistemic orientation lies beyond what is normally attributed to disciplines. Such post-disciplinary knowledge can no longer simply be "categorised" in terms of our traditional understanding of "study disciplines" or "subjects" in the university, and is a prerequisite for most forms of applied ethics.

I shall argue for trans- and post-disciplinary languages from two perspectives.

In part one I give a cursory and very general overview of the increasing fragmentation and specialisation of knowledge in the Western tradition – including the fragmentation of theology into various isolated disciplines. I will argue that theology's inter-disciplinary orientation should develop from its own encyclopaedic nature and from its openness to the rise in the study of religion.

---

1 This is a substantial shortening and reworking of an unpublished inaugural address held in 1996 at the University of Port Elizabeth under the title: "Is God hovering above the nineteenth floor?"
2 See the many disciplines involved in addressing the topics listed in the *Encyclopaedia of applied ethics* (2nd edition 2012, edited by Ruth Chadwick).

In part two I attempt to develop an argument which would provide a foundation for the cooperation amongst different disciplines and different sciences. I hope to demonstrate that such a coalition of the sciences is indeed possible. The basis for this is a radical hermeneutical self-consciousness in both the human and natural sciences that may open up the possibility of accepting "textuality" as the matrix for post-disciplinary studies.

PART ONE

THE FRAGMENTATION OF (THEOLOGICAL) KNOWLEDGE AND THE RISE OF RELIGIOUS STUDIES

The search for sure knowledge in Western philosophy and theology may be traced back to the classical Aristotelian distinction between *episteme* (knowledge) and *doksa* (opinion). This distinction, however, may be further refined: *episteme* (later translated as *scientia* in Latin) had an ambiguous meaning. It referred, on the one hand, to true knowledge as *habitus* – a habit or orientation of the soul, a cognitive disposition of what God reveals, and on the other, to knowledge as a result of a deliberate inquiry. This ambiguity entered the self-understanding of Christian theology and was still integrally part of a unified conception of *theologia* up to at the least the 11th century.

The establishment of universities in Bologna, Paris and Oxford (preceded by monastic and palace schools) gave rise to a sharper division between *habitus* and *scientia*. Under the influence of the Thomistic-Aristotelian method "theology was not simply the direct cognitive vision of something given to it, a cognitive habitus of the soul, but a deliberate and methodological undertaking whose end was knowledge" (Farley 1983:37). In this way, theology was no longer a mere *sacra pagina* but *sacra doctrina*, with a certain autonomy vis-à-vis canon law and medical science. At the height of the scholastic period it was Aquinas who assigned theology the honourable position as queen of the sciences: theology yields superior knowledge if compared to other disciplines because of the supernatural origin of its principles (Farley 1983:38).

The rise of the Enlightenment from the late 17th century onwards challenged traditional authority-orientated thinking in favour of critical and historical thinking. This led to the growth of independent disciplines such as philosophy and history and the pursuit of mathematical exactitude in physics and geometry (Toulmin 1990: x-xi). This in turn had a radical impact on theology in general, and on biblical interpretation specifically as can be seen in the work of Ernesti and Semler in the later part of the eighteenth century.

According to Farley, the impact on theology was a widening of the gap between theology-as-habitus and theology-as-science because the former was institutionalised in denominational seminaries whereas the latter formed part of the establishment of the first universities in the modern sense of the word. Theology, specifically systematic theology, became an independent discipline alongside law (no longer only canon law) and philosophy (no longer a mere introduction to theology).

From the middle of the eighteenth century the study of theology was construed as an "encyclopaedic" problem on the assumption that theology itself is an aggregate of relatively independent sciences. This led to the classical formulation of the so-called "fourfold pattern" (discussed in detail by Farley 1983:56ff) of theology, namely

Bible, church history, dogmatics and practical theology. The science of mission (missiology) developed later and the resultant encyclopaedic grouping forms the basis for separate faculties of theology at universities.

One could thus argue that the knowledge traditionally linked to "theology" was gradually fragmented in three senses: (i) the growth of independent disciplines historically subsumed under theology fragmented the body of knowledge originally related to theology; (ii) the term "theologia" acquired the limited meaning of systematic theology only; and (iii) theology in its broader connotation was no longer seen as a singular discipline. As a result of, *inter alia*, the special requirements of ministerial training, theology became a pluralised family of discrete scholarly pursuits (see Farley 1983:59-63).

This fragmentation of knowledge also influenced other disciplines. The formation of distinct "subjects" was decisively shaped by the European Enlightenment and the rise of modern universities referred to above. As time passed, a healthy tension arose "between the focused accuracy of specialisation, and the synthetic relationality that figures in the historical ideals of the university ..." (Farley 1988:29). This tension was, however, gradually reduced in favour of specialisation. Farley gives a number of reasons for this development which may be reconstructed as follows.

First, the reward system of modern universities has not been geared toward broad academic disciplines, but to speciality fields which are smaller units than what are known as "subjects" institutionalised in academic departments. To make rapid progress in academia, the only route is to become a specialist of some sort who can stake a claim executed by publications on a topic about which very few could (or want to?) question you.

Second, the professionalisation of the new sciences through universities (which themselves became professionalised: we are "professors"!), was the surest route not only to safeguard standards (the reason normally put forward), but to gain public legitimacy and status (with the concomitant ability to limit numbers and entrench a market share). We live in a culture of professionalism.

Third, the growing dominance of the quantitative (empirical) sciences with their spectacular technological success set the paradigm for research *überhaupt*. Farley suggests that the rise of speciality fields may historically be linked to the rise of empiricism to which many human sciences turned as a norm for "proper scholarship" (Farley 1988:42), where the focus is on a sufficiently restricted set of problems that yield the desired quantitative data.

It is important to note that this overview of fragmentation in knowledge is not directed against the proliferation of knowledge or the important advances in science made by specialists in their various fields or even the empirical paradigm *per se*. My uneasiness may be articulated in the following two points from which the urgent need for inter- and trans-disciplinarity arises.

First, the problem of isolation, and second, the problem of a reductionist ontology. Both these points are embedded in a view of "education", to which I will refer briefly below.

Isolation occurs at various levels. There is the isolation from the discipline itself, because the specialist loses the realisation that the specialist area is but an abstraction of the discipline. Teaching in departments may then degenerate into a "mere aggregate of speciality projects", because the professor "who embodies the larger learning is a fast-vanishing breed" (Farley 1988:47). There is also an isolation from colleagues, because speciality fields become epistemological territories over which the specialists rule. Imperialism becomes the primary academic transgression, i.e. the invasion of another's territorial integrity. To be an academic is akin to waging war.

These two forms of isolation imply that it becomes very difficult to transcend the speciality's framework in the direction of alternative interpretative frameworks. It is no wonder that Feyerabend suggests in his *Against Method* (1978, Chapter 16) that the traditions of the sciences are so rigid that we need at least a generation of "professional anarchists" to relativise these boundaries.

Let us turn to the issue of a reductionist view of reality. This relates specifically to the pervasive influence which the empirical method exerts over research. With growing specialisation, universities may superficially gain the aspect of a multi-versity or poly-versity but, epistemologically speaking, an ever growing paradigmatic uniformity is established. If the tension between other modes of knowledge and empiricism is reduced in favour of the latter, the result is a reductionist grasp of reality which is, however, understood as "the real".

This creates a one-dimensionality that distorts the complexity of reality and the problems facing our society. If intuitive imagination, a sense of tradition and insight into the complicity between "empirical science" and "power" is not honoured, for example, the university will retain only "a very anorexic version of the critical principle" (Farley 1988:12, see also 27). I will return to this point below.

The concerns about isolation and reductionism are imbedded in an ideal of university education. It is obvious that students in a degree programme undergo an increasing level of specialisation at postgraduate and especially doctoral level. But if an "educated person" implies *inter alia* a respect for the multi-dimensionality of reality and the complexity of (social) problems, the university has a moral and epistemological obligation to foster and institutionalise inter-disciplinary work. Specialists must not be allowed to create isolationist worlds of their own, but be involved in the inter- and post-disciplinary debate on shared problems in order to overcome a one-dimensional view of reality.

Universities will also have to guard against the temptation to (institutionally) discredit staff and departments that by their nature attempt to retain a synthetic view of academia such as, for example, philosophy, art and religion. That the rationalisation (i.e. scrapping) of the Linguistics Departments in some universities is a serious fatal blow to inter-disciplinary studies, will be evident from part two of this essay.

The impact of fragmentation in the form of "specialisation" in theology is severe. In the biblical sciences there is a constant revisiting of reading strategies, but in the process of this ever increasing ingenuity, it becomes impossible to speak about "the Bible". Excellent specialist work may be done on (for example) the waw-consecutive construction or the sources theories, but very few attempts at **theologies** of the Old or New Testament (the wider perspective) are written. One may reach a certain level of expertise in the various areas of the encyclopaedia, but it becomes almost impossible to speak of being a "theologian" except in the narrow sense of being a systematic or practical theologian.

The effect of independent, autonomous disciplines (i.e. specialisation "outside" theology) led to a de-canonisation of theological knowledge as privileged knowledge. Theology has no option but to relinquish its position as "queen of the sciences" and be incarnated as fellow servant in our human endeavour to approximate the truth. The growth of other human sciences such as history, psychology, anthropology and sociology, as well as the major advances in the natural sciences, will only be seen as an embarrassment or loss of power for a theology longing for an epistemic privileged position.

Instead of denying or lamenting these realities, the encyclopaedic nature of theology and its relative position to other disciplines open up an opportunity: it is precisely theologians who should be in the forefront of inter- and even post-disciplinary studies!

In the course of the past four decades a new phenomenon has come to the fore which yields special possibilities for an inter-disciplinary vision for theology. I refer to the growth of religious studies (science of religion, comparative religion) and the concomitant debate on theological pluralism (see Osborn 1992). Although the *Religionsgeschichtliche* school in both Old and New Testament Studies extended the religious basis of Biblical Studies, I refer to the independent study of religions *per se*.

Ninian Smart, in his inaugural lecture in 1991 at the Institute for Comparative Religion in Southern Africa (ICRSA at UCT), explains that the modern study of religion as a new and distinct discipline grew from the 1960s and came to the fore "as the **multidisciplinary**, plural, cross-cultural, empirical, and reflective study of religion and religions" (Smart 1991:3, my emphasis). How deeply this affects the South African situation becomes evident from the many departments of Biblical Studies – including our own – which in recent years opted for new or dual names expressing a focus on Religious Studies.

There are a number of factors which have contributed to this very significant development. Without elaboration, I merely enumerate a few with specific reference to the South African situation.

i. On a philosophical level, Western society has become radically pluralistic (Tracy 1987:47ff), shattering the grip of "universal reason" and the existence of "grand meta-narratives" (Lyotard 1984:xxiii). Although our situation can hardly be equalled to that of "the West", South Africa did not escape these conditions. Translated into socio-political terms, the demise of apartheid broke the enforced uniformity of our society, resulting in an acute realisation of the plurality of the South African situation – equalled by similar developments in the former Soviet Union and other East bloc countries. Where a certain intra-pluralistic awareness (differences within the Christian tradition, for example) did exist, this process now includes a realisation of the rich religious traditions ranging from Christianity and Judaism to Islam and African traditional religions. Chidester's excellent historical revisionist project (1992) shows the development of religious pluralism in South Africa from the Khoisan and other African religions to the situation of the 1980 census.

It is important to note that the formal establishment of religious pluralism took a long time to be realised. For political and economic reasons, the Dutch East Indian Company prohibited any other religious establishment in the Cape besides the Dutch Reformed Church for 126 years. The Lutherans built their first church only in 1778; the first Muslim mosque was built in 1789; the first Jewish synagogue in 1849 and the first Hindu temple in 1869 in Durban. The first formal declaration of religious tolerance was that of Jacob de Mist (1804) during the brief resumption of Dutch rule from 1803-6 (see Chidester's Preface and Chapter 5). The so-called "voluntary Act" by the Cape Parliament in 1875 ensured freedom of religion and a separation of church and state. But true religious justice – constitutionally guaranteeing our pluralist society – came about only in the Constitutional Principles of the 1993 Interim Constitution (see Prozesky 1995).

ii. In a general sense the struggle for justice in our country was a deeply religious struggle. Obviously the theological struggle was waged mainly between conflicting interpretations of apartheid from within the Christian tradition (see De Gruchy 1979). The previous political system collapsed not merely because of economic factors – the death blow was struck when it lost its moral (i.e. theological) legitimacy. And the role of other religious traditions – specifically from Jewish and Muslim perspectives – has been undervalued.3 That the major religious traditions can find common ground on global ethical issues is one of the most important factors for a growing awareness of religious diversity. See, for instance, the remarkable Assisi declaration on ecology issued in 1987.

iii. The establishment of a secular state in South Africa in 1994 withdrew the "unofficial" state support that Christianity had previously enjoyed. Christians now have no option but to come to democratic agreements with other faiths on issues such as the Preamble to the Constitution, meditation or prayers in Parliament, religious broadcasting and – more importantly – religious education in schools (see Smart's challenge with regard to the latter, 1991: 5). This obviously has an unsettling effect on Christian communities (hence the debate on the public role of the church), but enhances the imperative for proper studies of religion, and specifically the relation between religion and democracy.4

iv. South Africans – more than many other nations – know the explosive power of racial injustices. History has taught us, and is still teaching us, the lesson that if racial (or other) conflicts are couched in religious terms, the most vicious and prolonged wars follow (the Yugoslavian crisis, Northern Ireland, the Sri Lankan civil war, the Middle East and Rwanda are random examples). From this perspective South Africans intuitively know that inter-faith dialogue and respect need not be a complicating, but rather a healing, factor in the reconstruction of our country. But to unlock this healing resource we shall have to learn how to engage in real dialogue.5

---

3   See Moulana Esack's criticism of the Kairos Document as discussed by Peterson 1994:223.
4   See De Gruchy 1995 for an excellent study on Christianity and democracy.
5   See the prerequisites for dialogue as outlined by Tracy in *Dialogue with the other* (1990: 73ff) and in Paul Knitter's *No other name?* (1992: 208ff). For a broader, inter-disciplinary approach, see Charles Villa-Vicencio, *A theology of reconstruction*, 1992.

v. As a consequence of well-known historical factors, the study of theology and religion has been dominated by the Christian tradition (Thiemann 1991: 155). Da Costa argues that "the end of systematic theology" (1992) as traditionally understood has arrived. The reason is that Western theology has been intellectually and institutionally linked to two addressees: the secularists (apology for the Christian faith in the so-called post-Christian era) and the scientists (apology for the scientific nature of theology from the science of philosophy perspective).

This directedness of systematic theology is a "myopic Western assumption" which represents a diminished reality. What is the "other" reality? The simple fact is that Muslims, Hindus and Buddhists far outnumber Christians, atheists and scientists added together. Thus: "The future of Christian systematic theology lies with a whole range of new partners [the world religions], while not discounting older, familiar and mainly West European partners of scientists and atheists [and Jews]" (Da Costa 1992: 226). This implies that the hermeneutical spiral of systematic theology will involve "not only the Bible, tradition, teaching authorities or whatever, plus the modern world defined by scientists and atheists, but also, and equally as importantly as the latter, the Hindu and Buddhist world views" (331).

And, important for my overall argument for doing theology in an inter-disciplinary fashion, Da Costa spells out that the institutional implication of his viewpoint is the establishment of combined departments of theology and religious studies. This is an imperative for being a proper theology department, because theology can only retain its integrity if it is intellectually honest in facing the challenges put forward by other religions and non-religious worldviews (332). This will precisely resurrect theology in the modern world and, says Ninian Smart, liberate Christian theology from its compartmentalisation and shrunken identity (Smart 1991: 6).[6]

The factors mentioned above cumulatively constitute powerful reasons to take the study of religion seriously and to include the study of religion at university. If one accepts that "religiousness" is one of the fundamental aspects of humanity that is open to study from a variety of perspectives, it might be advisable not to institutionalise the study of religion in one department. I agree with Thiemann's suggestion: "Ideally, religious studies should have the status of area studies in which resources dealing with religion in various departments are brought together" (1991: 159, note 28). This would be roughly equal to "gender studies" or "cultural studies". Religion is what Stephen Toulmin calls a "field-encompassing field", i.e. a field of study that utilises methodological approaches from a variety of disciplines.[7]

In short: religious studies – itself subject to a great variation in approaches, including historical, comparative and phenomenological – extended the inter- and

---

6 I will not expand on the interesting question of the relation between Christian theology and religious studies. To merely scratch the surface, one may refer to the view expressed by Ronald Thiemann where he, with reference to Lindbeck's definition of religion, critically discusses the views of Schubert Ogden and Edward Farley. He proposes an integrated approach to religious and theological studies on the basis of a cultural-linguistic conception of religion (Thiemann 1991:142-159).

7 Quoted by Thiemann 1991: 156 note 1. See the multi-disciplinary nature of publications in *The Library of Religious Beliefs and Practices Series* edited by John Hinnells and Ninian Smart.

post-disciplinary possibilities of (Christian) theology. In collaboration with other sciences, theology addresses the perennial problem of language, methodology and theory formation developed in a way that honours the specific object of its study whilst retaining scientific integrity.

PART TWO

RADICAL HERMENEUTICAL SELF-CONSCIOUSNESS AND TEXTUALITY: THE BASIS FOR POST-DISCIPLINARY STUDIES

In what way could we build the basis for inter- and post-disciplinary work – not only in the study of religion, but in general terms throughout the university? The direction in which to search for an answer, as suggested earlier, lies in the radicalisation of all sciences' hermeneutical self-consciousness. I hereby situate my argument beyond metaphysics (Middle Ages) and epistemology (Enlightenment) and will argue for **hermeneutics** as a central mode of mediating our relationship with reality (See Van der Merwe 1994).

I shall develop this with an extended view of "text" as put forward by Paul Ricoeur in his *Hermeneutics and the Human Sciences* (1991) and by alluding to David Tracy's idea of conversation as mode of interaction between a text and an interpreter set out in his *Plurality and Ambiguity* (1987). After investigating the relation between "humanities" and "social sciences", I engage in a short discussion of the relation between natural and human sciences.

It is customary to distinguish between the text-based "Geisteswissenshaften" (the languages, biblical/religion studies and history) and the social sciences based on a study of human action/behaviour (sociology, anthropology, political science, psychology). In an interesting article "The model of text: Meaningful action considered as a text" (1971, published as Chapter 8 in Ricoeur 1981), Ricoeur, with reference to JL Austin and the speech act theory of John Searle, argues that the paradigm of a text is equally applicable to the study of meaningful human action. For the sake of brevity I extract what is essential for my overall argument.

First: As a written text objectifies discourse (i.e. the speech event as interlocution) so that a certain fixation occurs, the event of human interaction can also be objectified so that a dialectic between the actual event and the meaning of the event arises. Says Ricoeur: "My claim is that action itself, action as meaningful, may become an object of science, without losing its character of meaningfulness, through a kind of objectification similar to the fixation which occurs in writing" (1981: 203).

Second: As a text, once objectified, leads a life "of its own", i.e. no longer bound to the author, an action may be autonomised to have consequences beyond the intention of the agent. This is the essence of the social dimension of action: "An action is a social phenomenon not only because it is done by several agents ..., but also because our deeds escape us and have effects we did not intend" (1981:206).

Third: As a text, once objectified and autonomised, acquires meanings beyond the boundaries of the initial communication, "we could say that a meaningful action is an action the importance of which goes 'beyond' its relevance to its initial situation" (Ricoeur 1981: 207). It may thus be re-enacted in different social conditions transcending the meaning which it initially may have had (see Tracy's reference to a classic's excess of meaning which resists definitive interpretation, 1987:12).

Fourth: As a text may be "read" by an indefinite readership and is always open to new meaning, "human action is an open work, the meaning of which is in 'suspense'. It is because it 'opens up' new references and receives fresh relevance from them that human deeds are also waiting for fresh interpretations which decide their meaning" (1981: 208; see Tracy's reference to the radical instability of texts due to ever-changing receptions, 1987:14).

This cumulative argument thus constitutes the convergence of humanities and social sciences. The object of both, whether written document or human action/behaviour, is *text* in the broadened sense of the word. It would thus be more accurate to speak of *human* sciences encompassing the earlier artificial division and opening up possibilities for a multi-disciplinary orientation.

The objectivity of the object of human sciences is constituted by the four traits taken together: their fixation, autonomisation, transcendence of the original (speech or act) situation and universal range of addressees (see Ricoeur 1981: 210). This links with Van Niekerk's (1992: 163-4) observation that in this sense the human sciences are "more like" the natural sciences, which is a movement in the opposite direction to the post-positivistic understanding of natural sciences as being "more like" the human sciences.

But if the object is text, what about the methodology of human sciences? Is it not here that the roads part? To be practical: what methodological affinity would there be between, for example, research projects in psychology and English respectively? The answer is simple: in both, the *meaning* of "text" (whether written or objectified human action) is not a given; it is to be *construed*.

The laborious effort of interpreting the pluri-vocity of written texts is equally valid for social phenomena – exemplified in the vigorous debates amongst different "schools of thought" within the various disciplines. The methodology of the human sciences is thus fundamentally hermeneutical and the on-going research and debates are none other than procedures of validation to defend the probability of an interpretation.

Building on HLA Hart's notion that this procedure of validation resembles juridical argumentation with its polemical nature, Ricoeur attempts to explain the procedure through which the relative superiority of "readings" may be established (implicit rejection of post-modernist relativism). We have no option but to argue in defence of our interpretation (which is always a mutilation of the pluri-vocity of the text!). And, unlike in a court of law where a final judgement is handed down (the judge or jury makes a final choice between two contrasting interpretations of the law and events peculiar to the case), the results of validation in human sciences are always provisional. But as far as good reasons may be provided at any one time, and as far as some readings are seen as paradigmatic, interpretation is, apart from being an art, also a science.

The intention of this essay is to draw all colleagues from across the university into the question of multi-disciplinary investigations. We must therefore now ask whether textuality can be extended to also include the natural sciences. Are natural scientists busy investigating empirical reality "as it is", short-circuiting the interpretation which is the cumbersome fate of the human sciences? Scientism as a form of epistemic foundationalism does live in the illusion that its mode of inquiry is a-historical. Science, in its positivist notion, destroys its past (Kuhn) and its mode of rationality excludes the tradition or history of scientific endeavour and what may be termed creative imagination (Farley). Scientism further denies its own hermeneutical character on the assumption that the formal-symbolic expression of knowledge puts an end to conflicting interpretations – the clarity of the explanatory method makes questions of interpretation redundant.

But natural science – *inter alia* under the influence of its own areas of investigation such as quantum theory, astronomy, the new physics and environmental science – has entered a post-positivistic era. There is no need to repeat the well-known trajectory of the philosophy of science from Popper and Kuhn to Feyerabend and Toulmin (Bernstein 1983:1-59; Van Huyssteen 1986: 63-110). It is now clear that all data are theory laden; all paradigms are historical, and science is a slice of life. In short: post-positivistic science has come to understand its own historical and hermeneutical nature.

The hermeneutical nature of natural science (which is my concern here) dispels the idea that natural science is naturally scientific. Although positivism has been proven over and over again as intellectually bankrupt, the pervasive influence of this kind of thinking, with its technological (and political) power in our culture, has kept many human sciences under its spell. Its totalising effect is to be seen in, for example, Max Weber's search for a social-scientific method; Talcott Parsons's idea of a stable society; the reductionism in some forms of behaviourism and even in Roman Jakobson's structuralist theory of poetics (see Tracy 1987:32-33).

That positivism is alive and well in our university[8] is evident from two very innocuous examples. The first is the marketing publication in which the faculties are presented. The faculty of natural sciences is simply indicated as the faculty of "science", whereas the rest (wherever they fit –, for example, economics) are described as adjective sciences. This reminds one of the observation that Western theology is referred to as "theology" whereas the rest – e.g. liberation, African, womanist – are adjective theologies. The second example is my attempt to formulate a research philosophy on behalf of the research committee in which all faculties are represented. My reference to a post-positivist framework in the opening paragraph (and ensuing explanatory notes) was met with disregard (What nonsense is this? Let us get on with research!) and relegated to mere notification status so that "real decisions" on the creation of a research infrastructure could be taken.

Why is this question of hermeneutics so important? Because it serves no real (i.e. practical) multi-disciplinary purpose that philosophers, linguists and theologians understand post-positivism, while some of our colleagues in the human and natural sciences live in an a-historical and non-hermeneutical illusion. It is worthwhile noting Kuhn's remark that when he as a physicist discovered the word "hermeneutics" late in his professional life, its most immediate and decisive effect was on his view of science (Bernstein 1987:30-31).

---

8   A reference to the University of Port Elizabeth which later (2005) became the Nelson Mandela Metropolitan University.

This inescapable linguistic – and therefore interpretative – nature of natural science is illuminated by Mary Hesse's summary of a post-empiricist view of natural science (Hesse 1980:167-186). I refer to the first and second last of her five remarks.

> In natural science data are not detachable from theory, for what count as data are determined in the light of some theoretical interpretation, **and the facts themselves have to be reconstructed in the light of interpretation** (my emphasis).

> The language of natural sciences is irreducibly metaphorical and inexact, and formalisable only at the cost of distortion of the historical dynamics of scientific development and of the imaginative constructions in terms of which nature is interpreted by science.

By emphasising the hermeneutic character of natural sciences, I do not wish to deny the differences between human and natural sciences. The question of a "double hermeneutics" for human sciences is referred to by, for example, Anthony Giddens (see Bernstein 1987:236 note 38). Nor do I wish to assume an antagonistic position against these sciences from the position of a concealed romantic textualism (Rorty 1982:139ff). Throughout this address the basic concern has been to show the possibilities of multi- and post-disciplinary research and teaching on the basis of the radical hermeneutical self-consciousness of all the sciences in the modern university. It is precisely the positive rigour of natural sciences, the intimate relation between science and technology, and – perhaps most importantly – the indispensable contribution of natural sciences in ethical debates (for example ecology, political ethics and the diverse questions in medical ethics) that lie behind the imperative for a coalition of the sciences.

The hermeneutical argument must be viewed in the light of the linguistic turn (Rorty) which was set in motion by Wittgenstein's analytical philosophy (emphasis on the plurality of worlds constituted by language games), Heidegger's hermeneutical philosophy (every linguistic disclosure is in itself a concealment) and De Saussure's structuralist philosophy (theory of language as a system) (see Tracy's discussion 1987:50ff).

These developments have helped us to understand that there is no pre-linguistic reality. Lacan has shown, through his reading of Freud, that even our unconscious is structured like a language (see Tracy 1987:63-4). And in the highly formal languages of logic and mathematics, our so-called "facts out there" are linguistically facilitated interpretations. Reality should always appear in quotation marks (Nabokov as quoted by Tracy 1987:47), because it is what we name our best interpretation. "Reality is neither out there nor in here. Reality is constituted by the interaction between a text, **whether book or world,** and a questioning interpreter" (Tracy 1987:48, my emphasis. See his criticism of an instrumental view of language in both romanticism and positivism on pages 49-50).

A commitment to inter- and post-disciplinary teaching and research is thus based on the notion of humans as "language-sated beings" (Derrida) and the constitutive textual-linguistic nature of all understanding. This is thus a commitment to be continually involved in the process of conversation (Tracy) and juridical reasoning (Hart), establishing or refuting the validity of specific interpretations. In a sense, "we have all become lawyers constantly using such qualifier words as 'allegedly' [and] 'supposedly' ... (Tracy 1987:35), although the role of argumentation is limited by Tracy's preference for questioning as the heart of conversation (1987:20-26).

The court case is never over. The more inter-disciplinary witnesses we hear, the better are our chances of unravelling the complexity of reality reflected in the "text" under discussion. Our only appeal is to the openness of participants to yet again hear or put forward new arguments. Conversation in Tracy's mind is a kind of game where the movement *is* questioning itself. "It is a willingness to follow the question wherever it may go. It is dialogue" (1987:18). No one speaks the last word: "Neither in literary criticism, nor in the social sciences, is there such a last word. Or, if there is any, we call that violence" (Ricoeur 1981:215).[9]

In the context of this hermeneutical argument for a spirit of trans-disciplinarity, it is important to remain vigilant and suspicious in the tradition set by the "masters of suspicion", Marx, Nietsczhe and Freud. Suspicious of what and whom, one may ask?

First, we should be suspicious of the intellectual untouchables with their innate tendencies of isolationism and professionalism. In religious language we shall constantly remind them and ourselves that thou shalt have no other gods, nor make any images of gods – not even in the form of sedimented intellectual paradigms or a-historical constructs.

Second, we should be suspicious of those who live in the illusion that theorising is apolitical and ideologically neutral. As we DO theology and ethics – understanding that theory is a form of praxis – we shall constantly remind them and ourselves that faith without works is dead.

Third, we should be suspicious of all – including our own – self-indulgent, narcissistic post-modern reflection, whilst we remind ourselves that modernity was not merely followed by post-modernity, but also by **sub**-modernity. The ambiguity of the Enlightenment – from the French to the industrial and technological revolutions – is evident from the massive growth of the poor, the marginalised and the oppressed. In religious language we shall have to remind ourselves that love for the stranger is the perfect fulfilment of the law. A cup of cold water is sometimes worth more than an accredited article.

From a religious perspective, the fundamentalist temptation is to see "God" without inverted commas. This would deny the constructive nature of our very notion of God. We construct models of God whilst we have to accept that God is always beyond these very constructs. Our metaphors and interpretative schemes, however fragmentary, do however have a referential function.[10] Faith also means that these constructs, our God-talk, do refer to something rather than nothing. In the Jewish-Christian tradition it is implied that these references are to somebody, i.e. God. And She defies adequate description, inter alia because She is only accessible via the

---

9 Note the important notion of counterfactual ideal speech situations – expounded by Habermas 1987 – which may serve as regulative idea for all conversation, and the ensuing debate on consensus and dissensus with Lyotard 1984.

10 See Sallie McFague's work on metaphorical theology, 1982.

relative adequacy (Tracy) of classical texts (Scriptures and tradition), and the text of our human (religious) experience.

We interpret God and broader reality via our interpretation of the manifold "texts" which form the rich plurality of our investigations at university. Is there a special hermeneutical role for theology/religion in this coalition of interpretation?

This may be answered in the affirmative, because it belongs to the nature of religion to not only construct models of knowing God, but to construct a comprehensive view of reality. Lindbeck states that "religion can be viewed as a kind of ... linguistic framework or medium that shapes the **entirety** of life and thought" (1984: 32-33, my emphasis) and Ninian Smart links religions not to partial aspects of reality, but to **worldviews** (1991:7, my emphasis). This focus on the "whole" of reality does not give theology a "last word" or higher status, but it does constitute theology as a necessary partner in the trans-disciplinary search for knowledge, including ethical knowledge.

I close on a religious note in providing a motto for inter-, trans-, and post-disciplinary studies:

In the beginning was the "text", and the text was with "God", and the text was "God".

BIBLIOGRAPHY

Bernstein, J. 1983. *Beyond objectivism and relativism: Science, hermeneutics and praxis.* Philadelphia: University of Pennsylvania Press.

Chadwick, Ruth (editor) 2012. *Encyclopaedia of applied ethics* (2nd edition). London: Elsevier.

Chidester, David. 1992. *Religions of South Africa.* Oxford: Routledge.

Da Costa, G. The end of systematic theology. *Theology*, Vol. XCV, No. 167: 324-333.

De Gruchy, J.W. 1979. *The church struggle in South Africa.* Cape Town: David Philip.

De Gruchy, J.W. 1995. *Christianity and democracy: A theology for a just World Order.* Cambridge: Cambridge University Press.

Farley, E. 1988. *The fragility of knowledge.* Philadelphia: Fortress Press.

Farley, E. 1983. *Theologia: The fragmentation and unity of theological education.* Philadelphia: Fortress Press.

Feyerabend, P. 1978. *Against method: Outline of an anarchistic theory of knowledge.* London: Verso.

Habermas, J. 1987. *The philosophical discourse of modernity.* Cambridge, Mass: MIT.

Hesse, M. 1980. *Revolutions and reconstructions in the philosophy of science.* Brighton: Harvester Press.

Hollis, M. & Lukas, S. 1982. *Rationality and relativism.* Oxford: Basil Blackwell.

Knitter, P.F. 1992. *No other name? A critical survey of Christian attitudes towards the world religions.* New York: Orbis.

Lindbeck, G.A. 1984. *The Nature of doctrine: Religion and theology in a post-liberal age.* Philadelphia: The Westminster Press.

Lyotard, J.F. 1984. *The postmodern condition*. Manchester: Manchester University Press.

McFague, Sallie. 1982. *Metaphorical theology*. London: SCM Press.

Osborn, R.T. 1992. From theology to religion. *Modern Religion* 8 (1): 74-88.

Peterson, Robin. 1994. Theology and religious pluralism, in De Gruchy and Villa-Vicencio (eds.) *Doing Theology in Context*. Cape Town: David Philip, 219-228.

Ricoeur, P. 1981. *Hermeneutics and the human sciences*. (edited and translated by John B. Thompson). Cambridge: Cambridge University Press.

Rorty, R. 1982. *Consequences of pragmatism*. Brighton: The Harvester Press.

Rorty, R. 1985. Solidarity or objectivity? In John Rajchman and Cornwell West (eds.) *Postanalytic Philosophy*. New York: Columbia University Press, 3-19.

Smart, N. 1991. *Religious studies and religious education: Challenges for a new South Africa*. Inaugural address: ICRSA. Cape Town: University of Cape Town.

Thiemann, R.F. 1991. *Constructing a public theology: The church in a pluralistic culture*. Louisville, Kentucky: John Knox Press.

Toulmin, S. 1990. *Cosmopolis: The hidden agenda of modernity*. Chicago: University of Chicago Press.

Tracy, D. 1987. *Plurality and ambiguity: Hermeneutics, religion, hope*. San Francisco: Harper and Row.

Tracy, D. 1990. *Dialogue with the Other: The inter-religious dialogue*. Louvain: Peter's Press.

Van der Merwe, W.L. 1994. Die taalwending in die 20ste-eeuse filosofie en die vraag na 'n eeuwendingsgestemdheid. *Tydskrif vir Christelike Wetenskap* 30/2: 80-114.

Van Niekerk, A. 1992. *Rasionaliteit en relativisme: Op soek na 'n rasionaliteitmodel vir die menswetenskappe*. Pretoria: RGN.

Van Huyssteen, J.W. 1986. *Teologie as kritiese geloofsverantwoording*. Pretoria: RGN.

Villa-Vicencio, C. 1992. *A theology of reconstruction: Nation-building and human rights*. Cape Town: David Philip.

2.2 WHY IS A MULTIPLICITY OF CONFESSIONS PARTICULAR TO THE REFORMED TRADITION?[1]

The significance of the confession in the Reformed church consists in its essential non-significance, its obvious relativity, humanity, multiplicity, mutability, and transitoriness ... Reformed confession is confession of the truth of Scripture; as long as and to the extent that it is this, it has not ceased to exist (Barth 2002:38, 40).[2]

INTRODUCTION

In the Reformed tradition, the act of confession has developed as a particular response to questions of doctrine and, by implication, ethical matters confronting the church at any given time. In putting forward a confessional statement, the Bernese synod of 1532 provided a classic example of the Reformed view on confessions:

> If something would be brought forward to us from our pastors or others, which leads us closer to Christ, and which is, according to the Word of God, more conducive to general friendship and Christian love than the opinion recorded now, we are happy to accept it and do not want to block the way of the Holy Spirit.[3]

In the introduction to his vast collection of the major theological affirmations of the Christian churches John Leith (1973:1) makes the general observation that "Christianity has always been a creedal religion in that it has always been theological". When one compares the different traditions with one another, it becomes immediately apparent that the Reformed part of the Christian church has yielded a rich variety of creedal statements, far beyond the number and scope of the Catholic and Lutheran (and, lately, the Pentecostal) traditions. For Reformers, confessions have become a particular "mode of discourse" to express convictions about doctrine, ethics and life.

This is evident not only from Leith's inclusive volume, but also from the well-known collections by EFK Mueller (1902), which starts with the pre-Calvinist confessions (notably Zwingli's theses from 1523) and ends (54 statements of faith later!) with the American Congregationalist confession from 1883; the collection, *Reformed witness today* (1982), edited by Lukas Vischer, which includes confessional texts and statements of church unions from all continents; the collection and theological interpretation by Jan Rohls (1987) of the old Reformed confessional writings stemming from the Zurich reformation up to the Barmen declaration of 1934;[4]

---

1   Paper prepared for a conference on the Heidelberg Catechism at the Stellenbosch Faculty of Theology, 30 October 2013.
2   Karl Barth in *The theology of the Reformed confessions* from lectures held in 1923.
3   The text is found in G.W. Lochner (ed.), *Der Berner Synodus von 1532*, Vol. 1, 26, published in 1984 by Neukirchener Verlag. I found the reference and translation in Busch 2003:23. The full significance of this quotation will become evident from the discussions below.
4   See Rohls 1998:3-4 and 16 for references to other collections, including H.A. Niemeyer's collection of Reformed confessions, *Collectio confessionum in ecclesiis reformatis publicatarum*, published in 1840 (to which Müller also refers in his preface) and the more

and the more recent annotated commentaries published by Neukirchener Verlag, *Reformierte Bekenntnisschriften*, which will include confessions from 1523 until today (also the Belhar confession).

As we celebrate the most ecumenical of the Reformed confessions, namely the Heidelberg Catechism, it is appropriate to ask why the creeds of the Reformed churches show such a remarkable variety and multiplicity. The answer is sought below in a discussion of the nature of Reformed theology (Willie Jonker), the spiritual power of the church to declare and interpret doctrine (John Calvin), and the character of Reformed confessions themselves (Karl Barth).

1. JONKER: WHAT IS THEOLOGY?[5]

In an article "What is theology?" written for a 1976 consultation of the Reformed Ecumenical Synod, South African systematic theologian Willie Jonker (1976:3-7)[6] distinguishes four models of theology. These are (i) theology as mystical knowledge of God, constituting theology as "wisdom" (Augustine and the Eastern Orthodox tradition); (ii) theology as rational knowledge about articles of faith (Aquinas and Roman Catholic scholasticism); (iii) theology as knowledge of God through revelation in Scripture (the Protestant tradition inaugurated by Luther and Calvin); and (iv) theology as knowledge of God through human experience or religiosity (Schleiermacher, Neo-Protestant and Pentecostal theologies).

Jonker then makes a conscious choice for the Protestant model because – according to him – the Scriptures are taken as source, object and criterion of theology in a more adequate manner than in the other models or traditions. In the mystical tradition Scripture is important up to a point, after which mystical reflections may lead to a higher order knowledge of God beyond the revelation in Scripture. In the Catholic tradition the doctrines and traditions of the church are seen as equally important sources of revelation when compared to Scripture, and these doctrines (and not Scripture itself) are the actual object of theological study. He, interestingly, considers the model of experiential theology to be the least attractive, as he views this as an anthropocentric way of speaking about God in terms of religious experience, with only a relative position assigned to Scripture, thereby in fact deserting the very modus of theo-logical language (Jonker 1976:7).

---

    recent article by W. Neuser in the *Handbuch der Dogmen- und Theologiegeschichte* Vol. 2, 165-166 (edited by C Andresen, 1980). See Mueller 1903:xiii for an interesting list of older collections of Reformed confessions.

5   The following paragraphs on Jonker are extracts from a longer essay on his work accepted for publication by the journal *Verbum et Ecclesia* in 2014 under the title "A public theology from within the church?"

6   Jonker (1929-2006) taught Practical Theology in Kampen (The Netherlands) from 1968-1971 and Dogmatics at the Stellenbosch theological faculty from 1971 to his retirement in 1994. He played a major role in the church struggle from within the Dutch Reformed Church, always steering toward the Reformed roots of the church. For our current discussion his book on Reformed confessions (including a discussion of the Heidelberg Catechism), published as *Bevrydende waarheid* (Liberating truth) in 1994 is of specific significance.

Jonker goes further and positions himself in the specific Reformed tradition within broader Protestant theology.[7] He draws distinctions between Luther and Calvin, and argues that the valid insights from Luther should be maintained, but supplemented by the broader theological vision of John Calvin (Heyns and Jonker 1974:248-252).

Jonker works in broad strokes here. In depicting the relationship between God and humans, Luther would emphasise the holiness of God and sinful nature of the human being, whereas Calvin works on the basis of our Creator God in relation to fallen creation, including fallen human beings. Justification for Luther means being saved from sin, whereas for Calvin justification encompasses the recreation of all of reality and God's saving act from sin and all destructive powers. Luther interprets the rule of Christ through the "two kingdoms" view, where the law has as primary role the revelation of sin, whereas Calvin views Christ's rule as a rule over all of reality in the one kingdom of God, with the law as a guide to holiness and the transformation of society (Heyns and Jonker 1974:251-252). This last point – obedience to the law of God as revealed in the Bible for the whole political and social order – is put forward by Pelikan as "the most characteristic difference between Lutheran and Calvinist views of obedience to the word and will of God" (Pelikan 1984:217).

Already in the question as to what theology actually is lies the answer to why the Reformed tradition has given rise to a multiplicity of confessional statements: **because the revelation of God in Scripture is taken as the sole source and criterion of the Gospel truth which spans the whole of society and is proclaimed anew in and for each time.**

One can thus say that the Reformed churches adhere to an "open" rather than a "closed" confessional tradition, where the former holds a particular statement of faith to be adequate for all times and places, and the latter holds that statements of faith follow one another as a line of gospel proclamation in history, always expecting new confessions as may be required from time to time[8] (Stotts 1998:xi). Leith remarks that Reformed Protestantism "has been prolific in the production of creeds" over a long period of time and emanating from wide geographical areas.

> Hence the Reformed creeds exhibits a variety that is the nemesis of all those who would write *the* theology of *the* Reformed confessions (Leith 1973:127, original emphases).[9]

---

7   See Jonker's (1974:232-260) contribution in the Heyns and Jonker co-publication, *Op weg met die teologie*.
8   There are different reasons why confessions are adopted. These may vary from internal strife around specific doctrines, the needs of catechism and liturgy, statements accompanying church unification processes, or – in extreme cases – as a response to a *status confessionis* or situation in which it is judged that the very nature of the church and the very truth of the gospel are at stake.
9   There are indeed some distinctive Reformed doctrines in relation to (for example) Holy Communion, the third use of the law, and predestination, but "one of the hallmarks of Reformed theology is that no single creed or teaching office has been vested with the power to state definitively what the boundaries of Reformed opinion sought to be" (Johnson 2003: 66). See Smit (2010) for a good overview of the search for a specific "Reformed" identity, and note the remark by Eberhard Busch: "Apparently it belongs to the structure of the Reformed tradition itself to question its confessional identity" (2003: 20). He writes this just before he ventures to outline the specific profile of Reformed thought in relation, inter alia, to the Heidelberg Catechism (29-33).

Let us investigate this through a closer reading of Calvin's discussion of the spiritual power of the church to declare doctrine, and an examination of Barth's view on the nature of the Reformed confessions in contrast to Concordist Lutheranism.

2. CALVIN: NO NEW DOCTRINE?[10]

After discussion in his *Institutes* on the marks and government of the church, Calvin (IV.8.1) considers the spiritual power of the church in terms of doctrine, jurisdiction (legislation) and in enacting laws. It is the first of these powers that concerns us here: the authority to deliver dogmas and the power to interpret them.

Calvin (IV.8.2) enters into a broad discussion of the Old Testament prophets and makes clear that

> ... whenever they are called to office, they are enjoined not to bring anything of their own, but to speak by the mouth of the Lord.

Referring to the examples of Moses, Ezekiel and Jeremiah, Calvin (IV.8.3) reiterates that "none of the prophets opened his mouth unless preceded by the word of the Lord". Their power and authority rests solely on their being "organs of the Holy Spirit" in that the prophets were "strictly bound not to deliver anything but what they received" (Calvin IV.8.3).

The same holds for the apostles in the New Testament: their authority rests on the fact that they do not speak "their own pleasure, but faithfully deliver the commands of him by whom they are sent" (Calvin IV.8.3). Just as Christ relies on the Father for his doctrine (John 7:16), so the apostles are sent to teach the nations whatsoever is commanded by Christ, and "not what they themselves had at random fabricated" (Calvin IV.8.8).

The power of the church to deliver doctrine is therefore a limited power. It is not infinite, "but is subject to the word of the Lord and, as it were, included in it" (Calvin IV.8.4). The word of the Lord refers firstly to Christ as the only true manifestation of God. The Father appointed the Son as our teacher,

> ordering us to seek the whole doctrine of salvation from him alone, to depend on him alone, in short, to listen only to his voice (Calvin IV.8.7).

But God was pleased to commit and consign his word to writing, and the Scriptures therefore serve as source and yardstick of all doctrine. Under guidance of the Holy Spirit, the Spirit of Christ, the Church is to remember the teachings of Christ. The supreme power that pastors of the church carry is to boldly witness to the word

---

10 Note that Calvin uses the word "doctrine" in the general sense of "teaching" and in the more specific sense of "dogma" or "confession". See Opitz *Calvins theologische Hermeneutik* (1994), with a chapter on the preaching of the Word of God as "doctrina"), and also d'Assonville's doctoral dissertation, *Der Begriff "doctrina" bei Johannes Calvin – eine theologische Analyse* (2000) for a detailed analysis of Calvin's use of the word "doctrina".

of the Lord, and not to coin new doctrine or design new decrees which are mere "fictions of men" (Calvin IV.8.9). Yes,

> God deprives man of the power of production of new doctrine, in order that he alone may be our master in spiritual teaching, as he alone is true, and can neither lie nor deceive (Calvin IV.8.9).

Calvin (IV.8.12), however, does not deny that the church has the power to "deliver dogmas", but then such dogmas must be judged by the word of God to see whether "the word of the Lord is faithfully preserved and maintained in purity", or whether these are doctrines "extraneous to the word of God" (Calvin IV.8.13). He fiercely denies the Roman Catholic view that the promise of the Spirit to the Church automatically implies that the church cannot err. If a Council meets and acts in contempt of the word of God by coining dogmas contrary to the word of God, the church strays from the right path and misuses its authority to demand assent to those decisions (Calvin IV.8.14). In simple terms:

> … we cannot concede to the church any new doctrine; in other words, allow her to teach and oracularly deliver more than the Lord has revealed in his word (Calvin IV.8.15).

The word of the Lord is thus the source of dogma that may never state more than the word, and the word is the measure by which dogma is to be interpreted. Calvin is clear: this restriction does not mean that no new words or phrases may be designed to express the truth of the gospel. In Nicea we confess that the Son is "consubstantial" (*homo-ousios*) with the Father, and although this term does not appear in Scripture, it does "simply declare the genuine meaning of Scripture" (Calvin IV.8.16).

If the measure of the word of the Lord, the only "sure law of discrimination" (IV.9.9), is applied to the Councils, not all pass the test. If measured by the authority of Scripture, the councils of Nicea, Constantinople, Ephesus I and Chalcedon are to be affirmed, as "they contain nothing but the pure and genuine interpretation of Scripture" (Calvin IV.9.8). But Ephesus II and the Council of Nice are repudiated because the former confirmed the Eutychian heresy[11] (Calvin IV.9.13), and the latter condoned the setting up of images in the church, opening the door to idolatry (Calvin IV.9.9). The same repudiation holds for teachings on purgatory, priestly celibacy, intercessions of saints and auricular confession as "not one syllable can be found in the Scripture" (Calvin IV.9.14) to support them.

It is clear from this exposition of Calvin's thought that Christ as attested to in Scripture is the only basis for the authority of the church to formulate doctrine. The limits of the Scriptures in the confessions of the church are twofold: Scriptures are the source of doctrine and such doctrine is a mere interpretation of Scripture. And when the church does accept or proclaim doctrine, only Scripture acts as judge of its orthodoxy (Calvin IV.9.9).

This tendency to "relativise" dogma and subject it to the constant proviso of the Word of God is exactly one of the grounds for the multiplicity of confessions in the

---

11   Eutyches (380 – c. 456) was judged heretical in his view of the two natures of Christ by the Synod of Constantinople in 448, but was re-instated in 449 at Ephesus II (Calvin's reference here), and again deposed at Chalcedon in 451.

Reformed tradition. This is confirmed and further explained in Barth's discussion of the task of dogmatics and the nature of Reformed confessions.

3. BARTH: "... A PUZZLING AND PARADOXICAL PICTURE?[12]

In explaining the task of dogmatics Barth takes at least three factors into account that highlights the provisional nature of dogmatics and subsequently of confessions.

First, dogmatics as a science shares with all sciences the trait of always being "preliminary and limited" and merely an attempt at knowledge (Barth 1949:9). For Christian doctrine this "attempt" is specifically related to the gospel, which is "boundless, eternal and therefore inexhaustible", so that no doctrine is able to reproduce its fullness. The gospel of Jesus Christ relates to God's own perfect work and – measured by it – our human descriptions are always imperfect (Barth 1964:18).

Second, dogmatics does not fall from heaven nor does the Christian Church exist in heaven, but amid earthly and human circumstances, so that dogmatics that studies the "what" (content) of the church's proclamation always reflects knowledge "as it has been given to us today" – knowledge that is relative and liable to error (Barth 1949:11).

Third – and more directly relevant to our topic – the guidance of the confessions, the "witness of the Fathers" has to be taken seriously, but always keeping in mind that the confessions stand under Scripture and have a relative and non-binding authority.[13] "Holy Scripture and the Confessions do not stand on the same level. We do not have to respect the Bible and tradition with the like reverence and love, not even the tradition in its most dignified manifestations. No Confession of the Reformation or of our own day can claim the respect of the Church in the same degree that Scripture in its uniqueness deserves it" (Barth 1949:13).

The corpus of confessions within the Reformed tradition shows a marked fluidity and openness derived from its lived context-dependency, the specificity of its content, and its provisional authority.

The context-orientation refers to the fact that, if the church lives under the living word of God and is always being reformed according to the Word of God, there will always yet again arise occasions where the proclamation of the church is directed at a new situation requiring the Word of God to be spoken differently to be a word for that place and that time. This is why Barth defines a Reformed creed as a statement publicly formulated by a Christian community "within a geographically limited area", thereby providing one reason why a general or universal Reformed creed is simply not a good idea:

> I can believe with the most distant, with the ecumenical company; I can confess my faith only with my neighbours, that is with those known to me as fellow believers (Barth 1962:125).[14]

---

12 "Discerning the significance of the confession in the Reformed church has presented us with a puzzling and paradoxical picture." See Barth 2002:38ff.

13 See Georg Plasger's authoritative work, *Die relative Autorität des Bekenntnisses bei Karl Barth* (2000) for an interpretation of Barth's understanding of confessions.

14 See Naudé 2010:95ff for a discussion of Barth's definition of a Reformed confession as applied to the Belhar confession.

Reformed confessions "bear the marks of the occasional, of relatedness to a specific time and situation, of the unique" (Barth 2002:20)

This content-specificity is closely tied to the spatial limits of the creeds. A creed does not cover the whole of Scripture; it is not a general theological treatise, but addresses a specific aspect of the will of God. It refutes a specific lie or half-truth; it offers something definite in the name of God. To attempt writing a confession so that "as many as possible can rally under the banner of a very general 'yes' can happen only at the price of the 'yes'" (Barth 1962:129).

In his reflection on the Heidelberg Catechism (originally from 1948), Barth (1964:22) states clearly:

> Good (i.e. right) Christian doctrine does not take place in the vacuum of solitary thinking; it chooses its place in the fellowship of saints, in connection with the living, thinking, knowing of the whole Christian church …

He judges the positive impact of the Heidelberg Catechism from the fact that – unlike some other confessional writings – "it grew out of the immediate necessities of the life of a *church*" (Barth 1964:22; emphasis in original).

In his contribution to Martin Niemoller's Festschrift, Barth reflects as follows on the Barmen declaration:

> Barmen war darum (im Unterschied zu manchen kirchlichen Schriftstuecke, die so heissen) ein echtes, ein kirchliches Glaubensbekenntnis, weil seine Saetze nich im leeren Raum einer bloss theologischen Diskussion, **sondern in einem konkreten Akt und Bezug des Bekennens einer christlichen Gemeinde**, im Feuer eines handgreiflich konkreten Gegensatzes zu ihrem Zeugnis, als Theorie einer bestimmten praktisch notwendigen Verantwortung ausgesprochen wurden (1952:10; my emphasis).[15]

He goes so far as to say that the power of the Barmen declaration stands or falls with the presupposition that it was confessed and spoken in the church, as the church, and for the church at that specific place and in that specific context (Barth 1952:12).

The provisional nature of the confessions is at a more fundamental level to be derived from their position under the authority of Scripture. A creed is always formulated "until further action", because the on-going revelation of God in Jesus Christ as attested to in the Scriptures can never be fully and finally captured by our creeds, and the church always stands under the guidance of the Spirit of Jesus Christ, who allows and commands what should be confessed (Barth 1961:86). No matter how widespread the acknowledgement of a Reformed confession is, it is always intended as "merely provisional, improvable and replaceable offerings",

---

15   A translation of this (rich!) quotation may read: "That is why the Barmen declaration was (unlike some other church documents which go by the name) a real, a church creed, because its propositions were not declared in an empty space of a mere theological discussion, **but in a specific act and reference of a confessing Christian community**, in the heat of a palpable specific antithesis to its witness, as theory of a particular and necessary responsibility."

and always open to be corrected from Scripture (Barth 2002:24).[16] The significance of a Reformed confession, writes Barth, "consists in its essential nonsignificance, its obvious relativity, humanity, multiplicity, mutability, and transitoriness" (Barth 2002:38).

This is the basis of Barth's polemic about the significance of the confessions in the Lutheran church. He acknowledges that a "reasonable Lutheranism" could find resonance with the Heidelberg Catechism (Barth 1964:25) as the latter expresses the great truths, commonly recognised in the Reformation. But he returns to *The Book of Concord* (1580)[17] – and specifically the view expressed in the Formula of Concord on the Augsburg Confession – which for him is ambiguous about two important matters.

First, the Augustana is the one, final symbol of the Lutheran church, confessing the ancient faith (like Nicea) and serving as guideline for the interpretation of all other expressions of faith, not only for its own time but *ad omnem posteritatem* (Barth 1962: 115). This creates a closed hermeneutical frame that lacks the provisional nature of confessions in the Reformed tradition.[18]

Second, and for Barth even more unacceptable, is the fact that – although Scripture is confessed as "eternal truth" and as the "basis" of all truth standing in "brilliant distinction" from all other writings – the Augustana is brought into remarkable proximity to the Holy Scriptures. The Augustana is presented in some formulations as having a similar normativity in judging other writings as is accorded to the Scriptures. This places the Augsburg Confession beyond the questioning and criticism of Scripture, because "the dignity of Scripture" (Barth 2002:5) has been transferred to it, rendering it no longer a mutable but rather an "immutable entity" (Barth 2002:6).

The binding obligation put upon Lutherans by this authoritative confession has advantages. Against the Catholic church Lutherans now have their own authoritative understanding of the Bible (i.e. their own authoritative tradition acting as unitary norm of doctrine); and against the Reformed churches, which live in the uncertainty of always confessing anew under the judgment of Scripture, Lutherans have the certainty and dignity of a viewpoint promulgated as law.

---

16 See the reference to examples such as Zwingli's Sixty Seven theses, the Bern consensus and the Duisberg General Synod of 1610 (Barth 2002: 24-25).

17 *The Book of Concord* includes, inter alia, the Augsburg Confession (1530), the Apology of the Augsburg Confession (1531), Luther's Smalcaldic Articles (1537), Luther's Small and Large Catechism (1529), and the Formula of Concord (1577). See Leith (1973: 61ff) for introduction and texts.

18 Jan Rohls (1998:9) refers to the interesting impulse amongst Reformed churches – responding to Concordist Lutheranism – to also develop a standard set of confessions that could serve as unitary norm for all other statements of faith. A prime examples of such a (failed) project is the unionistic collection, *Harmonia confessionum fide, orthodoxarum et reformatarum ecclesiarum*, produced by Jean Salvard and published in Geneva in 1581.

But, argues Barth, these advantages could never be acceptable in the Reformed churches. Tradition – even the most highly venerated confessions – can never have the same authority or dignity as the Scriptures.

> The Reformed confessions are and desire to be nothing other than mere human confessional *acts, over against which* the revelation of God in Scripture also stands as a *given*" (Barth 2002:20, emphasis in original).

Reformed confessions – which should never be called "symbols"[19] – are indeed "sincere expositions of faith" (Calvin). They should be viewed with reverence and thankfulness for those who confessed before us, but there must be *freedom* in the communion of saints through a re-interpretation (and not mere repetition) of past confessions.

> Not to allow and require such freedom would mean that we in the church had returned to a kind of tradition which stands with equal honour alongside Holy Scripture (Barth 1964:21-22).

The confessions should, however, also not be viewed as permanent laws for interpreting Scripture (like a frozen river on which one could walk), because they are by their very nature open to examination and discussion, requiring time to prove themselves (like a flowing river in which one can freely swim) (Barth 2002:20, 27). "Gottes Wort und Luther's Lehr vergehen nun und nimmermehr" could, says Barth, "never be uttered by a Calvinist". It would be just as impossible to talk about "the Word of God and the Augsburg Confession" in the same breath (Barth 2002:21).

The so-called perceived "deficiencies" brought about by this understanding of the Reformed confessions must all be brought back to one fundamental point: The church is called to witness to the gospel of Jesus Christ

> ... not as the truth in our mouth but as the truth in God's mouth ... The witness (as person) stutters, and the witness (as content) is confused, but the Word of God will stand for ever (Isa. 40:8) (Barth 2002:39).

In short:

> Ultimately, the Reformed principle of Scripture[20] forces the Reformed confession against the wall and renders it so fragmented, so desecrated, so human and temporal, so minimally binding. 'Woe is me, I am lost', it says, and as by a devouring fire, the truth of Scripture that is confessed, attacks the truth of the confession, puts it in question, destroys it to the extent that it does not glow with the same fire that consumes it.

---

19 Barth, in his analysis of the HC, even avoids speaking about the Heidelberg **orthodoxy**, as that could be interpreted as an "unmoveable and unchangeable" doctrinal view (1964:21). He also stands firm against any attempt toward confessionalism, "one of the most questionable things which is happening today in German theology and in the German church" (1964:22).

20 There is no room in this paper to go into the complex dogmatic and hermeneutical questions related to the so-called "Scriptural principle". For an enlightening discussion by Michael Welker, see "Sola Scriptura? The authority of the Bible in pluralistic environments" (Welker 2002).

Reformed confession is confession of the truth of Scripture; as long as and to the extent that it is this, it has not ceased to exist (Barth 2002:40).

4. CLOSING REMARKS

This paper notes that a multiplicity of confessional statements is particular to the Reformed tradition. Examples of such collections from the Reformation up to the present were cited at the beginning.

It was then argued that the reason for this creedal plurality should be sought in the very understanding of theology as reflection on God's revelation in Scripture; in the limited power of the church to produce and interpret new doctrine, and in the radical proviso of confessions, which – though held in high reverence – always stand under the ultimate authority of Scripture and are therefore treated with marked freedom in the communion of saints.

Because the church stands in the power of the Spirit and the Word – as specifically interpreted in Reformed circles – there will always be further confessions. These confessions are gifts of insight into the gospel truth, given at a specific time and in a specific place, in response to burning questions of doctrine, ethics, and life.

Until further action is necessary…

BIBLIOGRAPHY

Barth, K. 1949. *Dogmatics in outline.* London: SCM Press.

Barth, K. 1952. Barmen. In Joachim Beckmann & Herbert Mochalski: *Bekennende Kirche. Martin Niemoeller zum 60. Geburtstag.* München: Chr Kaiser Verlag, 9-17.

Barth, K. 1956. *Church dogmatics I/2: The revelation of God.* Edinburgh: T&T Clark.

Barth, K. 1961. *Church dogmatics, III/4: The doctrine of creation.* Edinburgh: T&T Clark.

Barth, K. 1962. The desirability and possibility of a universal Reformed creed. In *Theology and church: Shorter writings, 1920-1928.* London: SCM Press.

Barth, K. 1964. *Learning Jesus Christ through the Heidelberg Catechism.* Grand Rapids: Eerdmans.

Barth, K. 2002. *The theology of the Reformed confessions 1923.* Louisville: Westminster John Knox.

Busch, E. 2003. Reformed strength in denominational weakness. In: W.M. Alston Jr and M. Welker (eds.). *Reformed theology. Identity and Ecumenicity.* Grand Rapids: Eerdmans, pp.20-33.

Calvin, J. 1975. *Institutes of the Christian religion.* Grand Rapids: Eerdmans.

D'Assonville, V.E. 2000. *Der Begriff "doctrina" bei Johannes Calvin – eine theologische Analyse.* Münster-Hamburg-London: Lit Verlag.

Heyns, J.A. & Jonker W.D. 1974. *Op weg met die teologie.* Pretoria: NG Kerkboekhandel.

Johnson, W.S. 2003. Theology and the church's mission: Catholic, Orthodox, Evangelical, and Reformed. In: W.M. Alston Jr and M. Welker (eds.). *Reformed theology. Identity and Ecumenicity*. Grand Rapids: Eerdmans, pp.65-81.

Jonker, W.D. 1976. What is theology? In: P.C. Schrotenboer (ed.): *Church and theology in the contemporary world*. Grand Rapids: Michigan, pp.3-15.

Jonker, W.D.1994. *Bevrydende waarheid*. Wellington: Hugenote Uitgewers.

Leith, J. 1973. *Creeds of the churches. A reader in Christian doctrine from the Bible to the present*. Oxford: Basil Blackwell.

Mueller, E.F.K. (Hrsg.) 1903. *Die Bekenntnisschriften der reformierten Kirche*. Leipzig: Deichert.

Naudé, P.J. 2010. *Neither calendar nor clock. Perspectives on the Belhar confession*. Grand Rapids: Eerdmans.

Naudé, P.J. 2014. A 'public theology' from within the church? A reflection on aspects of the theology of W.D. Jonker (1929-2006). In: *Verbum et Ecclesia* 35(1). DOI:10.4102/ve.v35i1.1136

Opitz, P. 1994. *Calvins theologische Hermeneutik*. Neukirchener Verlag: Neukirchen.

Pelikan, J. 1984. *Reformation of church and dogma (1300-1700). The Christian tradition, Vol. 4*. Chicago: University of Chicago Press.

Plasger, G. 2000. *Die relative Autorität des Bekenntnisses bei Karl Barth*. Neukirchen: Neukirchener Verlag.

Rohls, J. 1998. *Reformed confessions. Theology from Zurich to Barmen*. Louisville: Westminster John Knox.

Smit, D.J. 2010. Trends and directions in Reformed theology. *The Expository Times* 122(7),1-14.

Stotts, J.L. 1998. Introduction: Confessing after Barmen. In: J. Rohls 1998, pp. xi-xxiv.

Vischer, L. (ed.) 1982. *Reformed witness today. A collection of confessions and statements of faith issued by Reformed churches*. Bern: Evangelische Arbeitstelle.

Welker, M. 2002. Sola Scriptura? The authority of the Bible in pluralistic environments. In: B. Strawn (ed.). *A God so near. Festschrift for Patrick D Miller*. Winona Lake: Eisenbrowns, pp. 375-391.

2.3 CAN WE STILL HEAR PAUL ON THE AGORA?

An outsider perspective on the ethics of South African New Testament scholarship

Paul speaks at the house of Gamaliel, and Paul speaks in the house of the Lord, but he rarely speaks in the public house, the marketplace of ideas, the agora.

1. INTRODUCTION

1.1. The role of the outsider

I am obliged to call myself an outsider at this meeting of the New Testament Society of South Africa (NTSSA)[1] for various reasons. My general field of theological expertise lies in systematic theology and ethics.[2] I have never been a member of the NTSSA nor have I ever attended one of its conferences. (This is an indication – perhaps – of the insularity of systematic theology and NT scholarship in general, and of my particular inability to contribute towards forging closer ties). I am therefore ill-informed about the inner politics and ethos of NT scholarship in South Africa and, despite a fair knowledge of the biblical languages and a deep interest in exegesis, I am also ill-informed about the latest reading strategies and technical debates among New Testament scholars in general.

There are, however, two reasons precisely why an outsider might be useful to stimulate debate amongst the members of a learned society:

1. In social sciences research the value of an *etic* versus an *emic* view has been well established.[3] And the "outsider" perspective – because of greater distance and different pre-understandings – may yield new insights while looking at the same set of events as the "insiders";[4]

---

[1] Opening address at the NTSSA conference on 12 April 2005 in Bloemfontein, South Africa.
[2] The bias of my background is declared up front and will play a significant role in my interpretation of NT scholarship in this paper. I record my thanks to the reviewers for their comments, which aided me in preparing the final draft of the paper.
[3] This distinction stems from social anthropology and the study of "foreign" cultures, but has entered general research terminology in the social sciences. See Mouton and Marais 1988, Chapter 4.
[4] Thomas Kuhn's well-known paradigm theory (Kuhn 1970) was developed in the context of the natural sciences, but gained a wide heuristic function across disciplines. For a theological discussion, see Küng and Tracy (1989). A very important aspect of his theory is that a paradigm is constituted by a community of practitioners who share the same scientific commitments and view of reality (which is then later challenged by theories with apparently superior problem-solving abilities). One could interpret Kuhn as saying that to change the "ontology" you need to change the "sociology"; i.e. the composition of the community, in order to open the possibility of "an alternative view".

2. From narrative theory we have learnt the value of story-telling to reveal identity. German ecumenical theologian, Dietrich Ritschl,[5] has – for example – taught us how particularly revealing it can be not so much telling our own story, but listening without interruption as our story is being told to us by others. One tends to glorify or justify one's own story, and needs the view of "the other" to expose and explore the "implicit axioms" of one's own world view.

The NTSSA is therefore to be commended for establishing a tradition of opening addresses by persons from outside its ranks. I consider this invitation as a great honour and opportunity, as I have always viewed this society as one of the strongest in SA and as having an impeccable international standing.

1.2. The metaphor of Paul

A few notes about the topic: I am obviously not in a position to make a scientific contribution to "Pauline studies" as understood within NT scholarship – as will become evident from other papers over the next two days. The topic above wishes to engage in what one could call the reception of "NT scholarship" as a "text" in its own right in other publics than the public of the NT scholarly family. Can "Paul" – as metaphor for any NT genre or topic – "speak" through and beyond scholarly insiders? Can NT scholars follow Paul from Gamaliel to the *areios pagos* (Areopagus) and the lively, public interchange of ideas on the *agora*?

1.3. The notion of responsiveness

This kind of critical self-awareness is not new and has previously been addressed by NT scholars themselves (see references below). The present South African academic context forces upon us the urgent question of the reception of our work beyond the confines of our scholarly associations. This may be explained by the requirement to be "responsive" to the context of South Africa as part of the African continent.

The deep-seated and encompassing programme of transformation in Higher Education – from SAQA (South African Qualifications Authority) to the current mergers of tertiary educational institutions (2004) – was guided *inter alia* by the value of "responsiveness". This "indicates a shift away from academic insularity, a closed system governed primarily by the norms and procedures of established disciplines, toward an open higher education system which interacts more with its societal environment" (National Council on Higher Education [NCHE] 1996:76).

As **epistemological** category, responsiveness expresses the idea of an "open" knowledge system where universities create knew knowledge in partnership with others (civil society, business communities) and disseminate this knowledge beyond the confines of their own boundaries. In the spirit of so-called mode 2 knowledge,[6] there is a recognition of multiple sites of knowledge production, a blurring of the modernist boundaries between "theoretical" and "applied" knowledge, and

---

5   See Ritschl and Jones (1976) for one of the earliest systematic attempts at a "narrative" theology, and Ritschl's specific discussion in his own work, *Zur Logik der Theologie*, later (1984:45ff).

6   The "modes of knowledge" debate was largely informed by Gibbons et al. (1994). For a South African perspective, see Kraak 2000.

acknowledgment of the validation of knowledge by the users (and not the creators!) thereof. And in the context of "globalisation", the symmetry between local and global knowledge is to be promoted – as seen, for example, in the National Research Foundation's special funding for Indigenous Knowledge Systems and the recent report to minister Naledi Pandor on the promotion of indigenous languages.

As **social** category, responsiveness urges South African academics to reflect in the content and focus of their work the realities of this country in the context of Africa.[7] Ours is "a modernising country in a state of transition, emerging from the consequences of a dispensation of racial discrimination and oppression, and hopefully heading towards a free and open society" (NCHE 1996:79). Scholarship tends to move in the direction of money and prestige, and for now it has been the West that has set the agenda, determines the paradigms, yields sabbatical opportunities, owns the publishing houses and provides the social orientation. Theology is only expressed with a genitive if it is not mainline Western theology, making clear what is in the centre and what is marginal.

As a **political** category, responsiveness refers to the growing insistence that higher education is not so much a private but a public good. Academics, and the system as a whole, are "accountable to larger social and economic constituencies" and to "a larger community of interested parties" that include the taxpayer in a client/consumer relation of cost-effectiveness, quality and relevance (NCHE 1996, 80).

This interpretation of responsiveness ("knowledge", "sociality" and "politics") forms the basis of my paper, as I suggest three prerequisites for scholarship – specifically Biblical scholarship – to "speak" beyond its own boundaries in our present context. They relate to the philosophy of science ("knowledge"), an understanding of social location and ethics ("sociality"), and a commitment to the construction of a public theology ("politics").

2. THREE PREREQUISITES FOR A RESPONSIVE BIBLICAL SCHOLARSHIP

2.1. *New Testament scholars need to make their implicit epistemological assumptions explicit, and commit themselves to emancipatory cognitive interests*

Most of you know Habermas's theory of cognitive interests that, according to him, underlie our search for truth and the production of knowledge (see Habermas's classic exposition (1972:308- 310)):

- The technical interest, pursued by the empirical-analytical sciences, is promoted through observation and nomological hypotheses with empirical content that make predictions possible. This forms the core of science in a positivist framework;

- The practical or communicative interest, pursued by the historical-hermeneutical sciences, is promoted through interpretation and the construction of meaning. This forms the core of science in an interpretivist framework;

---

7   See the recent publication of a number of essays, edited by Sipho Seepe (2004), that attempt to define what an African identity for higher education would mean.

- The emancipatory interest, pursued by the sciences of social action, is enacted through self-reflection and ideological critique, and forms the core of science in a transformative framework.

Two crucial insights from Habermas are especially relevant for this paper.

First, he did not reject the technical and communicative interests in favour of the emancipatory. A mature social science, he argued, would not see these interests as mutually exclusive: they complement one another. In terms of biblical scholarship, this implies that the striving for more "objective" readings, where the empirical text as stable sign system is analysed as an autotelic, literary unit (like New Criticism and some forms of structuralism), need not refute more historical or reader-oriented approaches – on condition that the former do not fall into positivism and a narrow view of objectivity.

Second, keeping Habermas's roots in Marxist thought in mind, satisfaction with mere "Erklärung" (empirical-technical interest) and "Verstehen" (hermeneutical interest) would be epistemologically dangerous and obviously unacceptable. The emancipatory epistemic interest is not a luxurious extra that may or may not be pursued by the scientist. All knowledge production is embedded in socio-economic interests and subject to ideological manipulation, and either confirms or critically transforms power relations in society.

Although we need not all suddenly become Marxists, Nietscheans, Freudians, feminists, liberation theologians or deconstructionists in the Derridean sense, we need to engage in self-critical reflection on our social location and the interests served by our scholarship. In the absence of such reflection, the outcome is guaranteed: we will opt for interesting new technical methods of interpretation and will relish new hermeneutical insights that make alternative readings of the biblical texts possible. But we will rarely pursue radical emancipatory interests, as this would – in most cases – be contrary to our own social and economic interests.

The story of critical self-reflection in biblical scholarship now invariably starts with the almost classic SBL presidential address by Elizabeth Schüssler-Fiorenza in 1986. She noted an assumed value-neutrality oblivious to the political context of interpretation; an inability to translate meaning beyond the historical investigation of the text; and the creation of a closed world of expert inquiry which denies the interests and values underlying scholars' own communicative practices (Schüssler-Fiorenza 1988:4).

South African NT scholarship has been challenged in the same vein. Already in 1989 Pieter de Villiers had noted the lack of a specific (South) African perspective in the work of NT scholarly contributions. He refers to the social vacuum in which NT scholars operated due to a "contextless" lack of awareness of social location in their interpretative task (De Villiers 1989:122). In a number of contributions Dirkie Smit analyses the history of NT scholarship. He calls for a "responsible hermeneutics" that highlights the doctrinal and ethical implications of the text (1988); he discusses what the ethics of interpretation would mean in our context (1990); and he calls for readings that take the underlying interpretative interests seriously (Smit 1994:272-277), whilst engaging with other interpretative communities in a constructive dialogue (Smit 1994:277-282).

This self-critical orientation against what was seen as a "scientist ethos" flared up a few times between 1992 and 2003 in the pages of *Neotestamentica*. I put these contributions in chronological order.

- In 1992 Jan Botha calls on fellow scholars no longer to hide from pressing social realities behind literary and structural analyses. He argues for an ethics of interpretation that still takes reading the textuality of the text seriously (Botha 1992:185).

- JN Vorster reflects on the "rhetorical turn" that requires an analysis of the rhetoricity of enquiry itself. This prompts one to ask specific questions about interpretative interests, rhetorical situations, and a focus not so much on the object as on the purpose of inquiry (Vorster 1999:293, 316).

- Maretha Jacobs, in the light of feminist insights, defends a focus on the impact of Bible-reading on people's lives as an integral part of the hermeneutical task (Jacobs 2001:86).

- Gerald West develops an "indigenous exegesis" that takes the interpretative interests of ordinary African readers seriously, so that one may talk about indigenous hermeneutical forms (West 2002:159).

- Jeremy Punt calls attention to the potential of post-colonial biblical criticism as a form of ideological critique to shape interpretative discourses as counter-offensive against political, economic and cultural forms of imperialism (Punt 2003:60).

Why are these papers so significant? Because each one in its own right performs some form of decentring ideological critique, albeit from different angles: textuality, rhetoric, feminism, ordinary readers and post-colonialism. These relatively small voices are indispensable as it is always possible for a guild of scholars to be immensely critical, but still remain ideologically naive, i.e. blind to the unconscious interests that drive their cognition. The task of critical self-reflection on the philosophy of science underlying NT scholarship is an ongoing one. The hermeneutics of suspicion in its various forms,[8] and post-modern ideological critique should be applied first and foremost to the self, to one's own paradigm.

The question, however, is whether this critical self-reflection on the "knowledge" produced by NT scholars made any real difference to the form and content of that knowledge? To answer this, we to turn the next section on ethics.

2.2 New Testament scholars need to honour and act according to a multidimensional understanding of "the ethics of interpretation"

For the sake of clarity I wish to distinguish four senses in which "ethics" and "NT scholarship" may be linked, understood and practised.

2.2.1 Ethics firstly refers to the internal research – or **professional – ethics** of a scholarly society. This links with issues normally discussed in ethics pertaining to

---

[8] See the summary (with a somewhat OT bias) of approaches that would fall into the category of a "hermeneutics of suspicion" (including Freudian, Marxist, feminist, African and ecological approaches) in Jonker and Lawrie (eds) (2005:167-228).

qualitative research: transparent use and recognition of sources; ethical publication practices; obligation to donors; and the open dissemination of research results (see Mouton (2001) as well as Babbie and Mouton 2001:520-547).

2.2.2 Ethics may secondly refer to "**biblical ethics**" or in our case "NT ethics". This is a specific attempt to understand the moral world of the early Christian communities,[9] and a careful systematisation of what could be called "Pauline ethics"[10] or "the ethics of Jesus"[11] or even "NT ethics" seen in its inner complexities, but still as a canonical whole.[12]

2.2.3 Ethics could refer, thirdly, to the **ethicality of biblical scholarship**[13] as such. This is closely tied to the critical self-reflection referred to above. Questions about the following then arise: the social location of the scholar, the power of the academy and its effect on our context, the link between scholarship and interpretative communities (Fish), and the reception of the "scholarly text" beyond its own confines.

This reflection has in recent years been stimulated by forms of rhetorical criticism where the technical questions of implied author, persuasive literary devices and implied audience have been augmented by the vital question: At what is the rhetoric aimed?[14] Towards what attitude or action is the reader/listener spurred on? In terms of this section: Of what are receivers of NT scholarship rhetorically persuaded? Toward what action – if any – are we motivated? What vision of life and society – if any – is embedded in our scholarship?

2.2.4 Ethics may refer, fourthly, to **Christian ethics**.[15] In highly simplistic terms, Christian ethics is aimed at the resolving of moral dilemmas facing people or society by skilfully combining insights from biblical ethics, interpretative theological traditions and the contemporary context relevant to the moral question.

To understand a contemporary ethical issue one needs to read at least three texts as competently as possible: the biblical text; the text of the *Wirkungsgeschichte* and confessional tradition in which subsequent interpretations have occurred; and the

---

9   See the well-known publications of Wayne Meeks since 1983 and Theissen (1978) in this regard.
10 See, for example, Paul Sampley (1991) on Paul's moral reasoning and the older work by Victor Furnish on Pauline theology and ethics (1968).
11 See Allen Verhey's recent attempt (2002) to reconstruct a contextual ethics of Jesus based on the notion of the first Christian communities as communities of moral instruction.
12 This paper is not an attempt to provide an overview of all attempts at New Testament ethics. For me as an outsider, the older work by Schrage (1988, original 1982) remains a good example of letting all the voices of the NT speak from an ethical perspective.
13 I am aware of Daniel Patte's work on the ethics of interpretation, but readers will see that I use a slightly different approach here.
14 One thinks of the social implications of Derrida's critique of the inherent oppositional and hierarchical logocentrism of Western metaphysics. See Jonker and Lawrie (2005:150ff) for a discussion and literature.
15 One of the best examples that I recently read is Richard Hays, *The Moral Vision of the New Testament* (1996). Hays sets out a methodological framework of how to read NT texts "ethically". He moves from the descriptive task (textual analysis) through what he terms the synthetic and hermeneutical tasks to end with the pragmatic task. It is in the last section where he boldly moves to address issues such as violence, re-marriage, homosexuality, ethnic conflict and abortion in what I would call a "Christian ethics". This "pragmatic" concern is what I find lacking in South African NT scholarship.

text of the moral issue (ecology, bio-medicine, economics, human rights and so forth). There are more: the subtext of ideology and the unconscious; the text of the person or community that asks the question; and the text of the intertextual nature of ethical dialogue itself!

Let us evaluate New Testament scholarship in the light of the above senses of "ethics".

Most scholarly societies would almost naturally respond to and practise professional ethics. Biblical scholarship may also – as we saw above – every now and again engage in critical self-examination on the ethics of its own enterprise. And biblical ethics – although not as popular as designing new reading strategies – has also claimed a respectable academic place. The question is whether NT scholarship has engaged with the broader ethical issues facing (South) African society today? **Has NT scholarship made a significant contribution to a contextual Christian ethics?**

In very straight terms: In what way has the academically eminent *Neotestamentica* shaped and responded to the many serious issues facing our country and our continent from 1994 to 2004?

I scanned the articles published in the ten years from 1994–2004.[16] To "make the grade" an article needed to display a grappling with at least the text of the NT (Hays's descriptive task) in relation to the text of a moral issue in contemporary society (Hays's pragmatic task).[17]

There were a number of methodological reflections on a meta-ethical level worth mentioning. They do not strictly qualify as contributions to concrete Christian ethics as they still only "sharpen the knives without actually cutting the meat." The list is short.

Pieter Botha explores the link between narrative rhetoric and moral identity (1994); Andries van Aarde argues for the priority of the historical Jesus in the canon as a source of emancipatory living (1994:575); Dirkie Smit asks whether NT scholarship can give credence to an "ethics of being" (1996:181); and there is a discussion of Jan Botha's thesis on multiple interpretative strategies to deal with authority in Rom 13 (1997:195ff) without any specific attempt to draw implications for South African society (1997:220).

The list of ethical contributions in the narrower sense is equally short (and I omit Johan Degenaar's paper published in 1997 as he comes from outside the ranks of NT scholarship).

Pieter Botha's excellent analysis of gender relations in the first-century world is by his own admission not about "recovering the voices of women and the subjugated",

---

16 I am acutely aware of the limitations of this approach. Many NT scholars write in other journals too – such as the special edition of *Scriptura* ("Geloof en opdrag" S9, 1992) – and many have possibly done "ethical" work in non-academic genres published elsewhere. But if one assumes that the academic output and conference proceedings of the NTSSA specifically is reflected in *Neotestamentica*, and that a full decade of publications has been examined, it is not totally unreasonable to make inferences about the focal points of leading NT scholars in South Africa.

17 I have spared scholars the criterion of engagement with the theological reception of biblical texts.

but "first and foremost a critique of a bad way of doing 'background studies'…". There is a methodological bias here, but there is enough ethical flesh in his last two remarks[18] to consider this helpful in our understanding of violence against, and abuse of, women as "disturbing markers of our culture" (2000:32).

The only two other substantial ethical contributions are from women.

Elna Mouton explores how the Aristotelian *ethos*, *logos* and *pathos* contributes to a rhetoric of theological vision. In a wide-ranging "reading of the South African text," she proposes reconciliation as *logos*, biblical authority as healing *ethos*, and lament and praise in liturgy as *pathos* (2001:119-125).

It is significant in itself that the only focused ethical contribution over ten years of *Neotestamentica* issues that I could find appeared only last year and is written by Patricia Bruce.[19] The article deals with the issue of virginity testing in the context of HIV/AIDS and stands out as a genre on its own. She deliberately (?) says: "Before considering the biblical texts, I would like to say a few words about the wider context out of which I have posed questions to the texts" (2004:9). The first 5 sections of her paper are taken up with a reading of cultural texts before she returns to the text of the NT in section 6 (page 17ff), and some concluding remarks where she has the courage to write: "The texts dealing with virginity illustrate that biblical texts on a particular topic are not always useful or relevant to the contemporary debate about that topic…"

I sincerely invite members of this society to assist me in understanding this apparent avoidance of concrete ethical issues.

Can it be explained by a love for methodologies that hover above social issues, but rarely if ever approach them directly? Is it related to the internal organisation of working groups in the NTSSA? Is this a manifestation that ideological critique (see above) is in itself an isolationist technique, a mere rhetorical device to show "how serious we are about the effect of our reading" with no concrete consequences? Do we require an ideological critique of ideological critique? Is the problem, as Dirkie Smit (1996:180-183) has suggested, that NT scholars take over the language of ethics, but attach a different meaning to it?

My own provisional explanation is that Christian ethics is not high on the agenda of biblical scholarship for three reasons.

First, there is no commitment to what I will call public theology (see below).

Second, because ethics is more an art than a science, it does not fit well with notions of "science" and "objectivity" and "academically acceptable research". It therefore requires the biblical scholar to make his/her hands dirty with uncomfortable trans-disciplinary work related to some practice "outside the text". It further requires academics to take a stand – sometimes in highly emotional and politically charged contexts. And there is nothing academics fear more than to be vulnerable,

---

18   Due to a small editorial oversight, they are numbered 4 and 4.
19   On the basis of Kuhn's paradigm theory, I suspect that she is not (yet) deeply steeped in the "normal science" and ethos of New Testament scholarship. But I obviously stand to be corrected.

except where "vulnerability" and "uncertainty" are part of the post-modern, deconstructionist academic language game itself.

Third, there might be a general cynicism about the ability of the biblical text to enlighten contemporary moral texts. There might be a restriction to "intertextuality" or to cross-references among written texts, but not an attempt to engage with "extra-textual" texts. Perhaps NT scholars simply do not see addressing Christian ethics as part of their academic role, despite compelling internal grounds to the contrary. Has ethics been handed over to "the ethicists", whilst biblical scholars stick to an analysis of the biblical text only?

Let us turn to the third broad argument to assist scholarship to move towards social responsiveness.

2.3 New Testament scholars need to contribute to the construction of a public theology in (South) Africa

The term "public theology" is in its origin a technical term referring to those systematic theologies (mainly from the West) that overtly address the loss of public space by theological discourse in a post-Enlightenment context.[20] This context is marked by the privatisation of religion, the growing separation of church and state, and the epistemological isolation of theology as a result of both internal specialisation and the inability to engage in the trans-disciplinary public discourse of the day.

In response to this, Lynn Cady (1987), linking with various other theologians, identified three marks of a public theology.

1. An **open form of argumentation** ensures that theologians accept general terms of rationality such as internal consistency and clarity of thought as equally applicable to them as to other social and human sciences. Theology does not speak a secret language and its truth claims must be open for others to investigate and critically assess.

2. **Accessible forms of communication** ensure that theologians make a concerted effort to translate their scientific work into other forms than merely the genre of the conference paper or academic book, exactly to make these results accessible to other audiences than scholarly colleagues (further restricted to those sharing the same specialisation!).

3. A **focus on the public issues of the day** ensures that theologians show in what way theological knowledge contributes to a better understanding and possible resolution of these issues in the public eye and mind.

This links up with David Tracy's well-known distinction of the three "publics" that are addressed by the theologian: the publics of the academy, the church (and I would add: non-institutional faith communities) and wider society (including various spheres such as politics, the economy, the arts and law) (see Tracy 1981).

---

20 See the contributions of Thiemann, Bellah, Tracy, Stackhouse, Moltmann, Neuhaus and many more. For three South African contributions, see Conradie (1993), Bezuidenhout and Naudé (2002) and Smit (2003).

As an ill-informed outsider, I would suggest that NT scholarship is clearly a public enterprise in the first sense, and partially so in the second sense outlined by Cady. But from my restricted perspective I do not see NT scholars active in both identifying and shaping public issues in the South African context today (and issues of religion and hermeneutics are indeed part of that).

In Tracy's terms, the public of the academy – relating to the internal discourse of NT scholarship and cognate disciplines – is adequately addressed. Whether NT scholars actively engage with the "public" of other theological disciplines like missiology, practical theology and systematic theology is an open question (the pot calling the kettle black!). The faith communities are also partially served by those scholars who attempt to translate technical knowledge into generally accessible faith language – either to confirm, broaden and strengthen faith, or (like the *Nuwe Hervormers*) to unsettle and critically question faith assumptions.

Cady's "public issues" and Tracy's "third public", however, are a matter of grave concern. **Paul speaks at the house of Gamaliel** (at least with others who study rhetoric, history and languages), **and Paul speaks in the house of the Lord** (synagogue and early house communities), **but he rarely speaks in the public house, the marketplace of ideas, the** *agora.*

What are these public issues? The selection itself would reflect one's preferences, but should not prevent us from at least talking about it. My random list[21] would include the following issues.

- The question of moral identity in a transitional society. (Is there nothing to learn from the life-in-between of Paul himself as reflected in Phil 3 and Gal 2, and of the struggle about conflicting moralities as evident in the question of circumcision or eating meat in the first churches?)
- Questions related to justice in its many forms of procedural, retributive, distributive and cultural justice. (What does justification in Romans 1-8 imply for justice in Rom 12-15? And how does that affect our view on restorative forms of justice such as affirmative action and land distribution?)
- How can we break the restricted mould of a bio-medical focus on the HIV/AIDS pandemic in developing a theology of sexuality and understanding taboos and marginalisation? (Is AIDS indeed the leprosy of our time,[22] and how did early faith communities deal with that affliction?)
- The nature of work and the effect of unemployment. (Is there anything useful for today in Eph 4 and 1 Tim 6?)
- How can we live peacefully together and create institutions that "celebrate" diversity despite our gender, class and cultural differences? (Do Eph 2, Col 3 and Gal 3:26-28 help at all?)

The silence of Paul on the market place is no simple matter and the reasons lie both "outside" and "inside" NT scholarship.

---

21 Biblical scholars will note that issues about the "historical truth" of passages like creation, Noah, Jonah, and the miracles and resurrection of Jesus are not listed here as public issues.
22 See the book by Saayman and Kriel with this title.

Reasons "outside" NT scholarship

NT scholarship finds itself in the same boat as theology in general. The acceptance of a liberal constitution in the classical sense has hastened the effects of modernity on South African society: the individual's right of choice as reference point in resolving ethical issues; a clearer *de facto* division of church and state; a loss of the privileged position of the Christian faith despite its huge demographic majority; the promotion of entrepreneurship and the ideals of the free market as regulative value orientation.

In the minds of many religion was useful in the struggle for liberation, but has now receded from its public space to be of use to pious individuals, other-worldly charismatics and "secretive" African Independent Churches. Central stage has now been occupied by economics, politics and law (in that order of importance), and it is a very complex process to regain such space, or to speak from the margins into the public space.

Reasons "inside" NT scholarship

The internal reasons for NT scholarship's inability to shape a public theology lie both in its history and in the cumulative effect of the factors mentioned above. Let us turn to two examples from history first.

Historically speaking, NT scholarship up to the 1990s shared the profile of the SA academy in general: highly elitist and white male dominated. It strikes one that the apartheid system received its moral legitimacy from theology where missiologists (followers of Warneck), NT scholars (e.g. Groenewald (1947) and Snyman (1957)) and systematic theologians (neo-Kuyperians like JD du Toit and FJM Potgieter) provided both a biblical and theological rationale for separate ethnic churches and a political system of separation.[23]

The early white prophets against apartheid in the period 1955-1965 came from systematic theology (Bennie Keet, Ben Engelbrecht, Willie Jonker, Beyers Naudé) and missiology (David Bosch). These protest voices were joined only much later by NT scholars who decisively argued for the unity of the church (from 1988 onward) and started to address socio-political issues.[24]

Biblical scholars were generally slow to openly criticise the system, because – and this is an assumption based on later reflections – the way they understood themselves, and the role of the academy, precluded active participation in such debates.

A second example relates to the unwillingness or apparent reluctance of NT scholars to engage in systematic theological debates about the Bible. One can understand this reluctance from the misuse of Scripture by some systematic theologians who would seek "proof-texts" of prior accepted doctrines and then proudly claim an adherence to *sola scriptura*. A confessional standpoint is, it seems, the deadly enemy of "unbiased" biblical research.

---

23 The classic analysis of Johann Kinghorn and others in 1986 (*Die NG Kerk en apartheid*) still stands as important milestone in unravelling the past. A very useful recent contribution is found in the collection of papers edited by Wolfram Weisse and Carl Anthonissen, published in *Scriptura* 76 (2001) and in Weisse and Anthonissen (2004).

24 See the excellent contributions at various occasions after 1988 by scholars such as Breytenbach, Nicol, Combrink and Lategan.

But on two very important occasions in our recent history one would have expected at least some involvement in a broader theological debate about how we understand and confess Scripture.

The first refers to the highly influential report, *God met ons* (1979), by the Dutch Synod of Delft, where a relational notion of truth was defended against a correspondence theory. This had both a devastating and enriching effect on traditional understandings of "truth" and the Bible as "God's authoritative Word". It was left to systematic theologians and philosophers (see Van Huyssteen and Du Toit (1982)) to engage with these crucial theological issues, whilst a biblical scholar such as Prinsloo could only write: "It is my basic presupposition that the Old Testament is the authoritative Word of God" (Prinsloo 1985:410).[25]

The second relates to the formulation (1982) and acceptance (1986) of the Belhar confession[26] as fourth confession of the former Dutch Reformed Mission Church, the first confession in South African Reformed circles since 1618! I stand to be corrected, but I have up to this day not seen a scientific analysis of the many NT references in Belhar by a reputable biblical scholar, nor any engagement to argue the case for or against Belhar's consonance with Scripture. Is the anti-confessional bias so strong, and is the lack of focus on the religious/theological dimension of the text so weak, that not even internal arguments about text reception (of which confessions are important milestones) can break this silence?

This historical trend (if one can indeed call this a "trend') may now be reinforced by the cumulative effect of the factors discussed above.

- Insofar as scholarship – in the good name of autonomy and academic freedom – confines accountability to itself and the members of the guild, and judges "responsiveness" as a code word for political interference, there will be no internal drive toward shaping public discourse. This even excludes a voice of criticism against politicians' ever lurking tendency to rein in the "politically dangerous" organs of civil society such as trade unions (Cosatu [Congress of South African Trade Unions] and Solidariteit), churches (SACC [South African Council of Churches] and the Catholics), NGOs (the TAC [Treatment Action Campaign] and the Transvaalse Landbou-Unie), and universities.[27]

- Insofar as scholarship is satisfied with a scientist ethos, positivist orientation and mere interpretative knowledge, it undermines its philosophical ability to move toward transformative interests linked to the public issues of the day.

- Insofar as scholarship is blind to its own ethos and implied effect (or non-effect) on public ethical issues, and insofar as it does not see the latter as really part of "pure and proper" scholarship, it will not miss these questions from its agenda.

---

25 It is impossible to know everything that has been published, but the only later contributions on this topic by NT scholars that I could find are those by HJB Combrink and AB du Toit (both published in 1990).
26 For the text and discussion, see Cloete and Smit (1984).
27 Universities are so overwhelmed by multiple policy interventions that they have lost their nerve in the public sphere, except perhaps for a few voices such as those of Jonathan Jansen (formerly University of Pretoria, now University of the Free State) and William Makgoba (University of KwaZulu-Natal).

The safety of high science is just too comfortable to exchange for the heat and dust of public debate in an open space.

3. CONCLUSION

This paper is not intended to single out NT scholars as being alone in their unresponsiveness. It could probably be read with different examples at some of the other academic communities making up the field of theological scholarship in South Africa. I know too little about history and sociology and other the social sciences to make a bold claim about them. Perhaps my paper is but a symptom of the same types of questions facing the academy in general in our country at the moment.

If NT scholars accept that Paul can indeed speak beyond his own context, and beyond his own texts, the possibility exists in principle at least that we may meet him at the *agora*. That meeting will chiefly depend on your struggle with, and commitment to, emancipatory interests, ethical scholarship and the design of a public theology in our country.

May God, the mother of us all; Jesus, our incarnate brother; and the Spirit of truth who has blessed you with considerable knowledge resources, lead you on this exciting path.

See you at the market!

BIBLIOGRAPHY

Babbie, Earl and Mouton, Johann. 2001. *The Practice of Social Research*. Cape Town: Oxford University Press.

Bezuidenhout, Ronell & Naudé, Piet. 2002. Some thought on 'public theology' and its relevance for the South African context. *Scriptura* 79, 3-13.

Botha, J. 1992 The ethics of New Testament interpretation. *Neot* 26.1:169-194.

Botha, P. J. J. 1994 Moral Possibility and Narrative Rhetoric. *Neot* 28.2: 495-510.

Botha, P. J. J. 1997. History, rhetoric and the writings of Josephus. *Neot* 31.1: 1-20.

Botha, P. J. J. 2000. Submission and violence: exploring gender relations in the first-century world. *Neot* 34.1: 1-38.

Bruce, P. 2004. Virginity: Some Master Myths a study of Biblical and other ancient references to virginity in the context of HIV/AIDS in South Africa. *Neot* 38.1: 7-27.

Cady, L. E. 1987. A model for Public Theology. *HTR* 80:193-212.

Cloete, D. and Smit D. J. 1984. *A Moment of Truth*. Grand Rapids: Eerdmans.

Combrink, H. J. B. 1990. Die krisis van Skrifgesag in die gereformeerde eksegese as geleentheid. *NGTT* 31.3: 325-335.

Conradie, E. M. 1993. How should a public way of doing theology be approached? *Scriptura* 46: 24-49.

Degenaar, J. 1997. Religious discourse, power and the public. *Neot* 31.1: 39-58.

De Villiers, P. G. R. 1989. New Testament scholarship in South Africa. *Neot* 23: 119-124.

Du Toit, A. B. 1990. Die toekoms van Skrifgesag in die moderne eksegese. 'n Hoofsaaklik Nuwe Testamentiese perspektief. *NGTT* 31.4: 509 -517.

Furnish, Victor. 1968. *Theology and Ethics in Paul*. Nashville: Abingdon.

Gibbons, M. (et al.) 1994. *The New Production of Knowledge*. London: Sage.

Groenewald, E. P. 1947. Apartheid en voogdyskap in die lig van die Heilige Skrif. In *Regverdige rasse-apartheid*. Edited by G. Cronje. Stellenbosch: CSV, pp. 40-67.

Habermas, J. 1972. *Knowledge and Human Interests*. London: Heinemann.

Hays, R. 1996. *The Moral Vision of the New Testament*. Edinburgh: T & T Clark.

Kinghorn, J. (ed.) 1986. *Die NG Kerk en apartheid*. Johannesburg: Macmillan.

Kraak, A. (ed.) 2000. *Changing Modes: New Knowledge Production and its Implications for Higher Education in South Africa*. Pretoria: HSRC.

Kuhn, TS 1970. *The Structure of Scientific Revolutions*. 2nd edition. Chicago: Chicago University Press.

Küng, H & Tracy, D. 1989. *Paradigm Change in Theology: A Symposium for the Future*. Edinburgh: T & T Clark.

Jacobs, M. M. 2001. Feminist Scholarship, Biblical Scholarship and the Bible. *Neot* 35.1-2: 81-94.

Jonker, Louis & Lawrie, Douglas (eds.) 2005. *Fishing for Jonah (Anew)*. Stellenbosch: Sun Press.

Meeks, Wayne. 1983. *The First Urban Christians: The Social World of the Apostle Paul*. New Haven: Yale University Press.

Mouton, E. 2001. A rhetoric of theological vision? On Scripture's reorienting power in the liturgy of (social) life. *Neot* 35.1: 111-127.

Mouton, Johann 2001. *How to Succeed in your Master's and Doctoral Studies*. Pretoria: Van Schaik.

Mouton, J en Marais HC 1988. *Metodologie van die geesteswetenskappe: Basiese begrippe*. Pretoria: RGN.

National Commission on Higher Education 1996. *A Framework for Transformation*. NCHE: Pretoria.

Punt, J. 2003. Postcolonial Biblical Criticism in South Africa: Some Mind and Road Mapping. *Neot* 37.1: 59-85.

Ritschl, Dietrich und Jones, Hugh. 1976. *"Story" als Rohmaterial der Theologie*. München: Kaiser.

Ritschl, Dietrich. 1984. *Zur Logik der Theologie*. München: Kaiser.

Saayman W. and Kriel J. 1992. *Aids – the Leprosy of our Time?* Pretoria: Unisa.

Sampley, J Paul. 1991. *Walking between the Times: Paul's Moral Reasoning*. Minneapolis: Fortress.

Seepe, Sipho (ed.). 2004. *Towards an African Identity of Higher Education*. Pretoria: Skotaville.

Schrage, Wolfgang 1988 (1982). *The Ethics of the New Testament*. Edinburgh: T & T Clark.

Schüssler-Fiorenza, E 1988. The ethics of interpretation: De-centering biblical scholarship. *JBL* 107: 3-17.

Smit, D. J. 1988. Responsible hermeneutics: A systematic theologian's response to the readings and readers of Luke 12:35-48. *Neot* 22: 441-484.

Smit, D. J. 1990. The ethics of interpretation – and South Africa. *Scriptura* 33: 29-43.

Smit, D. J. 1994. A story of contextual hermeneutics and the integrity of New Testament interpretation in South Africa. *Neot* 28.2: 265-289.

Smit, D. J. 1996. Saints, disciples, friends? Recent South African perspectives on Christian ethics and the New Testament. *Neot* 30.1: 169-185.

Smit, Dirkie. 2003. Openbare getuienis en publieke teologie vandag? Vrae oor verskeie vanselfsprekende voorveronderstellings. *Scriptura* 82: 39-48.

Snyman, W. J. 1957. Rasseverhoudinge in die Skrif. (In besonder in die Nuwe Testament). *Koers* 25: 161-173.

Theissen, Gerd. 1978 [1977]. *The Sociology of Early Palestinian Christianity.* Philadelphia: Fortress.

Tracy, David. 1981. *The Analogical Imagination. Christian Theology and the Culture of Pluralism.* New York: Crossroad.

Van Aarde, A. G. 1994. The epistemic status of the New Testament and the emancipatory living of the historical Jesus in engaged hermeneutics. *Neot* 28.2: 575-596.

Van Huyssteen, J. W. V. and Du Toit, B. J. 1982. *Geloof en Skrifgesag.* Pretoria: NGKB.

Vorster, J. N. 1999. Reflecting on the rhetoric of biblical rhetorical critics. *Neot* 33.2: 293-320.

Verhey, Allen. 2002. *Remembering Jesus. Christian Community, Scripture, and the Moral Life.* Grand Rapids: Eerdmans.

Wolfram Weisse & Carel Anthonissen (eds.) 2004. *Maintaining Apartheid or Promoting Change? The Role of the DRC in a Phase of Increasing Conflict in South Africa.* Berlin: Waxmann.

West, G. 2002. Indigenous Exegesis: Exploring the Interface between Missionary Methods and the Rhetorical Rhythms of Africa – Locating Local Reading Resources in the Academy. *Neot* 36.1-2: 147-162.

2.4 "BUT YOU, WHO DO YOU SAY I AM?"[1]

How the Christian faith turns into an ideology of power

This is a reading of the gospel of Mark, introducing contextual creativity from a South African perspective.[2] Written by a systematic theologian, ethicist and preacher, the "proclamation" or "homily" below will not meet all the demands of technical New Testament exegesis, nor reflect the status of current scholarship on Mark. It is sincerely hoped, though, that the exposition will provide some insight into how a well-meaning Christian people can do inhuman things in the name of God; how a seemingly orthodox belief system may in fact harbour and support systemically unethical systems, attitudes and action, but also how the gospel can liberate from ideological blindness.

1. SEEKING THE GROUNDS OF AN IDEOLOGICAL FAITH

One perennial question faced those of us who were born under apartheid and later studied theology during the time that South Africa struggled to liberate itself from her past: **How was it possible to not only grant Christian legitimacy to an inhuman, racist system, but actually to co-design such a system with a direct and pious appeal to God and the Scriptures?**

Many books and articles were written to analyse the ideologising of the gospel by white Reformed churches in South Africa. This ideology was built on the deadly combination of nationalistic power and an enabling religious hermeneutics, resulting in an Afrikaner civil religion.[3] The rise of Afrikaners after their defeat in the Anglo-Boer War (1899-1902) and formation of the Union of South Africa (1910) was the engine that fuelled a fervent nationalism that upheld itself with strong "in-group" (Afrikaners) and "out-group" (English, blacks and communists) boundaries. Coupled to this was the appropriation of Scripture by some that identified Afrikaners as God's chosen people,[4] with a mission in Africa, based on a differentiated pluralism

---

1 A reference to Mark 8:29. See the exposition below. This essay has its origin in a sermon, published in an Afrikaans collection, *Brug na môre. 'n Kruisevangelie vir gewone mense*. Lux Verbi: Kaapstad (1995). It was later re-worked into a more academic text for the Festschrift for Michael Welker. See "'But you, who do you say I am?' A homily on ideological faith from the Gospel of Mark." In Andreas Schuele and Günter Thomas (eds.): *Who is Jesus Christ for us today? Pathways to contemporary Christology*. Louisville, Kentucky: WJK (2009), 134-149.

2 These contextual comments are added in the footnotes for two reasons: to allow the Markan narrative to proceed uninterrupted, and to allow for other appropriations beyond the South African context. I can imagine a German, Latin American or US reader who might find illumination from the text quite differently from what is presented here.

3 "There can be hardly any doubt that religion and nationalism were the main ideological forces that impacted on the Afrikaners during the twentieth century. The two were interrelated." The exact relationship between the two is a matter of debate, however. For a discussion, see Giliomee (2003:221-226), a foremost South African historian who published a major and widely acclaimed work, *The Afrikaners* (2003).

4 With reference to O'Brien's distinction between a "holy nationalism" and limited self-understanding as a "holy people", Giliomee gives strong evidence that, unlike Germans

assuming that from creation onward God assigned each people (*Volk*) its own land and development potential.

It is possible – to show the complex pro- and counter-theological currents in the years between 1935 and 1990: the roots of apartheid theology lie in an interesting combination of neo-Calvinist Kuyperianism, the missiological thinking of Gustav Warneck, Scottish Pietism and German Romanticism, combined with a naïve hermeneutics that shielded itself from critical scholarship.[5] The counter-currents were inspired inter alia by Barth's critique of religion,[6] Bonhoeffer's notion of a confessing church,[7] historical-critical exegesis,[8] and the rise of a critically minded, indigenous, black Reformed theology[9] that presented a credible alternative to what was accepted as "Reformed" at that stage.

My generation of theologians knew that all these intricate and important analyses were crucial to a theological interpretation of the situation. But this was not enough. What was required was to use the counter-ideological insights to preach differently. Proclamation is the form of God's Word that reaches ordinary people – black and white. One does not engage in a direct political or moral argument. One just allows the Word to take its course, believing that this Word will not return empty, but in fact "prosper in the thing for which I sent it" (Is. 55:10-11).

What follows is one such example of proclamation amongst many.[10] The sections below are reconstructed from an actual sermon, but provided with some exegetical[11] and theological comments, and adapted to speak beyond one situation only.

---

    under National Socialism, Afrikaners never claimed an exclusive right to God's favour, though there was a strong sense of God's providential hand in their history (Giliomee 2003:224).

5   For a short summary of these theological currents, see Naudé (2005). For a more elaborate account, see the excellent essays in Kinghorn (1986), and for a classic historical overview, read the anniversary edition of *The church struggle in South Africa* (De Gruchy and De Gruchy 2004).

6   See Willie Jonker's seminal essay on Barth (Jonker 1988) and the thorough analysis (with extensive literature) of Barth's significance for understanding justice – also in South Africa – by Dirkie Smit (2004).

7   Nobody did more than John de Gruchy to appropriate Bonhoeffer's insights for the church in South Africa. See specifically his essays in De Gruchy (1984). Under the able leadership of Dirk Smit, then professor of dogmatics at the University of the Western Cape, young scholars such as Russel Botman and Johann Botha wrote theses on Bonhoeffer, and played an important part in the confessing church movement in South Africa.

8   The academic and popular work by internationally acclaimed scholars such as Ferdinand Deist (OT) and Bernard Lategan (NT) played an enormous role in reclaiming the Bible for an anti-apartheid reading.

9   Under the leadership of people such as Allan Boesak, ABECSA (Alliance of Black Reformed Christians in Southern Africa), which issued its *Charter and Declaration* in October 1981, played a major role in reclaiming the Reformed tradition in SA to include Black members.

10   Some of my sermons have been collected in popular Afrikaans publications. See footnote 1 and *Drie maal een is een. 'n Besinning oor God vandag*. Vereeniging: CUM (2004); *Onder die skewe reënboog. 'n Evangelie van hoop vir gewone mense*. Lux Verbi: Kaapstad (1999) and *Geesgedrewe gelowiges. Terug na die grondwaarhede van jou geloof*. Wellington: LuxVerbi.BM (2005).

11   References to the original Greek text were removed for this publication to make it more accessible to readers without a technical knowledge of the Greek language.

2. "BUT YOU, WHO DO YOU SAY I AM?"[12]
A READING OF MARK

It has been argued by both narrative and structural analyses that Mark 8:27-30 (the confession of Peter) is a turning point in the gospel narrative. This passage is the "hinge" of the gospel story that tells of Jesus' ministry up to that point (the road to Caesarea Philippi), and then recounts his journey to the cross (the road to Jerusalem).[13] Mark states his aim quite clearly in 1:1 "The beginning of the gospel about Jesus the Messiah, the Son of God",[14] and what follows is a narrative in which Mark attempts to reveal the true identity of this Jesus, the Christ.

In this regard, the disciple group – those closest to Jesus – is of particular interest. At the point of Jesus' question to them in the narrative – "But you, who do you say I am?" – they have been in His presence for quite some time (1:17-20; 2:13-14; 3:13-19; 6:7-13). They have heard his remarkable teaching – from reinterpreting the Jewish law in general (7:1-23) and more specifically on fasting and the Sabbath (2:18-28) to explaining his mission and the nature of God's kingdom with parables.[15] The disciples also witnessed many of Jesus' miracles: these include examples of physical healing, exorcism of devils, as well as the resurrection of Jairus' daughter from death (5:21-43). They witnessed Jesus' power over nature by his stilling of the storm (4:35-41) and walking on the sea (6:45-52), and were intimately involved in the two events narrated as the miraculous multiplication of the bread (6: 30-44; 8:1-21).

2.1 The question of Jesus' identity

A recurring theme in the gospel up to this "confession" pericope is the vexing question of understanding who Jesus really is. There are numerous clues to this in the text.

The authority of his teaching and power over unclean spirits in Capernaum lead those present to the question: "What is this? A new teaching! With authority he commands even the unclean spirits, and they obey him" (1:27). The exorcised devils on that occasion are not permitted to speak, "because they did not know him" (1:34), leaving Jesus' true identity open for further enquiry.

After declaring the lame man's sins forgiven, the question arose: "Who can forgive sins but God alone?" (2:7), attesting to some divine power at work in this man from Nazareth.

Despite Jesus' remark that to the disciples is given to know the mystery (the secret) of the kingdom of God (4:11), they are unable to interpret his parables (4:13) and are taught separately from the public at a level that they would understand (4:33-34). That this is a great struggle emerges after the disciples' question about Jesus'

---

12 In the discussion of the Markan text below, most English translations will taken from the RSV and occasionally the NIV, whilst in some cases I attempt my own translation.
13 The division of the gospel into a short prologue (1:1-13) followed by two major sections, 1:14-8:30 and 8:31-15:47, is based on clear textual markers and is reinforced by the narrative structure. For the textual divisions with extensive literature, see Moloney 2002:16-22, and for the narrative structure, see Juel (1999) and Rhoads et al. (1999).
14 Textual critics agree that "the Son of God" is a later addition.
15 See 4:1-34 for parables of the sower, lamp, seed and mustard seed.

teaching on traditions and inner cleanliness (7:1ff): "Are you also then without understanding?" Jesus asks (7:18), before explaining again that impurity comes from inside, from the heart, and not through what you eat, i.e. "from outside".

After the stilling of the storm, the disciples are overwhelmed by a great fear and they ask: "Who is He then ... that even the wind and the sea are subject to him?" (4:41). Jesus' walking on the sea later in the narrative is situated in the same "identity question" context. They think they see a ghost, scream loudly, and are clearly upset. He identifies himself (6:50), gets into the boat and calms the winds. This leaves the disciples "extremely astonished and perplexed" (6:51), and the narrator inserts the clue that the real issue is understanding who Jesus is: the disciples are astonished now, it is explained, "because they did not understand about the bread, as their heart was hardened" (6:52).[16]

This identity confusion is reinforced after the second multiplication of the bread.[17] They do not understand Jesus' reference to the leaven of the Pharisees and Herod, and interpret his words as a rebuke that they forgot to bring bread into the boat, resulting in their quarrelling amongst themselves. Jesus then asks: "Why do you argue that you have no bread?[18] Are your hearts hardened? Having eyes do you not see, and having ears do you not hear?" He reminds them of the earlier multiplication of bread, and ends the conversation: "Do you still not understand?" (see 8:17-21).

In his home town the question of Jesus' true identity is posed with even greater perplexity as they obviously "know" him: "Is he not the carpenter, the son of Mary, and the brother of James?" they ask in 6:3. But where does he get these ideas and what wisdom is given to Him? Whence the power that acts through his hands? (6:2). Mark is clear: they do not recognise Jesus and rather consider him a shame and a scandal (6:3).

The other actor in this drama of identifying Jesus is King Herod. He is reported to have heard about the healings in Jesus' ministry (6:14). Whereas some identify Jesus as Elijah, or another prophet, Herod himself is convinced that Jesus is a resurrected John the Baptist (6:16).[19]

---

16 The passive use of the "hardened hearts" creates a difficult problem of interpretation as it might suggest that the disciples did not choose to misunderstand Jesus, but were mere passive objects of a divine hardening of the hearts. If one reads this passage in the context of Is 6:9-10 (already referred to in 4:12), and link it to Jesus' rebuke of their hardness of heart later (8:17) and after his resurrection (16:14), there is no justification to diminish the disciple's agency and responsibility. In the same way, Jahwe's hardening of Israel's heart in the time of proto- Isaiah was in no way glossing over their own breaking of the covenant. For discussion and literature, see France (2002:273-274).

17 The reason why the bread miracles are singled out by Mark as the signs of Jesus' true identity – more than the other miracles – might, according to Hooker, be because they are reminiscent of the miraculous provision of manna during the exodus (see France 2002:273, footnote 73).

18 "Are you thus without understanding also?" The *asunetos* has a ring of being dull or foolish to it.

19 This recognition of Jesus by the heathen king is an ironic twist, remarks Edwards (2002:185): he holds Jesus in higher regard than his own people in Nazareth do! This may be part of the wider irony – see discussion later – that the "lower" the agent (e.g. unclean spirits and Roman officer), the "higher" their knowledge of Jesus. For an extensive study, see J Camery-Hoggat: *Irony in Mark's Gospel: Text and subtext*. Cambridge: CUP (1992).

"Who do the people say I am?" in 8:27 is therefore not a question out of the blue. The various audiences – the disciples, the Pharisees and teachers of the law, the crowds in different locations, king Herod and the impure spirits – all struggled to "pin down" the identity of Jesus.

It is ironic that up to that point the only replies close to the truth came from the least likely sources. The man with the unclean spirit explicitly confesses: "I know who you are: the Holy One of God" (1:24).[20] On two other occasions the demons see Jesus and it is reported that they call out: "You are the Son of God!" (3:11), and "Son of the Most High God" (5:7), echoing the very first verse (1:1), which serves as superscript for the whole gospel.

Jesus' self-identification before this question to the disciples is twofold: He calls himself "the Son of Man", able to forgive sins (2:10), and "Kurios": the Lord of the Sabbath (2:28), and the Lord who healed the devil-possessed man from Gerasene (5:19).

The disciples' answer about the peoples' perceptions link Jesus to John the Baptist, Elijah, or one of the other prophets (8:28). The crucial question, perhaps expecting a more informed reply from insiders than outsiders,[21] is then raised in 8:29: "But who do you say that I am?"

Peter's[22] answer that Jesus is the Christ, does for the first time – in the context of the narrative – repeat the announcement at the beginning (1:1). Jesus is identified as the Messiah, the eschatological king who was promised from the Old Testament times (Jer 23:5). Judged purely on its orthodoxy, its theological correctness, the reader is relieved to find that all Jesus' struggles to lead the disciples to a deeper understanding of Him bear good fruit. At last they got it right, we think. Is He not – indeed – the Messiah?

2.2 Why the disciples could not comprehend the suffering Messiah

At this point the narrative takes on a more dramatic turn: Jesus begins his final journey to Jerusalem and makes three passion announcements in 8:31-33, 9:30-32, 10:32-34 that are structurally roughly the same. Each of these announcements (varying slightly in content) is followed by a reaction from the disciples (showing yet again their profound misunderstanding of Jesus' person and mission) and a counter-reaction from Jesus (as an attempt to open the disciples' minds).

---

20 What happens here is that "the demon displays a supernatural insight as yet denied to human actors in the story. The reader is expected to note it..." (France 2002:10). To call Jesus "holy" is to emphasise the contrast with his "unclean" opponent, and might also refer to Jesus possessing the "Holy Spirit" (1:8) that empowers his messianic ministry.

21 "Jesus' comrades are asked to render a judgment about his remarkable *exousia*, his divine authority, which they have witnessed and experienced... The disciples must move from the status of passive recipients to active participants" (Edwards 2002:248).

22 Although Peter replies, the context where Jesus addresses the disciples in vv 30-31 suggests that he serves as spokesperson for the disciples. This role of Peter as group representative is repeated in 10:28, 11:21 and 14:37. See France (2002:329).

Jesus does not confirm or deny Peter's confession. He starts to teach them that the Son of Man[23] (not the Christ) must suffer and will be rejected by the elders, that he would be killed and rise after three days (8:31). Peter's reaction is one of total disbelief: he takes Jesus aside and rebukes Him. Jesus on his part turns around and rebukes Peter in the presence of the disciples: "Get behind me Satan! You do not have in mind the concerns of God, but merely human concerns" (NIV) This last sentence may be translated as "Because you do not think about the things of God, but those of the people" or more aptly (but less literally) "You are thinking not as God thinks, but as human beings do" (8:33). This is immediately followed by the call to cross-bearing: "Whoever wants to follow me must deny himself, take up his cross, and follow Me" (8:34).

In Peter's and the disciples' minds the confession of Christ, on the one hand and the announcement of a *suffering* Son of Man, on the other, created a total dissonance, an impossible possibility. The popular conception of the Messiah in Jesus' time was that this Anointed One would destroy God's enemies by the word of his mouth, deliver Jerusalem from the Gentiles, gather the faithful from dispersion, and rule in justice and glory.[24] And the popular notion of the Son of Man is – according to Jewish Scriptures (Daniel 7) – an apocalyptic figure who would descend from heaven to destroy evil kingdoms and establish the reign of God.[25] The idea of a suffering, rejected and dying Son of Man – missing the point that he would rise after three days? – was just incomprehensible.

The question arises: Why could the disciples not comprehend Jesus' person and mission? The answer emerges from a close reading of the other two passion announcements.

After Jesus announces his passion, death and resurrection in 9:31, the narrator clearly tells us: "But they did not understand the saying, and were afraid to ask Him" (9:32). They therefore sensed some danger in the announcement, but could not actually comprehend its meaning. The reasons for the disciples' closed minds are hidden in the following few verses.

The disciples were not open to the meaning of Jesus' passion, because they were talking along the road about who were the greatest amongst themselves (9:34). The same self-interested power paradigm that led to a dissonance between "You are the Christ" and the "suffering Son of Man", or between following Jesus in his glory and

---

23   This self-identification (used fourteen times only by Jesus) might be ambiguous, but was in the time of Jesus largely free from the political and military connotations of the Messiah. Son of Man is used in three contexts: an *apocalyptic* context as in Daniel and 1 Enoch (8:38; 13:26; 14:62), *authority* to forgive sins and rule over the Sabbath, and predominantly in the context of *suffering* (nine times, as in all the passion announcements). For the disciples, the apocalyptic connotation would be most in line with their own expectations.
24   See the short but insightful excursus with further literature on "Christ" in Edwards (2002:249-252).
25   The fact that Jesus calls himself the Son of Man indicates that He will indeed establish the Kingdom of God. This is clear from his opening sermon as reported in Mark 1:14. The problem lies in *the means* to establish the Kingdom: not via military or political victory as understood in an apocalyptic framework, but through suffering and resurrection. This reinforces the point: the title or description of Jesus *per se* is not the issue, but its interpretation! For the complex interpretation of the Son of Man in technical literature, and a clear position based on Daniel 7, see Moloney (2002:212-213).

carrying a cross (quite literally), now emerges: instead of being child-like, the last, and being everybody's servant (9:35-37), they were arguing who was the greatest, the ruler, the first.[26]

This inward focus on retention of power is reinforced when John[27] proudly announces that they have seen someone casting out demons in Jesus' Name, but prevented him from continuing. The reason, given twice, is not that the exorcism had been unsuccessful,[28] but rather: "because he was not following us" (9:38). Jesus opens up their closed, sectarian mind-set[29] and explains that who is not against us is for us (9:40), and that even the smallest gift for the sake of Christ (a cup of water) will be rewarded (9:41).

The paradigm of power and glory is revealed most clearly in the third passion announcement: Jesus explains in the greatest detail thus far that suffering and death await him in Jerusalem (10: 33-34). James and John – as if no word about suffering was ever mentioned[30] – clearly expect a crowning, glorious future in which they wish to secretly secure their stake: "Grant us to sit, one at your right hand and one at your left, ... in your glory" (10:37). That the other ten also hoped for some glory

---

26 What we see here is a juxtaposition "between Jesus' humility and the disciple's desire for distinction and recognition" on the assumption that Messiahship entails privilege, not suffering (Edwards 2002:285).

27 John's solo role here should be read as part of the narrator's skilful suggestion that it is precisely the inner circle of the disciples (how close can you be to Jesus!) that misses the point of the suffering Son of Man. See the role of John and James (10:35ff) as discussed below.

28 See a similar event with less satisfactory results in Acts 19:13-16. The "protection" of Jesus' name after his resurrection must have been in the forefront of John's mind, though he expresses this in terms of the exclusive disciple group and not so much as concern over Jesus' honour!

29 Ideological faith is by its very nature sectarian. Where nationalistic interest and pious belief intersect, a strongly denominational church (in the negative sense) is the inevitable result. As the tension between "us" (who are right and are not properly understood) and "them" (who are out to discredit us) grows, ecumenical isolation increases. But the isolation in turn is not interpreted as Christian exhortation, but exactly as vindication of the truthfulness of one's own position. It may take years to change. The ecumenical church in the form of the WCC and SACC (Cottesloe 1961, *Message to the People of SA* 1968), the Lutheran World Federation (*status confessionis* 1977) and the World Alliance of Reformed Churches (*status confessionis* 1982) all played this ambiguous role in the life of the Afrikaans Dutch Reformed Church. The story of the DRC's ecumenical relations between 1960-1990 could be described as a move from wilful isolation to re-establishment of ties in full communion. For an overview of critiques from the ecumenical church, see De Villiers (1986); for the constructive role of the ecumenical church, see Naudé (2003).

30 The heretical nature of self-serving, ideological faith is rarely (if ever) an open denial of orthodoxy. As is clearly the case with John and James here: it is a hermeneutic at work that renders reading the "unacceptable" parts of the gospel impossible, and framing that gospel to fit your own agenda. They just do not hear the explicit predictions of "suffering", but do hear "Son of Man", and that is enough to cling to the apocalyptic notion of a glorious kingdom. To call apartheid a theological heresy was not based on any explicit doctrinal denial by those supporting the system, but the implicit, unsaid "doctrine" that resulted from a racist, pluralist reading of the gospel. See the essays in De Gruchy and Villa-Vicencio (1983).

emerges from their upset reaction when they heard about the request from James and John (10:41).[31]

This is followed by yet another attempt by Jesus to release them from the paradigm of power, dominion and being "great men" with authority, and instead understand that in God's kingdom that order is precisely reversed. To be the first, you must be everyone's slave (44).[32] He ends this passage by reinforcing his passion announcements and self-identification: "For[33] the Son of man also came not to be served but to serve, and to give his life as a ransom (*lutron*)[34] for many" (10:45).[35]

In a brilliant ironic twist the narrator inserts the healing of the blind Bartimaeus here. Jesus asks him exactly the same question as he had earlier asked James and John: "What do you want me to do for you?" (compare 10:51 and 10:36). The disciples asked for glory, the blind man for sight; the disciples were obstructing the way, Bartimaeus "followed him on the way" (10:52).

The entry into Jerusalem that follows here is – in line with the struggle to understand identity thus far – a confusing event. The readers know that Jesus enters to suffer and die, and that his kingdom is of a different order. But He nevertheless enters with the symbolism of a king, riding a colt on which no one has sat (Gen 49:11; Sech 9:9), whilst clothes and branches are spread before him as with a royal inauguration (2 Kings 9:13). The mainly Jewish crowds are swept up in nationalistic fervour: "Hosanna! Blessed is he who comes in the name of the Lord![36] Blessed is the kingdom of our father David that is coming! Hosanna in the highest!" (11:9-10).[37]

---

[31] This is the only case in this gospel where James and John are mentioned separately from the twelve. One can easily imagine their intention to side-line Peter, the other member of the inner circle. There are only two positions of glory, but three (if not twelve) contenders.

[32] "The preeminent virtue of God's kingdom is not power, not even freedom, but service." *Diakonos* is the ordinary Greek word for waiting on tables, and *doulos* was in ancient society the least and the last. That a slave could be first is an absurd paradox (Edwards 2002:236). Barth beautifully describes theological work as service: "Since theology is called to serve, it must not rule. It must serve both God in his Word… and the man loved by God and addressed by God's Word. It may rule neither in relation to God nor in relation to men" (Barth 1963:187-188).

[33] The Greek *gar* must be read purposively here and introduces service and giving as the very way of the Son of Man.

[34] In the Hellenistic and Roman periods *lutron* refers to "transactions between human beings and gods in which sins were forgiven and offenses expiated" (Collins as quoted by Edwards 2002:328, footnote 67).

[35] There are indications that Mark draws on the Servant of Lord from Is 53 here. This Servant will give his life as guilt offering (Is 53:10) and bear the iniquities of many (53:11), in the same way that Jesus describes the Son of Man here. For a discussion, and with literature presenting alternatives, see Moloney (2002:213-214).

[36] A direct quotation from Psalm 118:25-26 as a reference to pilgrims' entering Jerusalem.

[37] For the sake of my specific reading, i.e. to uncover the traits of ideological faith, I am less open to Edwards's suggestion that the crowds did not harbour messianic expectations from Jesus, but merely welcomed him as a pilgrim (2002:336-7). In line with the narrator's emphasis on "misunderstanding", the shift from "the kingdom of God" (Jesus) to "the kingdom of our father David" (crowds) is highly significant. **This identification of political interests with divine interest is the deepest core of an ideological faith.** That the Markan account of Jesus' entry is significantly "down-scaled" when compared with Matthew and Luke is true, but this does not detract from the misreading of Jesus' purpose and identity by those present.

The rest of the gospel emphasises the failure of the twelve to both understand the significance of the events and their inability to support their Master in his ordeal. this reinforces the tragic truth set out from the beginning: those closest to Jesus do not know: Judas is shown to be the traitor (14:18ff); Peter is warned that he would deny Jesus three times (14:27-31); and in the garden the disciples are found sleeping three times, failing to comply with Jesus' request to stay and remain wake (14:32-42). After Judas' betrayal, Jesus is captured by people sent out by the high priests, scribes and elders – echoing the exact actors of his passion announcements. The end of the discipleship journey – apart from Peter who still follows from afar and denies Jesus – is only a terse sentence: "And they all forsook him and fled" (14:50).

2.3 The confession of the Roman soldier and the messianic secret

The question of identity prevails even unto the cross. Jesus is crucified under the ironic script: The King of the Jews. The high priests and law scholars ironically acknowledge his messianic status: "Let the Christ, the King of Israel, come down now from the cross that we can see and believe!" (15:31). When Jesus calls out in Aramaic (Eloi, Eloi,...) some – in line with earlier speculation – mishear him as appealing to Elijah[38] for help.

The question: "Who do you say I am?" remains urgent right up to the end. Our hope might be pitched on the women. At least they followed up to the end and are present at the cross. The news of the resurrection is later told to Mary Magdalene, Mary the mother of James and Salome. They are requested by the young man in white clothes to go and tell others to meet Jesus in Galilee. The original text of the gospel, however, ends in disappointment: "And they said nothing to any one, for they were afraid" (16:8).

We saw earlier that – contrary to expectation – the unclean spirits knew Jesus. When everyone else was struggling to understand, they confessed: "You are the Son of God" (3:11). At the end it is left to the Roman soldier, an officer with command over a hundred men, who had no other exposure to Jesus but to witness the crucifixion,[39] to say: "Truly, this man was the Son of God" (15:39).[40] What no one could fully comprehend during Jesus' life and ministry becomes possible through his death.

---

38 It was believed that Elijah had been taken to heaven without dying (2 Kings 2 :11) and that he could return to help the righteous in times of crises.

39 In the Matthew version (27:54) the centurion's confession is a reaction to the signs accompanying Jesus' death; here the confession is a direct response to the death of Jesus itself. See the good argument by Davis (1989) that 15:39 should not be seen merely as the climax of the gospel, but as the governing key to interpret the gospel as such. What we find is not merely a narrative climax, "but the Christological climax as well" (Davis 1989:14).

40 There are no grammatical grounds for the assertion (*inter alia* by Johnson 1987:14) that, because of the absence of a definitive article before Son of God, the centurion only made a general confession about a son of god, i.e. a special person. As Edwards rightly points out, a definitive predicate nominative in Koine Greek omits the article when it precedes the verb (2002:480). What we have here – according to the narrative – is a full confession in line with the intention of the gospel as set out in 1:1.

This exposition may aid us in understanding two interesting remarks in the first encounter between Jesus and Peter after the latter made his confession. The one is the command to keep quiet, and the other is the reference to Peter as a Satan.

Jesus' strong insistence that they should tell no one that he is the Christ has become known in scholarship as the messianic secret.[41] This is a complex theme recurring in contradictory modes in the narrative: Sometimes someone is urged to go and tell (e.g. the man from Gadarene in 5:19), but mostly people who are healed are asked not to tell (e.g. 1:44; 5:43; 7:35 and 8:26).

If one reads the identity question of the Markan narrative as playing itself out in the tension between two radically opposing paradigms (reminiscent of Luther's theologies of glory and the cross), the insistence not to tell anyone about the Christ in 8:30 specifically is explained: Jesus is well aware of the nationalistic and self-indulgent misinterpretation of his mission. He understands that his disciples are following him because of their expectation of dominion and glory. This type of Christ is dangerous: "Do not tell others about Him".

The problem lies not in the words of the confession. Jesus is indeed the Christ. The problem – as we saw earlier – lies in the interpretation of this Christ and the consequences it has for the practical choices made by the disciples. They were dogmatically correct, but were still standing in God's way, closing out others in a sectarian mind-set, struggling to be the most important, involved in a secret politicking for positions of glory, and clearly over-estimating their own religious loyalties to Christ.

Seemingly orthodox statements are shattered by heterodox attitudes and actions. Theology is constitutively verified or falsified through ethics.

By rebuking Jesus for the announcement of his passion, Peter is acting "naturally". He tries to defend his prevailing paradigm of Christ. His mind is thinking like the minds of the people and he cannot think the way God thinks. He wants to avoid the cross; he wants to save himself. That is equivalent to being Satan (8:33). By opposing God's will for his Messiah, Peter and the disciples "are acting as spokesmen of God's ultimate enemy" in his role as taking away the word of God (see Mark 4:15; France 2002:338). What we see here are "incompatible ideologies" at work, where a human perspective is incapable of grasping divine purpose (France 2002:339).

History teaches us: **Where this paradigm of power becomes institutionalised and moves beyond individual notions of Christ for the sake of myself and my in-group, we find the deadly combination of nationalistic politics and the Christian religion.**

---

41 Modern scholarship on Mark was set in motion by the ground-breaking work by Wilhelm Wrede, *Das Messiasgeheimnis in den Evangelien*, in 1901. His enduring legacy is that Mark is a theological work (not a mere biographical account), and that Christology forms the centre of that theology. For a discussion of the reaction to Wrede and major viewpoints up to the mid-1960s, read David Aune's instructive article, *The problem of the messianic secret* (1969), specifically pp 1-8 with discussions on major scholars from Schweitzer to Bultmann. My fairly straightforward explanation of the messianic secret stems from the specific hermeneutical angle from which I chose to read Mark, and is perhaps a good illustration of Bultmann's work on presuppositions!

The most dramatic 20th-century examples are National Socialism in Germany and apartheid theology in South Africa. Both linked a people (*Volk*), a specific land and God in an ideological triangle in which the church and ordinary people confessed Christ in an orthodox manner, whilst dehumanising others in their narrow pursuit of privilege, power and racial self-glorification. You could kill in the Name of the One you confess. By God's grace, the alternative truth, the rejection of ideological faith, was also spoken in both countries as represented by Barmen (1934) and Belhar (1982/86). An emerging 21st-century example is the pre-emptive wars initiated by the USA, exhibiting in some respects the same ideological structure of a Christian God identified with Western political values, and the protection of American interests and security.

Over against this Satanic temptation to seek power, influence and glory stands the utter foolish paradigm of the cross.

3. IS THERE HOPE FOR LIBERATION FROM AN IDEOLOGICAL FAITH?

The urgent question that now arises is whether there is hope. Is there a possibility that Peter and the disciples can indeed come to an understanding of who Jesus is and shape their lives accordingly? In the context of prevailing Christian ideologies: Is there an expectation that those caught up in a paradigm of power, legitimised by theology and supported by political and military means, can indeed turn around?

The story of Peter (as representative of the disciples, and for that matter all followers of Christ) gives us the clue. Conversion to a radically new insight is possible through divine intervention.

First, Peter's religious self-confidence had to be shattered by a practical realisation that he – despite his good Messianic intentions – has been betraying Christ. A simple maid in the house of the high priest and a cock that crows twice are the instruments[42] of shaking the ideological foundations of Peter's faith. (It is yet again ironic that Peter denies knowledge of Jesus whilst confessing and protesting all along that he does know Him!) In a fleeting moment he realises who he really is himself: a follower and defender, but at the same time a traitor to Christ. The narrator tells of the effect: "And he broke down and wept" (14:72).[43]

---

42 Sometimes – God forbid – the "instrument" to destabilise an ideological self is war and destruction to the point of no return. In other cases you only realise those moments when you look back. In the South African case two seemingly simple events that contributed to insight into the ideological faith of Afrikaner Christians were the rejection of the prohibition of mixed marriages on Scriptural grounds by leading ethicists like De Villiers and Kinghorn in the late 1970s, and the declaration of apartheid theology as a matter of *status confessionis*, accompanied by the draft Confession of Belhar by the "coloured" Mission Church in 1982. It still took some time, but these two viewpoints eroded the moral legitimacy of the system in the minds of ordinary white Christians.

43 This happens at an individual level – sometimes like here with Peter – in an instant. Bonhoeffer writes in *Sanctorum Communio* (published 1930) that ethical responsibility may be assigned not only to individuals, but to the whole people of God. There is something like "ethical collective persons" (Bonhoeffer 1998: 118) and a collective guilt that may gradually dawn. Chances are slim that self-realisation reaches everyone at the same time: "Breaking down and weeping", expressions of guilt and sorrow are mostly expressed not by all, but vicariously by some on behalf of all – even if not each and every

The readers, and the later addition to the ending of the Markan gospel (16:9-20), know the second part of the radical conversion: the destruction of the previous religious edifice, the revelation of the true self and the breaking down of all spiritual self-confidence make room for a fresh meeting – this time with the resurrected Christ.[44] Again Jesus reprimands them for their hardness of heart and disbelief.[45] But then – in a gesture of radical grace and acceptance – He empowers them, the very ones who did not understand and at first did not believe, to go into the world and "preach the gospel to the whole creation" (16:15). Because they then knew the whole gospel. They understood for the first time that the suffering Son of Man is indeed the resurrected Christ.

In the words of Michael Welker, "Reformed theology must engage in a variety of ways in the effort to renew a theology of the word of God, and above all, **it must make clear that the church of Christ lives in the presence of the risen Christ**" (1999a:141, my emphasis). We have the promise that – no matter what our past – the risen Christ will work with us and confirm our message by the signs that attend it (Mark 16:19).

Whilst we follow Christ in his command, let us be aware of the ever present danger of new ideological faiths: the rise of Islamic and Christian fundamentalism in the Middle East, Africa and the USA; the link between neoliberal capitalism and a prosperity gospel; the rapid growth of spiritualities that utilise the mass media to turn the Christian gospel into anthropocentric and pleasing entertainment.

"Who is Jesus Christ for us today?" (Bonhoeffer) might be the most important question to answer.

---

one is convinced at the time, and even whilst they fiercely resist and refuse to accept the radically other picture of the collective self. The confession of Willie Jonker on behalf of Afrikaners and the DRC at the ecumenical Rustenburg conference (read the text in Jonker (1991)), as well as the DRC's own confession of guilt in 1990, stand out as crucial markers on the road towards proper insight into "Christian" policies of apartheid. The role of the Truth and Reconciliation Commission – accompanied by many tears and personal confessions – has been described by some as a national catharsis, a deep look into our own hearts of darkness (Pauw); a view into the skull of our country (Krog).

44 "The good news does not say: Jesus is simply here again! The pre-Easter Jesus of Nazareth is here again! Instead, the good news, the gospel, says: here is the risen and exalted Christ, who is present in a wholly new way." For that reason the gospel is also called the "gospel of the *resurrection*" (Welker 1999a:148, emphasis original).

45 This is quite instructive: Jesus does not gloss over, but in fact reminds them of, their past **in the very act of commissioning them**! Much has been written about historical guilt. Theologically speaking, the only guilt that is both painful and empowering to remember is guilt covered by the grace of God according to his promise in 1 John 1:7-9, and repeated every Sunday after the reading of the law. The recommissioning of the church in SA – those who designed and supported apartheid, together with those who fought against the system – can only happen on the basis of remembered grace. In a country ravaged by the Aids pandemic, violent gender crime and a growing poverty gap, there is so much that needs to be done theologically and in practice.

BIBLIOGRAPHY

Aune, David E 1969. The problem of the Messianic secret. *Novum Testamentum* 11, 1-31.

Barth, Karl 1963. *Evangelical theology: An introduction*. New York: Holt, Rinehart and Winston.

Bonhoeffer, Dietrich 1998. *Santorum Communio. A theological study of the sociology of the church*. Minneapolis: Fortress.

Childs, Brevard S 1993. *Biblical theology of the Old and New Testaments. Theological reflection on the Christian bible*. Minneapolis: Fortress.

De Gruchy, John W 1984. *Bonhoeffer and South Africa: Theology in dialogue*. Grand Rapids: Eerdmans.

De Gruchy John W (with De Gruchy Steve) 2004. *The church struggle in South Africa. 25th Anniversary edition*. London: SCM.

De Gruchy John and Villa-Vicencio Charles (eds.) 1983. *Apartheid is a heresy*. Cape Town: David Philip.

Davis, Philip G 1989. Mark's Christological paradox. *JSNT* 35:3-18.

De Villiers, Etienne 1986. Kritiek uit die ekumene. In Johann Kinghorn (ed.), 144-164.

Edwards, James R 2002. *The gospel according to Mark*. Grand Rapids: Eerdmans.

France, RT 2002. *The gospel of Mark*. Grand Rapids: Eerdmans.

Giliomee, Hermann 2003. 'The weakness of some': The Dutch Reformed Church and white supremacy. *Scriptura* 83: 212-244.

Johnson, Earl S 1987. Is Mark 15:39 the key to Mark's Christology? *JSNT* 31, 3-22.

Jonker, Willie 1988. Some remarks on the interpretation of Karl Barth. *NGTT* 29:29-40.

Jonker, Willie 1991. Understanding the church situation and obstacles to Christian witness in South Africa. In Louw Alberts and Frank Chikane (eds) *The road to Rustenburg. The church looking forward to a new South Africa*. Cape Town: Struik, 87-98.

Juel, Donald H 1999. *The gospel of Mark*. Nashville: Abingdon.

Kinghorn, Johann (red.) 1986. *Die NG Kerk en apartheid*. Johannesburg: Macmillan.

Moloney, Francis J 2002. *The gospel of Mark. A commentary*. Grand Rapids: Eerdmans.

Naudé, Piet 2003. The theological coherence between the Belhar confession and some antecedent church witnesses in the period 1948-1982. *Verbum et ecclesia* 42 (1): 156-179.

Naudé, Piet 2005. From pluralism to ideology: The roots of apartheid theology in Abraham Kuyper, Gustav Warneck and theological Pietism. *Scriptura* 88: 161-173.

Oberdorfer, Bernd 1998. Biblisch-realistische Theologie: Methodologische Überlegungen zu einem dogmatischen Programm. In S Brandt und B Oberdorfer (Hrsg.) *Resonanzen: Theologische Beiträge*. Wuppertal: Foedus, 63-83.

Rhoads, D, Dewey, J & Michie, D 1999. *Mark as story: An introduction to the narrative of the gospel*. 2nd ed. Philadelphia: Fortress.

Smit, Dirk J 2004. '...The doing of the little righteousness': On justice in Barth's view of the Christian life. In Michael Welker & Cynthia A Jarvis (eds): *Loving God with our minds. The pastor as theologian*. Essays in honor of Wallace M Alston. Grand Rapid: Eerdmans, 120-145.

Welker, Michael 1999. *Creation and reality*. Augsburg: Fortress.

Welker, Michael 1999a. Travail and mission: Theology reformed according to God's Word at the beginning of the third millennium. In David Willis and Michael Welker (eds.): *Toward the future of reformed theology. Tasks, topics, traditions*, Grand Rapids: Eerdmans, 136-152.

Welker, Michael 2000. The task of Biblical Theology and the authority of Scripture. In Wallace Alston (ed.): *Theology in the service of the church: Festschrift for Thomas Gillespie*. Grand Rapids: Eerdmans, 232-241.

Welker, Michael 2001. Das vierfache gewicht der Schrit. Die missverständliche Rede vom "Schriftprinzip" und die Programmformel "Biblische Theologie". In Doris Hiller & Christine Kress (Hg.): *"Dass Gott eine grosse Barmherzighkeit habe". Konkrete Theologie in der Verschränkung von Glaube und Leben*. FS für Gunda-Schneider. Leipzig: Evangelische Verlaganstalt, 9-27

Welker, Michael 2007. What is Biblical Theology? Unpublished paper presented on 24 January at the Centre for Theological Inquiry, Princeton NJ.

Wenham, David & Walton, Steve 2001. *Exploring the New Testament* (volume 1: Introducing the Gospels and Acts). London: SPCK.

PART 3 –
ETHICS AND MORAL DISCOURSE

3.1 WHAT HAS ACCRA TO DO WITH NEW YORK?

An analysis of moral discourse in the Accra Confession

1. BACKGROUND TO THE ACCRA CONFESSION

The Accra Confession (AC) was adopted by the World Alliance of Reformed Churches (WARC) during its 24th General Council held in Ghana, Africa. This confession was the final outcome of a long consultation process that followed the Debrecen (Hungary) meeting in 1997, where churches were invited to enter a process of recognition, education and confession (*processus confessionis*) on their way to covenant for justice in the economy and the earth (as reflected in the subtitle of the confession).

This confession is itself not the result of purely internal WARC initiatives and must be read in the context of the important focus emanating from the World Council of Churches (WCC) Vancouver assembly in 1983. This assembly urged member churches to engage "in a conciliar process of mutual commitment (covenant) to justice, peace and the integrity of creation," subsequently leading to the well-known Justice Peace and the Integrity of Creation studies and reflections.[1] The world convocation in Seoul (Korea) in 1990 made strong affirmations on JPIC, and the concrete issue of a just economic order and liberation from the bondage of foreign debt was firmly put on the agenda of the following WCC assemblies in Canberra (1991) and Harare.

From a South African perspective, it is interesting to note that the Accra Confession has its direct antecedent in a Southern African constituency meeting of the WARC at Kitwe in 1995. But further back in history, the Belhar Confession of 1986 also played a significant role in the final formulations on justice in the Accra Confession.[2]

Apart from the introduction (AC 1-4), the Accra Confession is developed in three subsections: reading the signs of the time (a form of contextual analysis in AC 5-14), a confession of faith in the face of economic justice and ecological destruction (AC 15-36 with 17-35 normally seen as the actual core of the confession) and covenanting for justice (AC 37-42) on the commitment of the churches in the future.

2. THE NATURE OF THE ACCRA CONFESSION

Before we analyse the value and limitations of the AC as a moral argument with respect to economic justice, we need to clarify the exact nature of the document. This is not a trivial or marginal issue, and council members were clearly divided on whether to include a *status confessionis* in the declaration. Although the strong religious condemnations of the current economic system as "idolatry" and worship

---

1   See the successive contributions by D Preman Niles (1989, 1992, 1994).
2   See the close relation between AC 24-26, 31, 34-35 and Belhar's statement on justice (section 4) and obedience (section 5). For the Belhar text, see Cloete and Smit (1984).

of "Mammon" point in the direction of announcing a state of confession, two considerations seem to have prevented this.

The WARC itself is of the view that an assembly of churches cannot adopt a confession in the classical doctrinal sense of the word. That is the task of local and regional churches. By nevertheless calling the statement a confession, the assembly had in mind "a faith stance" that expresses the necessity and urgency of the situation (AC 15). If one takes the "covenanting" notion into account, one could also speak of a "common recommitment of faith" in the Old Testament sense of a covenant renewal between God and God's people.

The second consideration relates to the 20th-century history of *status confessionis*.[3] In both the situation of National Socialism and apartheid we were confronted with an exclusive relation between truth and lie, light and darkness. It was impossible to support either system on the basis of the gospel, and a line was drawn in the sand to distinguish the false church from the true church.

The complexity of the global capitalist system does not make such a clear line possible. The AC admits openly: "We recognize the enormity and complexity of the situation. We do not seek simple answers" (11). The relations of inter-dependence and complicity imply that the churches themselves "consciously or unconsciously benefit from the current neoliberal economic global system". This situation calls for a confession of sin, but might not allow for a *status confessionis* in the strict sense of the word.

To call the AC a "confession" in the tradition of Barmen and Belhar may therefore be misleading and confusing: Accra is a powerful "stance in faith", an urgent "faith response" to the signs of our time, a "covenantal recommitment" to live in a right relationship with God, our covenant partner, for the sake of the poor and the earth. But it is not a confession in the doctrinal sense, emerging spontaneously[4] from the knife-edge of a *status confessionis*.

3. THE ACCRA CONFESSION IN THE LIGHT OF JAMES GUSTAFON'S VARIETIES OF MORAL DISCOURSE

If one accepts the genre of AC as "faith commitment", the question arises whether it persuades as a moral argument. To evaluate the AC, I recall the well-known typology of moral discourses developed by James Gustafson (see Gustafson 1988, 1996).[5] He suggests a fourfold variety of moral discourse – prophetic, narrative, ethical and policy – and is of the opinion that a full moral argument should do justice to each of these discourses. He suggests that "if too exclusive attention is given to any of the

---

3   For a more elaborate history and conceptual clarification of *status confessionis*, there is hardly a better exposition than the one by Dirk Smit, written in 1984 already (see Smit 1984).
4   Karl Barth reminds us that the "spontaneous" nature of a Reformed confession is a fundamental theological and not a psychological description. See Barth (1961:77-80) and Naudé (2007) for a more extensive discussion of Barth's view on the nature of church confessions in relation to the Belhar Confession.
5   For an interesting contextualisation of Gustafson's typology in South Africa at the time of our transition to democracy, see De Villiers and Smit (1994).

types, significant issues of concern to morally sensitive persons and communities are left unattended" (1996:37). In other words, for a morally persuasive argument one needs due attention to each of the discourses.

Let us embark on a close reading of the Accra Confession in the light of this typology.

3.1 Prophetic discourse

It is clear that the AC understands itself as a prophetic critique and condemnation of an unjust economic system (see AC 39).[6] This is an important form of moral discourse steeped in many biblical traditions. As we learn from Gustafson's analysis, the strength of prophetic discourse is its emotive and radical exposure of the roots of what is perceived to be fundamentally and systematically wrong in a particular situation. It calls for repentance and a turn from unfaithfulness to faithfulness.

There is little doubt that Accra considers the global unjust economic system as the root cause of massive threats to both human and ecological life (AC 6). This economic system is then called a policy of unlimited or limitless growth (8, 23); neoliberal economic globalisation (9, 12, 16); a neoliberal ideology (14) that claims sovereignty over life and therefore amounts to idolatry (10); it carries the character of Mammon (14); it is a system of rampant consumerism and competitive greed and selfishness (21) that is equated with the wolves who come to steal kill and destroy (John 10:10, AC 29). This is an "immoral economic system" that is defended by strong nations with all their might (AC 11).

Who are the agents driving this unjust system? Against whom specifically is the prophecy directed? The answer is clear: "The United States of America and its allies, together with international finance and trade institutions (International Monetary Fund, World Bank, World Trade Organisation)" Although the confession later attempts to generalise its focus to "any other economic system, including absolute planned economies" (19, see also 21), the overwhelming critique is of global capitalism as root cause of death and injustice, creating "a scandalous world that denies God's call to life for all" (7).

A complementary dimension of prophetic discourse is its utopian vision of a future that raises human aspirations. This is exactly what the AC does as it espouses a vision of "changing, renewing, and restoring the economy and the earth, choosing life, so that we and our descendants might live" (AC 42).

3.2 Narrative discourse

One can also detect elements in the AC of what Gustafson calls narrative ethical discourse. This refers to the fact that moral communities are shaped by formative narratives that determine their identity, ethos and values (1999:49). Narratives are interpreted descriptions of the past that serve as argument for moral stances in the present, although such argument may be cast in the form of illuminating stories and not necessarily in a rigorous casuistic form (1988:269).

---

6 De Villiers and Smit (1994:232-234) consider the *Kairos Document* of 1985 as a predominantly prophetic discourse, whereas *The Road to Damascus* (1989) is written in a more narrative style.

In the AC, narrative discourse is exhibited in four ways: The first "story" is that of the WARC itself. In fact, the first two paragraphs of the AC relates the road that the WARC has walked to reach Accra, based on a previous commitment to engage economic injustice through a process of recognition, education and confession, and wide consultation all over the world. The second "story" is the slave history of particularly West Africa, vividly recalled by delegates' visits to the slave dungeons of Elimina and Cape Coast. Solidarity with this oppression is then directly used as an argument against "the ongoing realities of human trafficking and the oppression of the global economic system (AC 3).[7]

The third "story" is that of the poor and the earth in our current situation as told in the AC's reading of the signs of the time. The groaning of creation and the cries of people destined to poverty and death are combined to serve as argumentative base in exposing the ideological nature of the current economic system. Look, for example, at how AC 5-7 moves from description of a situation to exposing the oppressive nature of that very situation in the paragraphs that follow.

Narratives are the building blocks of the Christian faith as well. One would therefore expect a fourth "story" in the confession: the story of God as told in Scripture and tradition. The AC draws on powerful biblical traditions to explicate God for the specific context it addresses. This is especially evident in the more directly confessional or theological section of AC, namely paragraphs 17-36, where the identity of God is described as creator, sustainer, initiator of a covenant with the earth, and as defender of justice. Jesus is – in the theme of the Accra assembly – remembered as the good shepherd who lay down his life so that we might have abundant life, and as the One who chooses for the marginalised (AC 20, 28-29). The Spirit is God who calls us to account for the hope that is within us (AC 32), and – in line with the structure of Nicea[8] and the Apostolicum – the identity of the church and its task (AC 29, 31, 33) is drawn from the preceding theology.

The blending of these narrative strands renders an immanent persuasive power to the Accra Confession, and gives further credence to the prophetic critique. The question is whether the AC – read as moral argument – includes what Gustafson called "ethical" and "policy" discourse?

3.3 Ethical discourse

Whereas prophecy moves on a macro level ("the neoliberal economic system") ethical discourse moves on the micro level as it provides modes of appropriate reasoning through conceptual clarification and by making important distinctions, "which lead to greater precision and stronger backing for what Christians … think is the right thing to do" (Gustafson 1988:33). Whereas narrative discourse calls forth symbols and ethos-shaping stories, ethical discourse lies closer to moral philosophy with a more "logical-argumentative" approach.

---

7   See Berger's interview with German theologian, Ulrich Duchrow, who considers the visit to slave castles and dungeons as "the transformative moment" where delegates from the North understood some of the anguish of their Southern brothers and sisters (Berger 2005: 33).
8   See the many ethical passages in the WCC interpretation of the Nicene creed (WCC 1991). For ecology read paragraphs 84-89, and for economic justice read paragraphs 225-6, 238, and 277.

There are at least three overt attempts at conceptual clarification or "ethical" discourse in the AC.

- Paragraph 15 is an example of healthy self-reflection as the WARC explains what it means by "confession" and – by implication – why *status confessionis* is absent from the final text. This was discussed earlier in this paper.

- A very emotive term like "empire" is used as a description of the current global situation, and is – in my view – convincingly explained with greater precision: "In using the term empire we mean the coming together of economic, cultural, political and military power that constitutes a system of domination led by powerful nations to protect and defend their interests" (AC 11).

- The core focus of the AC is on the economy. One would therefore expect to find a description or more precise outline of what precisely is meant by "neoliberal economic globalisation". This is indeed set out in paragraph 9 where the beliefs or core assumptions of the current global system are enumerated. The description ranges from unlimited economic growth and deregulation of the market to unrestricted movement of capital and a subordination of social obligations to capital accumulation. Classical liberal economies were re-shaped in the course of the 20th century to include protection of workers and according crucial welfare functions to the state. We now have neoliberalism, where "the purpose of the economy is to increase profits and returns for the owners of production and financial capital, while excluding the majority of the people and treating nature as a commodity" (AC 12).

One may differ from AC regarding these conceptual clarifications, and could ask for more and greater precision. But this would indeed invite rational debate and would confirm the argumentative dimension of the confession at the level of "ethics" discourse.

A specific critique could, for instance, be levelled at the AC for its overtly biased analysis of the effects of global capitalism. There is enough empirical evidence to show the Janus-face or ambiguity of the current economic system,[9] and the AC would have gained in persuasive power if it had signalled these ambiguities in its reading of the signs of the time. Although AC recognises "the enormity and complexity of the situation" and the confessors "do not seek simple answers", there is the danger of fighting ideology with equally ideological language and losing credibility along the way.

It is not enough to just indicate that even churches benefit consciously or unconsciously from the current system – there are many other achievements of the system that have benefited and are benefiting even the poor. This ranges from the communication revolution to preferential trade agreements and the development of generic drugs. Every dollar of aid or debt write-off has been earned in the system. That does not exonerate the system for its weak features such as skew distributive

---

9 See, for example, the very well written analytical work on globalisation by Held and colleagues (1999) and the more defensive stance of Bhagwati (2004, especially sections I and II).

patterns[10] and asymmetrical power relations, but it is one thing to denounce a system in its entirety and quite another to make suggestions for its radical reform.

The confession of sin in paragraph 34 is quite appropriate (and reminds one of the Belhar Confession and its accompanying letter). What is missing from this confession is the complicity of poor nations' leaders (specifically in Africa) in misusing the system to enrich themselves, clinging to power through war on their own people, and intensifying human misery to the point where a reform of the economic system might not even benefit the poor. A prerequisite for escaping the trap of poverty is to empower the poor to take their future into their own hands and negotiate their place in the world from at least a position of equality, if not preference.[11] The question of how such social transformation could take place, may be addressed by referring to Gustafson' policy discourse.

3.4 Policy discourse

Gustafson succinctly describes policy discourse as determining "what is desirable within the constraints of what is possible" (1988:270). This links closely to an ethics of responsibility, because the persons involved in actual policy decisions are – unlike prophetic theologians or theory-driven economists! – accountable for the actions and outcomes of their policy decisions (1988:46). Agents of policy development are in the difficult position that they need to connect with centres of political power to ensure that their policies are executed, and they have the task of translating prophecy, narrative and ethical analyses into concrete realities.

As a stance of faith, the AC is weakest on the policy level. Prophetic discourse is notoriously weak on finer analysis and may itself show strands of ideological language. Narrative discourse may suffer from one-sidedness, depending on whose story is told and by whom, or from lack of intellectual clarity insofar as it calls on metaphors and symbols not always accessible to outsiders. Ethical discourse may get entangled in conceptual analysis, but end up with totally impractical suggestions on the way forward. That is why Gustafson's warning is to be heeded: one type of discourse is not sufficient in itself. If – for the moment – we understand ethics also as the translation of theology into achievable social goals (the so-called middle axioms of a responsible society), we as theologians cannot rest with denouncement and narratives, and leave the messy work of implementation to others in the real world.

One may argue that a "faith stance" does not aim at policy. The counter-argument may run as follows: it is understandable that a confession in the classical sense

---

10 For theories of distributive justice see the informative overview by Roemer (1998), and for a more specialised version of justice as fairness see Rawls (1971, 1999).
11 See the interesting observation by Bedford-Strohm (1994:169, 308) that "fehlende Teilnahme" (a lack of participation) is often the source of remaining in poverty. This echoes Rawls's view that burdened societies need sound political institutions to realise the potential of development. "What must be realized is that merely dispensing funds will not rectify basic political and social injustices (though money is often essential)." A focus on human rights and establishment of a democratic political culture is more important (1999:108-109). Rawls takes his cue from *inter alia* Sen's case studies of famine that show the political and economic factors are mostly more important than "natural" factors such as droughts. This reinforces Rawls's view that assistance for peoples must carry political consequences, i.e. the creation of just institutions.

(Barmen, Belhar) does not include an overt policy dimension, although they give strong clues about action and discipleship. These confessions were spontaneously born in the *kairos* of a specific situation with little time for reflection on policy.

However, a faith stance or covenanting for justice that is the result of many years of reflection and consultation owes the world a fuller moral argument. It is indeed important to show the ideological nature of the current economic system and call people to see its devastating effects on the poor and the environment. A confession can lead to insight and guilt, but unless further work is done to move from prophecy, narrative and ethics to policy, millions of Christians (and others of goodwill) in the system are left with no clarity on what they could/should actually do. The situation is compounded if the critique is systemic – as it should indeed be. But how to change and dismantle a system on which you also rely is – as the AC rightly states – a complicated matter and normally beyond the immediate expertise of the institutional church and theologians.[12]

An inclusion of some guidelines from the Public Issues Committee of WARC (referred to in paragraph 40) in the actual text of the AC, would have significantly heightened its persuasive moral argument. If you witness against an economic system, and if you convince others of that system's pervasive power, you need to make some suggestions on economic policy and practice that are not blue-sky visions, but – as Gustafson reminds - "within the constraints of what is possible."

That is why the relation between theology and economics is of such importance in the 21st century.[13] If the current global economic system is the key source of the threat to social stability and our actual survival on this planet, then debates about restructuring this system require that theologians and ethicists take the work of leading economists seriously. The same energy that we spent through the ages to learn the language of philosophers (from Plato to Habermas), sociologists (from Comte to Luhmann), psychologists (from Wundt to Freud) and linguists (from Socrates to De Saussure) in order to construct our theologies and hermeneutics, is now required to make theological sense of our radically "economised" context (from Adam Smith to Amartya Sen and Joseph Stiglitz).[14]

---

12   The transition from apartheid to democracy is an interesting case in point. The liberation struggle was led by church leaders. But once negotiations started, we needed political and constitutional experts to give flesh to the preceding prophetic critique. Following Gustafson's wisdom, however, one should be careful not to isolate policy from the other discourses.

13   As far as I know, the collection of essays edited by AJ van der Walt (2005) is one of the rare occasions where theologians in South Africa participated in a discussion on theories of economic justice. See chapter 4.4 for a broader discussion of the relation between theology and economic policy.

14   The choice of Joseph Stiglitz was initially quite arbitrary and was more the result of his status and best-selling books than actual insight into his views. Looking back, I am satisfied that this choice did yield the required results I aim at in this essay. The work of Amartya Sen – specifically his focus on the link between ethics and economics (Sen 1988) – is equally influential and should provide a fertile base for policy reflection. There are more radical choices such as Ulrich Duchrow, but also authors that would broadly support the tenets of Stiglitz, such as the Australian economist, Graham Dunkley (2004).

4. FROM ACCRA TO NEW YORK? A FEW POLICY SUGGESTIONS

I am quite aware that there is a degree of incommensurability between AC and many modern-day economists on their respective basic orientations to the current global economic system (not that economists agree amongst themselves!). But there are also common sentiments such as the moral unacceptability of skewed distributive justice and a serious questioning of neoliberal doctrines of economic growth, market liberalisation and the welfare role of the state. We must therefore accept the challenge to outline some implications that could be derived from a translation of AC into policy-type proposals.

For illustrative purposes, one could list the following ideas that might have been included in the AC's last section on covenanting for justice or could be part of practical implementation guidelines:[15]

> We, the participants of the WARC, commit ourselves, and call on all Christians and persons of good faith, to commit themselves to the following policy guidelines:
>
> - Instead of vigorously pursuing free trade as goal in itself, we join hands with the fair trade movement to ensure the empowerment of groups excluded from the current economic system. All trade agreements should be assessed to ensure that the net incidence of benefits accrues to developing and poor countries. The WTO should exercise extreme care to ensure that the principle of special and differential treatment – already accepted by all members – informs both its procedures and the outcomes of its activities. Where current under-development is the result of past oppression like colonialism or discrimination against indigenous peoples, equity demands that a greater share of benefits of trade agreements should flow to countries/peoples affected in this way.
>
> - Trade liberalisation, if agreed to, should be preceded by a general equilibrium incident analysis and phased in according to the adjustment capacity of the country or region concerned, with some compensation for transition costs and the greater risk associated with deregulated markets.
>
> - The state should retain an important social welfare function and privatisation only implemented if there are guaranteed service delivery at optimal costs and protection of the poorest segment of the population.
>
> - The Millennium Development Goals embody a global commitment to seriously address poverty and under-development. Progress to achieve these goals should be assessed each year and public commitments that are enforceable by the WTO must ensure that we half poverty by 2015.

In this way one can proceed to address the most urgent policy areas in a responsible and practical manner. These are merely suggestions and an illustration of the interplay between theology and economics. These statements are obviously built on the assumption that the neoliberal system can be reformed and its excessive negative effects stemmed. If, however, that assumption is not shared, more drastic policy

---

15 See, for example, the guidelines for implementing the AC by the Council for World Mission, 2008.

suggestions will have to be formulated to ensure the dismantling of the current global economic system and its replacement with another more just and humane system.

5. CONCLUSION

The Accra Confession is an important stance of faith. From the perspective of moral argumentation, it succeeds at the levels of prophetic and narrative discourses. There may be questions about the fairness of its ethical analysis – though clarification of core concepts is satisfactory. As the document reads now, it fails to provide a moral argument that could be classified as policy discourse. This is a deficit in a document that was carefully drafted over many years and through many consultations. Such policy directives should be developed in multidisciplinary consultation with economists and become an integral part of the church's mission and ongoing prophetic critique.[16]

BIBLIOGRAPHY

Barth, Karl 1961. *Church Dogmatics III/4. The doctrine of creation*. Edinburgh: T & T Clarke.

Bedford-Strohm, Heinrich 1993. *Vorrang für die Armen. Auf dem Weg zu einer theologischen Theorie der Gerechtighkeit*. Gütersloh: Chr. Kaiser Verlag.

Berger, Rose Marie 2005. The miracle at Accra. *Sojourners Magazine*, July, Vol. 34, No.7:33-36.

Bhagwati, Jagdish 2004. *In defense of globalization*. Oxford: Oxford University Press.

Cloete GD and Smit DJ 1984. *A moment of truth*. Grand Rapids: Eerdmans.

Council for World Mission. 2008. *Living out the Accra Confession*. http//www.cwmission.org.uk retrieved on 25 May 2008.

De Villiers, DE and Smit, DJ 1994. Hoe christene in Suid-Afrika by mekaar verby praat. Oor vier morele spreekwyses in die Suid-Afrikaanse kerklike konteks. *Skrif en Kerk*, 15/2:228-247.

Dunkley, Graham 2006. *Free trade. Myth, reality and alternatives*. London: Zed Books.

EKD 2006. *Gerechte Teilhabe. Befähigung zu Eigenverantwortung und Solidarität*. Gütersloh: Güthersloher Verlagshaus. Gustafson, James 1988. *Varieties of moral discourse: prophetic, narrative, ethical, and policy*. Michigan: Michigan Press.

Gustafson, James 1988. *Varieties of moral discourse: prophetic, narrative, ethical and policy*. Grand Rapids, MI: Calvin College and Seminary Press.

Gustafson, James 1996. *Intersections. Science, theology, and ethics*. Cleveland: The Pilgrim Press.

Held, David, McGrew, Anthony, Goldblatt, David and Perraton, Jonathan 1999. *Global transformations. Politics, economics and culture*. Stanford: Stanford University Press.

Naudé, Piet 2007. Would Barth sign the Belhar confession? *JTSA* 129, 4-22.

---

16 In my view, successful examples of faith stances on the economy that include policy discourse are the Catholic Social Doctrine on economic life issued by the Pontifical Council for Justice and Peace (2004) as well as the influential study guide, *Gerechte Teilhabe*, by the EKD in Germany (EKD:2006). In fairness it must be stated that these two examples are more study documents than confessions.

Niles, DP 1989. *Resisting the threats to life: Covenanting for justice, peace and the integrity of creation.* Geneva: WCC.

Niles, DP (ed.) 1992. *Between the flood and the rainbow: Essays interpreting the conciliar process of mutual commitment (covenant) to justice, peace and the integrity of creation.* Geneva: WCC.

Niles, DP (ed.) 1994. *Justice, peace and the integrity of creation: Documents from an ecumenical process of commitment.* Geneva: WCC.

Pontifical Council for Justice and Peace 2004. *Compendium of the social doctrine of the church.* Nairobi: Paulines Press

Rawls, John 1971. *A theory of justice.* Oxford: Oxford University Press.

Rawls, John 1999. *The law of peoples.* Cambridge, Massachusetts: Harvard University Press.

Roemer. John E 1998. *Theories of distributive justice.* Cambridge, Massachusetts: Harvard University Press.

Sen, Amartya 1988. *On ethics and economics.* Oxford: Blackwell.

Smit, DJ 1984. What does *status confessionis* mean? In Cloete and Smit 1984, 7-32.

Van der Walt AJ (ed.) 2005. *Theories of social and economic justice.* Stellenbosch: Sun Press.

World Alliance of Reformed Churches 2004. *The Accra Confession. Covenanting for justice in the economy and the earth.* Geneva: WCC.

World Council of Churches 1991. *Confessing the one faith. An ecumenical explication of the Apostolic faith as it is confessed in the Nicene-Constantinopolitan Creed (381).* Geneva: WCC.

3.2 IS PROPHETIC DISCOURSE ADEQUATE TO ADDRESS GLOBAL ECONOMIC JUSTICE?

1. INTRODUCTION

This chapter[1] commences with an outline of five possible features of 'prophetic discourse'. This is a short but important part of this essay (section 2), as the rest of the arguments are based on the notion established at the beginning. The key strength of prophetic discourse relating to economic justice is then analysed through a case study of the so-called 'preferential option for the poor' (section 3). After that four key weaknesses of prophetic discourse are shortly set out (section 4), before the chapter closes with a summary and conclusion (section 5).

2. OUTLINING PROPHETIC DISCOURSE

Distilling the defining characteristics of prophetic discourse is by no means simple. The difference in prophetic personalities, periods of prophetism in the Old Testament, the intra-canonical interpretation of the prophets, and developments and changes of emphases in interpreting the prophets, make this a challenging endeavour (cf. e.g. Seitz 2007).[2] The interpretative challenge is further exacerbated by the term itself. When speaking of 'prophets' the interplay between modern understandings and expectations of the word and its use in the Old Testament does not necessarily aid one in the search for a definition.[3]

Fortunately the complexity of interpreting and contextualising the prophets' message does not mean that we should refrain from interpreting and even systematising their message. Indeed, we are confronted with a basic challenge of theology, which we must accept with the same prophetic freedom Von Rad ascribed to the prophets themselves in his seminal *The Message of the Prophets* (Von Rad 1968:50-59).

In this article I shall identify, develop and apply certain biblical characteristics of prophetic discourse without implying that these impulses exhaust the message of the prophets.

It is clear, firstly, that prophetic activity in the Old Testament more often than not uncovers perceived economic injustice (Von Rad 1968:53).[4] Amos is a clear example.

---

1   It is an honour to dedicate this reflection to one of South Africa's foremost New Testament scholars, Andries van Aarde, who has always inspired me as a systematic theologian and ethicist to take the Bible in its historicity and complexity seriously.
2   Seitz illustrates this complexity by examining developments in the interpretation of the prophets, different periods of prophetism (Mosaism, Prophetism and Old Testament) (Seitz, 2007:79), differences in prophetic personalities (Seitz, 2007:82ff) as well as the way they are interpreted in the context of their canonical status (Seitz, 2007:85).
3   Wilson (1980:21-28) gives a very helpful description of modern, classical and biblical meanings of "prophet" and their influence on understanding prophetism in ancient Israel.
4   Von Rad regards the role of the prophet's own interpretation of the situation as of crucial importance for the communication of God's will: "It is hardly possible to overrate the importance of the prophet's share, for without it the word the prophet receives does not reach its goal and therefore cannot be fulfilled. What makes it such a tremendous

The "houses adorned with ivory" and the "mansions" will be destroyed (3:12), those who only want more to drink (4:1), those who "dine on choice lambs and fattened cows" (6:4) are actually oppressing the poor and crushing the needy (4:1, 5:11). Amos' prophetic activity exposed the injustice and inequality ingrained into the societal structures of his time.

The prophetic uncovering of unjust societal structures is often connected, secondly, with a moral denouncement in the name of God (cf. e.g. Wittenberg 1993).[5] One of the most memorable examples is Nathan's denouncement of David's murder of Uriah and his relationship with Bathsheba in 2 Samuel 12. Nathan states plainly that it is the Lord himself (12:7-11) who denounces David's sin. David fittingly replies by acknowledging that he has "sinned against the *Lord*" (12:13).

Closely connected to the denouncement from God is, thirdly, the prophets' call to repentance or judgement. This can be seen, for example, in Hosea: God's anger "burns" against Israel (8:5) and they will be "swallowed up" (8:8). Jonah's reaction to God's command that he should go to Nineveh and "preach against it" (1:1) illustrates the close bond between repentance and judgement in prophetic discourses in the Old Testament. The citizens of Nineveh respond with repentance and Jonah becomes angry, as he knew that prophetic preaching of judgement often leads to repentance and a change of fortunes – because God is "gracious and compassionate" and "slow to anger" (4:2).

Prophetic discourse is characterised, fourthly, by its pronouncement of a utopian alternative to current realities. Prophetic discourse "portrays an alluring vision of the future, of possibilities for life in the world in which the forms of strife and suffering we all experience are overcome" (Gustafson 1988:13). The prophet in Trito-Isaiah speaks lyrically of a time when there will be no hunger or thirst (49:10), as does the prophet in proto-Isaiah, where he speaks of a time when God will "settle disputes for many peoples" and they will "beat their swords into ploughshares and their spears into pruning hooks" (2:4). This characteristically utopian alternative one also sees in Ezekiel – albeit in even more metaphorical language – when he speaks of the "dry bones" of Israel that will one day be made alive by the breath of God (Ezekiel 37:1-14).

When viewed more broadly, one can say, lastly, that prophetic discourse is aimed at expressing the will of God (cf. e.g. Gene Tucker's account of the role of God's "own words" in prophetic speech (1987:30ff)). Uncovering unjust structures, making strong moral denouncements, calling for repentance and bringing a utopian alternative are aimed at nothing less than articulating God's will in reaction to very specific circumstances. Jeremiah's critique against the prophecies of Hananiah may suffice as a last example. God instructs Jeremiah to tell his people not to listen to their prophets, diviners and interpreters of dreams (27:9, 16), but that they should seek the will of God (28:9).

---

    responsibility is the fact that the prophet is thus puts the will of Yahweh into effect: Yahweh thereafter commits himself to stand by the decision of his ambassador."

5   Wittenberg (1993) frames these moral denouncements as "protest", and identifies the protest against idolatry (23-32), oppression (33-46), the politics of security (47-62), false prophecy (63-77) and despair (96-112) as the most important dimensions of their protest.

These five broad traits of prophetic discourse form the basis upon which the applicability and efficacy of this discourse in relation to economic justice are evaluated below.

3. THE STRENGTH OF PROPHETIC DISCOURSE ON ECONOMIC JUSTICE

On the basis of the biblical impulses set out in previous section, it can be said that a key strength of prophetic discourse is that it focuses unambiguous attention on a specific dimension of justice (cf. Naudé 2008:208). Gustafson describes the strength of prophetic discourse as both indictments that expose the perceived root of evil (Gustafson 1988:8) and a "powerfully attractive vision of a future which positively moves us to approximate it" (1988:13). According to Gustafson's analysis, prophetic discourse is passionate language "proclaimed against the moral evil and apostasy of the world and societies" (1988:8).

Characteristic of prophetic discourse is that its unambiguous focus on a dimension of justice – proclaimed against a specific 'moral evil and apostasy' – may over time diffuse through to mainstream thinking and in this way affect public opinion and policy far beyond its initial scope or intentions. This is a multi-directional, transformative, spontaneous and at times even contradictory process.

In this section the extension of justice understood as the 'preferential option for the poor' will be analysed. It will demonstrate how the prophetic cry emanating from Latin American liberation theologies (notably Gutiérrez) permeated political philosophy (Rawls), economic theory (Stiglitz), and later co-determined practical policy decisions (Doha ministerial declaration).[6]

3.1 Latin American liberation theologies: the preferential option for the poor

Gutiérrez famously described God's 'preferential option for the poor' as follows:

> The very term preference obviously precludes any exclusivity; it simply points to who ought to be first – not the only – objects of our solidarity. … [What option emphasises] is the free commitment of a decision. The option for the poor is not optional in the sense that a Christian need not necessarily make it, any more than the love we owe every human being, without exception, is not optional. It is a matter of deep, ongoing solidarity, a voluntary daily involvement with the world of the poor (1993:239).

'Poverty' is used as a comprehensive term, "a universe in which the socio-economic aspect is basic but not all-inclusive" (Gutiérrez 1988: xxi). In Gutiérrez's understanding the term 'the poor' denotes at least three forms of poverty, namely the material poverty of the physically poor, the social poverty of those who are marginalised as a result of racial, cultural or gender oppression and the spiritual poverty of those who are not open to God's will and solidarity with the poor (Gutiérrez 1993:235-237).

---

6   The discussion below draws extensively on an earlier article (see Naudé 2007) and is an abbreviation of the fuller discussion contained in chapter 1.2 above.

Early signs of the terminology could already be seen in *Gaudium et Spes*, originating from Vatican II (1965).[7] But long before Vatican II God's preferential option for the poor was developing in the 'roots' of liberation theology, i.e. the theologies practised by the poor in their base communities.[8] The starting point of theology is understood not as "doctrine" but "reality" (Sobrino 1984:2).[9] It paved the way for the discussion at the Second General Conference of Latin American Bishops at Medellin in 1968 and a chapter devoted to the terminology in the final document of the Third Bishops' Conference in Puebla (1979) (cf. Bedford-Strohm 1993:151-166). According to Sobrino, the poor are the "authentic theological source for understanding Christian truth and practice" as the poor "pose the problem of seeking God without presupposing that the Church possesses him once and for all", whilst at the same time offering to the church "the place for finding him" (Sobrino, 1984:93).

Within Latin American liberation theologies the terminology related to the preferential option for the poor gradually grew in importance and started to develop into a multifaceted prophetic framework for seeing, judging and acting on perceived injustice. The experience of the poor served as methodological starting point; hermeneutically the readings of "suspicion", especially by ordinary people, were taken as point of departure; the Trinity as a community of justice and charity opting as separate persons for the poor was understood as the fundamental theological motive; and an ecclesiology that connected the sanctification of the church with solidarity with the poor shaped the vision of the church (Naudé 2007:167-178).

By uncovering and pronouncing God's judgement on injustice by means of 'the preferential option for the poor', Latin American liberation theologies at the same time also provided a utopian vision on forms of justice that "conform" to the "reign of God" (Sobrino 1984:40). Sobrino expresses these forms of justice as

> the kind of love that seeks effectively to humanize, to give life in abundance to the poor and oppressed majority of the human race. Justice is thus a concrete form of love in which account is taken of the quantitative fact that its recipients form majorities and of the qualitative fact that they are poor and oppressed.

Stated in other terms we can say that this terminology responds to the injustice of material poverty with demands for a radical distributive justice, namely a form of socio-economic justice that regulates the distribution of goods and services based on a specific theory of justice in a particular geographical arrangement (cf. Roemer 1998). It also responds to socio-political injustice with demands for cultural justice,

---

7   According to Gutiérrez himself, the "name and reality" of liberation theology came into existence at Chimbote in Peru (July 1968), a few months before the bishops' conference in Medellín (1988:xvii).
8   Clodovis Boff views liberation theology as consisting of three forms of theology, namely popular liberation theology done by Christians in base communities (the "roots"), pastoral liberation theology done in ecclesial communities (the "trunk") and the liberation theology done by professional theologians by means of rigorous academic arguments (the "branches"). Cf. Boff & Boff (1984:5-11, 49-55) and Boff & Boff (1987:24ff).
9   Sobrino continues to qualify this provocative conviction: "Doctrine is of course necessary and important. But in itself, apart from the concrete reality of the Church and apart from the present manifestation of God in the Church, it cannot take any real historical shape. It can be true, but it will remain ineffective and irrelevant."

namely a form of social justice that regulates the relationship amongst individuals from different cultural backgrounds or amongst cultural groups themselves (cf. Kwenda 2003).

3.2 John Rawls: prioritarian distributive justice

A few years later, on a different continent and in a very different context, impulses similar to the demand for justice by Latin American liberation theologians can be recognised in the work of the North American political philosopher John Rawls. In *A Theory of Justice* (1971), arguably one of the most – if not the most – important works on justice of the 20th century, Rawls develops the concept of justice as fairness in a theory of prioritarian distributive justice (Rawls 1971:60-90). Central to Rawls's theory is his difference principle: redistributive policies may allow for social and economic inequalities only when they servethe least advantaged members of society (Naudé 2007:179).

Rawls conceptualised an "original position of equality" – a hypothetical situation where all are "similarly situated" – where people are required to choose the principles "which are to assign basic rights and duties" and to determine the division of "social benefits" (Rawls 1973:11) without knowing what their positions in this society will be, i.e. behind a "veil of ignorance" (Rawls 1973:136-142).

From this position Rawls develops his egalitarian conception of justice. Although based on the principle of equal rights and most extensive equal liberties to all, it acknowledges the existence of social and economic inequalities. It is therefore aimed at redressing "undeserved inequalities" by giving "more attention to those with fewer native assets and to those born into the less favourable social positions" (Rawls 1973:100). It is not egalitarian in the radical sense of requiring that all should ideally have an equal share of all social goods. Although the difference principle itself is not to be equated with the ideal of redress (Rawls 1973:101), it nonetheless gives expression to the prioritarian thrust of his understanding of distributive justice: inequalities in "rights and liberties, opportunities and powers, income and wealth" (Rawls 1973:101) must always be distributed in a manner that improves the situation of society's least advantaged.[10]

In his later work, *The law of peoples* (1999), Rawls broadens his work on "justice as fairness" to include the reality of an increasingly globalised international society, composed of people with "distinctive institutions and languages, religions and cultures, as well as different histories" (Rawls 1999:54-55). He conceptualises a second original position where representatives of all people meet behind a veil of ignorance (Rawls 1999:32-33) and eventually choose eight principles as the "Law of the Peoples" (Rawls 1999:37). Also in this 'internationalised' version of his work he develops a prioritarian sense of distributive justice.

Rawls formulates eight principles of justice of free and democratic peoples.

1. Peoples are free and independent, and their freedom and independence are to be respected by other peoples.

---

10 In terms of this understanding injustice is "simply inequalities that are not to the benefit of all" (Rawls 1973:62).

2. Peoples are to observe treaties and undertakings.
3. Peoples are equal and are parties to the agreements that bind them.
4. Peoples are to observe a duty of non-intervention.
5. Peoples have the right of self-defence but no right to instigate war for reasons other than self-defence.
6. Peoples are to honour human rights.
7. Peoples are to observe certain specified restrictions in the conduct of war.
8. People(s) have a duty to assist other peoples living under unfavourable conditions that prevent their having a just or decent political and social regime (Rawls 1999:37).

Principle 8 in particular marks Rawls' egalitarianism as prioritarian in character. He views those living under unfavourable conditions as citizens of "burdened societies" because they "lack the political and cultural traditions, the human capital and know-how, and often, the material and technological resources needed to be well-ordered" (Rawls 1999:106). This does not mean, however, that Rawls accepts a global difference principle. The principle of distributive justice is not necessarily the best or the only way to "regulate economic and social inequalities among societies" (Rawls 1999:106). His three guidelines for the duty to assist clarify this aspect of his theory (Rawls 1999:106-113).

Burdened societies are not assisted in order for them to reach greater equality in, for example, economic wealth, but rather tot assist them "to establish reasonably just basic institutions for a free constitutional democratic society and to secure a social world that makes possible a worthwhile life for all [their] citizens" (Rawls 1999:107).

3.3 Joseph Stiglitz: a differential option for poor countries

The renowned – and in some circles infamous! – economist Joseph Stiglitz may come from a completely different intellectual tradition than Latin American liberation theologians, and from a different discipline than Rawls, but his work nonetheless has moments of prophetic intensity that match those of the liberation theologians and of Rawls. One could contend that Stiglitz proposes an understanding of justice that shares at least some of the basic thrusts of the 'preferential option for the poor' or the least advantaged representative person/burdened societies discussed above.

Stiglitz continues to be committed to the free market, but has serious criticisms of some of its traditional basic tenets. He rejects, for example, two long-standing premises of trade liberalisation (Stiglitz 2006: 99, 23; Stiglitz, 2006a:18-21). First, Stiglitz is not of the opinion that the liberalisation of trade will necessarily lead to more trade and higher economic growth. Second, he does not believe that growth will necessarily 'trickle down' to the benefit of all. According to his research and reading of economic history and current economic theory, neither of these 'truths' is supported by the facts. Furthermore, he rejects the separation of efficiency and equity considerations. He argues that efficiency cannot be the sole criterion of economic performance, but that so-called non-economic values such as "social justice, the environment, cultural diversity, universal access to health care and consumer protection" should be co-determinants of economic success (Stiglitz 2006:xvii, 17, 22).

In a revealing reference to Rawls, Stiglitz asks how the economic system might have looked if those in power had to choose the fairest system from behind a veil of ignorance (Stiglitz 2006:296, footnote 15). In this context he integrates his critique with his allegiance to the current system and suggests a "differential option for the poor and the judgement of trade regimes by the criterion whether it does not make poorest countries relatively even poorer" (Stiglitz 2006:58). He is of the opinion that after the World Trade Organisation (WTO) replaced the General Agreement on Tariffs and Trade (GATT) in 1995, an asymmetrical system with uneven implementation evolved, with the result that developing countries became even worse off (Stiglitz 2006:48).

He therefore suggests a reform of international trade, which he calls "fair trade for the poor". This reform would entail that the current system of so-called reciprocity for and among all countries would be replaced by the principle of "reciprocity among equals, but differentiation between those in markedly different circumstances" (Stiglitz 2006:83). In practice this means that countries should trade with one another in a three-tier system of rich, middle-income and poor countries (Stiglitz 2006a:83). In such a system the rich countries open up their markets to all three tiers – reciprocally to other rich countries, but without reciprocity or political conditionality to middle-income and poor countries. Middle-income countries open their markets to other middle-income and poor countries without conditionality, and are not expected to open their markets to rich countries. Stiglitz suggests that this differential treatment towards developing countries should not be voluntary, but should be a necessary part of WTO trade negotiations.

Stiglitz defends his position from both a utilitarian and a deontological base. He is of the opinion that a differential option for poor countries would, firstly, serve the self-interest of developed countries as it would contribute to greater stability and security in these countries (Stiglitz 2006:59). Such a trade regime can stem the flow of immigrants to developed countries, and in the long run it will diminish the need for development aid and debt write-offs.[11] Secondly, Stiglitz motivates his position on the principle of the moral unacceptability of the scale of continued global poverty (Stiglitz 2006:100-101, 59). Although he does not argue this case at length, it is clear that the humanity of developed countries is connected to the humanity of their attempts to address global poverty.

Let us turn to the last phase of this development from theologically motivated prophecy to policy formulation.

3.4 Doha ministerial declaration: special and differential treatment for poor countries

The (often subversive) conviction that those in structurally disadvantaged positions should be treated in a differential manner in order for injustice to be undone is not evident only in the work of theologians from developing countries, academic

---

11 Stiglitz reminds us that rich countries cost poor countries three times more in trade restrictions than they give in development aid (2006:78).

philosophers or somewhat dissenting economists. The Doha Development Round of the WTO trade negotiations (which commenced in 2001) included strong statements recognising the need for the differential treatment of less-developed countries.

In this document it is agreed that "special and differential treatment for developing countries" forms an integral part of negotiations aimed at "substantial improvements" in market access, reducing and ultimately phasing out "all forms of export subsidies" and "substantial reductions" in domestic support (World Trade Organisation, Doha Ministerial Declaration Article 13). Differential treatment for poor countries is based on the premise that international trade "can play a major role in the promotion of economic development and the alleviation of poverty" (World Trade Organisation Doha Ministerial Declaration: 2).

Even in this document one recognises the implicit acknowledgement that current injustices are – at least partly – the result of a hierarchical, uneven and asymmetrical system (cf. Held et al. 1999:213, 224). In Article 2 the declaration rather candidly states:

> We recognize the particular **vulnerability** of the least-developed countries and the special structural difficulties they face in the global economy. We are committed to addressing the **marginalization** of least-developed countries in international trade and to improving their effective participation in the multilateral trading system (author's emphases) (World Trade Organization Doha Ministerial Declaration: 3).

These notions from the Doha Declaration understandably continue to receive strong support from developing countries, specifically from the African Union. The support is not, however, unqualified.

Whilst the African Union accepts the principles of a market economy, it has a wider theoretical frame of reference than a narrow mercantilist view of trade negotiations. A comprehensive theoretical framework in which "economic efficacy and solidarity, efficiency and equity, growth and sustainable development, short-term gains and long-term prospects" must be combined should inform trade negotiations (African Union Commission 2004:10). It also adopts a qualified stance regarding trade negotiations themselves. At this stage Africa still has low negotiation capabilities both in terms of human resources and technical knowledge. Although Africa is in the process of developing its trade negotiation capacities, the assistance of the WTO will be needed to participate effectively (Economic Commission for Africa 2007:90).

Africa has been the recipient of many forms of forced political and economic interventions. Whilst therefore understanding that trade liberalisation is the general aim of trade negotiations, the African Union continues to emphasise that allowance for trade liberalisation should be made according to the development needs and adjustment capacities of a particular country or region (Economic Commission for Africa 2007:87). It also supports the notion of aid specifically aimed at meeting the adjustment costs of trade liberalisation – given that it is not misused as a political weapon in negotiations or as replacement for current trade commitments (Economic Commission for Africa 2007:87).

4. WEAKNESSES OF PROPHETIC DISCOURSE

In the previous section the 'preferential option for the poor' that characterises Latin American liberation theology was used to illustrate the legitimacy and strengths of the prophetic discourse. But this legitimacy does not mean that prophetic discourse is sufficient (cf. Gustafson 1988:15). In fact, the discussion above points precisely to the inherent weaknesses of prophetic discourse, if taken by itself or if isolated from other forms of moral discourse. As Gustafson reminds us, prophetic discourse is but one 'variety' of moral discourse. According to him, prophetic discourse must necessarily be supplemented by identity-sustaining narratives (1988:19-27), rigorous logically coherent ethical arguments (1988:31-44) and the choice and planning of particular courses of actions (1988:45-53).

4.1 Failure to provide full moral argument

Prophetic discourse fails to provide a full moral argument. Moral discourse is aimed not at simply talking, but at reaching a decision (Tödt 1988:22). Uncovering the roots of perceived injustice with prophetic passion in the name of God, calling for repentance and inspiring with a utopian vision of the future are but a dimension of moral discourse.

Although some proponents of the exclusive use of prophetic discourse rightly argue that it can also be logically rigorous, this still does not mean that it provides a full moral argument. In distinction to the sometimes conceptual impreciseness of prophetic discourse, one finds more precise forms of argumentation, such as Tödt's theory of moral decision-making (see especially Tödt 1988:21-84). To appreciate the flow and extent of moral argumentation we shall investigate the main movements of his theory.

Tödt distinguishes between six step-like *Sachmomente* in a moral argument. The first is the recognition and acceptance of the moral problem. Only when the moral dimension of such a situation is recognised can the process of moral argumentation commence (Tödt 1988:30). The analysis of the situation in which this moral problem arose is the second step. It is, of course, impossible to come to a complete understanding of the context, therefore this step is characterised by the selection of what is perceived as the salient features of the situation (Tödt 1988:31). It is characterised, furthermore, by the acceptance of the risk of error (Tödt 1988:32).

The third step requires considering the different actions that prove themselves applicable and morally required. Tödt deliberately diverges from the typical casuistic order (from norm to action) as norms can only be considered in concrete situations, and connected to concrete options (Tödt 1988:62). In the same way he develops this step not as merely a functional decision, but connects the ultimate action that needs to be taken intimately with the identity and integrity of the decision-making agent, as well as the situation in which such an agent finds him/herself (Tödt 1988:34-36). Only after possible actions have been considered can the norms, perspectives and other resources relevant for making the moral decision be applied, in a fourth step (Tödt 1988:53).

Before making the moral decision in a last step, Tödt adds a fifth step. Because the moral agent is not alone on earth, and because moral decision-making is a supra-individualistic endeavour, each moral decision should have a "communicative bindingness" (in German: *kommunikative Verbindlichkeit*) (Tödt 1988:74). This means that any moral decision should be able to be generalised in order to transcend the subjectivity of the particular moral agent. Only after this generalising step can the moral decision be taken as an "integrated – i.e. cognitive, voluntary and identity-relevant – act" (Tödt 1988:77-78).

When compared to a moral argument such as proposed by Tödt, it is clear that a passionate and unequivocal moral indictment in the name of God fails to provide a full moral argument. In this sense, the greatest strength of prophetic discourse at the same time gives birth to one of its greatest weaknesses.

4.2 Weak on moral analysis

A second weakness of prophetic discourse is that it tends to be weak on moral analysis. The exclusive, or at least primary, use of prophetic discourse often leads to a totalising and one-dimensional view of the particular situation. Such a totalised view easily disables dialogue and misses the opportunity for interdisciplinary attempts at understanding the perceived injustice and formulating policy.

The Accra Confession, accepted by the General Council of the World Alliance of Reformed Churches in 2004 (World Alliance of Reformed Churches 2004a), serves as illustration of how the overriding use of prophetic language weakens its capacity for comprehensive moral analysis.[12]

The confession understands itself as a prophetic critique[13] against the unjust global economic system as the root cause of massive threats to human life and non-human forms of life on earth.[14] This economic system is identified as the "neo-liberal ideology" (Accra Confession, Article 14) that claims sovereignty over life and is therefore idolatry (Accra Confession, Article 10). It promotes policies of limitless growth (Accra Confession, Articles 8 and 23) and promotes rampant consumerism and competitive greed and selfishness (Accra Confession, Article 29). In classic prophetic style the Accra Confession also identifies the agents driving this unjust system: "The United States of America and its allies, together with international finance and trade institutions (International Monetary Fund, World Bank, World Trade Organisation)", who make use of "political, economic, or military alliances to protect and advance the interest of capital owners" (Accra Confession, Article 13).

Although it is very clear in its identification of the perceived injustice and those responsible for these injustices, the Accra Confession lacks a convincing moral

---

12   Already the Accompanying Letter use very emotive language and makes use of (prophetically) charged phrases such as the division between "those who worship in comfortable contentment and those enslaved by the world's economic injustice and ecological destruction"; "If Jesus Christ is not Lord over all, he is not Lord at all"; "dethrone the false gods of wealth and power" (World Alliance of Reformed Churches, 2004b).
13   Cf. e.g. Article 39: "The General Council calls upon member churches ... to undertake the difficult and prophetic task of interpreting this confession to their local congregations."
14   Cf. Article 6: "The root causes of massive threats to life are above all the product of an unjust economic system defended and protected by political and military might. Economic systems are a matter of life or death."

analysis on which to base these very strong statements. Like many prophetic documents it runs the very real risk of self-ideologisation. By the ideologisation of its own position it creates "a huge barrier … between prophetic voices and those that speak in more precise and rational modes of argumentation" (Gustafson 1988:16-17) and in this way misses the complexities and importance of inter-disciplinary dialogue. Economists – even those who are Christian and wish to eradicate injustice – feel silenced by this mode of discourse for two reasons: there are factual and perception distortions, and the black-white dividing lines make rational interaction difficult, if not impossible.

4.3 Silent on transitional measures

Closely connected to its weak moral analysis is the fact that prophetic discourse is likely to be silent on how exactly to bridge the gap between its judgement and its proposed utopian future. In a sense it is unfair to pronounce the principles and envisioned future without contributing to the transitional measures *en route*. These transitional measures can also be described as policy suggestions. Prophetic discourse indeed "does not concern itself with incremental choices that have to be made by persons and institutions in which good and evil are intricately intermingled" (Gustafson 1988:16).

Gustafson identifies two strengths of a policy discourse that may help us to understand this weakness of prophetic discourse better (Gustafson 1988:46-47). Policy discourse, firstly, is not conducted by 'external observers', but by those who have the responsibility to make the choices and carry out actions. Responsibility and accountability are central to formulating policy decisions. The tendency to self-ideologisation not only weakens prophetic discourse's moral analysis, but also hampers its proponents from contributing to formulating and enacting transitional measures, and impedes them from taking responsibility for the role they should play in reaching the envisioned future.

According to Gustafson, the second feature of policy discourse is the "particularity of conditions" in which policy should be developed. These conditions at the same time "limit the possibilities of action" and also "enable them". Prophetic discourse may easily be located in the abstract world of its utopian future without ever acknowledging the concrete realities within which its vision should necessarily take form. Ironically, denouncing and dreaming in the name of God can easily remain disconnected from realising God's will – and prophetic discourse may be a way of speaking that is most prone to this irony.

We may refer to the Accra Confession to illustrate this weakness of prophetic discourse. Virtually nothing is said on ways in which the transition from the sinful global economic system to God's future may be managed. Although the document understands itself as 'prophetic' and it presents a theological argument, there are no "clues about action and discipleship" (Naudé 2008:211).[15]

---

15   For a document with both a strong theological argument and strong clues on policy and an openness to dialogue, see the EKD's discussion paper *Gerechte Teilhabe* (EKD 2006).

4.4 Unable to dislodge itself from the system that is under judgment

A fourth and last weakness of prophetic discourse relevant for our discussion is that it often does not adequately recognise that it cannot dislodge itself from the system that is under judgement. Prophets indeed often

> do not help responsible Christian persons who seek to gain political and economic power as a means to serve the public good within the constraints of political, economic, medical or other institutions (Gustafson 1988:17).

Prophets often fail to recognise that also they benefit from, and make use of, the very system they regard as being under God's judgement. In his theory of moral decision-making Tödt recognises that moral decision-making is much more than simply applying certain universal principles to certain situations. Principles can only be understood in combination with "institutions, roles, social arrangements of relationships and routine chains of interactions" (Tödt 1988:37).[16] This means that persons who address a moral problem should always recognise that they always in a sense act from the inside rather from the outside of the situation.

When prophets do not recognise their own position within the system they denounce, it is very difficult to appreciate the strengths and avenues for reform present within the system. An interesting example is the pursuit of "enlightened self-interest", which attempts to curb the social and ecological excesses of the "neo-liberal empire" (Accra): Increasingly individuals and enterprises are realising that it is possible to do well by doing good (Vogel 2008:184-188). According to the influential Global Compact of the United Nations, "financial markets are starting to recognise that environmental, social and governance issues can be material to long-term performance" (United Nations Global Compact 2007:4). Globally business enterprises are putting into action business practices that ensure both sustainable profit and a sustainable use of natural and human capital. As businesses generally have "the greatest pools of human and monetary capital" (Institute of Directors in Southern Africa 2009:8), they are in a strong position to contribute to a more humane global order.

This is especially clear in the promise of corporate social responsibility in the activities of businesses. Although there are many definitions of corporate social responsibility, at least six core characteristics make evident how businesses are increasingly understanding themselves as in a position to bring about social change and create a capitalism with a human face (Crane et al. 2008:7-9). In essence it is the **voluntary** actions undertaken by businesses to both **manage externalities** and **move beyond philanthropy by aligning social and economic and social responsibilities**. This is done by internalising certain **values and philosophies** and by *e*ngaging a variety **of different stakeholders**. According to a survey done by PricewaterhouseCoopers, 70% of global chief executives already believe that corporate social responsibility is vital to their companies' profitability (quoted in Vogel, 2008:185).

The link between doing good and doing well is also clear in the growing trend of businesses to invest responsibly. Following the example of the FTSE's 4Good Index,

---

16 The original German is: "Sittliche Normen sind im Zusammenhang von Institutionen, Rollen, sozialen Beziehungsgefügen, regelmäßigen Interaktionsabläufen zu verstehen."

the Johannesburg Stock Exchange launched its Socially Responsible Investment Index (SRI Index) in 2004. It was launched in order to reach at least four key objectives, namely to identify companies that integrate the principles of the triple bottom line and good governance in their business practices, to provide a tool for a holistic assessment of companies based on local realities and international standards, to enable responsible investment by providing non-financial risk variables, and to contribute to responsible business practices in South Africa (Johannesburg Stock Exchange & Ethical Investment Research and Information Service 2007:2). Since its inception the SRI Index has grown to become one the JSE's most prestigious products, with 34 of its top 40 companies on the Index in 2009 (Johannesburg Stock Exchange 2009).

But in their blanket denouncement of the neoliberal system as such, prophets will – if they are consistent – also have to denounce all these efforts as driven by merely 'postponed' self-interest, and a seeking of public approval for the sake of business reputation. The question then arises: What is to be done as an alternative? And prophetic discourse on its own is not equipped to answer this important question, unless it wishes to dismantle the system as such. How such dismantling is to happen in practice is then a legitimate follow-up question.

5. SUMMARY AND CONCLUSION

This article gives an outline of key features of prophetic discourse. It then asks the question whether prophetic discourse – understood in this particular way – is an adequate mode of moral language to address issues of global economic injustice.

The strength of prophetic discourse is its ability to unambiguously denounce a specific situation of injustice, and at the same time announce a God-willed alternative future. This rhetorical power is not be underestimated as it has the potential over time to influence public debate beyond theological discourse and even lead to concrete policy formulation not intended by the original prophets. The case study of a preferential option for the poor demonstrated how, over a period of more than 40 years, the insights of Latin American liberation theologians found tentative expression in the Doha Round of trade negotiations.

The core weaknesses of prophetic discourse are its incomplete moral argument, weak moral analyses, silence on transition measures, and its inability to take a positive stance on reforms in the system from which it benefits itself.

The conclusion is that prophetic discourse plays an indispensable role in addressing issues of global economic justice, but – taken by itself – it is not an adequate form of moral discourse to actually address concrete matters of justice.

6. BIBLIOGRAPHY

African Union Commission, 2004, *Strategic Plan of the African Union Commission Vol. 1-3*, Addis Ababa: African Union Commission.

Bedford-Strohm, H. 1993. *Vorrang für die Armen: Auf dem Weg zu einer theologischen Theorie der Gerechtigkeit*, Gütersloh: Chr. Kaiser.

Boff, L. & Boff C. 1984. *Salvation and Liberation*, New York: Orbis.

Boff, L. & Boff, C. 1987. *Introducing Liberation Theology*, New York: Orbis.

Crane, A., Matten, D. & Spence, L.J. (eds) 2008. *Corporate Social Responsibility: Readings and Cases in a Global Context*, London: Routledge.

Economic Commission for Africa, 2007, *Economic Report on Africa 2007*, Addis Ababa: African Union.

Evangelische Kirche in Deutschland 2006. *Gerechte Teilhabe: Befähigung zu Eigenverantwortung und Solidarität*, Gütersloh: Gütersloher Verlagshaus.

Gustafson, J.M. 1988. *Varieties of Moral Discourse: Prophetic, Narrative, Ethical and Policy*, Grand Rapids, MI: Calvin College and Seminary Press.

Gutiérrez, G.1988. *A Theology of Liberation*, London: SCM.

Gutiérrez, G. 1993. "Option for the poor", in I. Ellacuria & J. Sobrino (eds.), *Mysterium Liberationis: Fundamental Concepts of Liberation Theology*, pp. 235-250, New York: Orbis.

Held, D., McGrew, A. & Perraton, J. 1999. *Global Transformations: Politics, economics and culture*, Stanford, CA: Stanford University Press.

Institute of Directors in Southern Africa 2009. *Third King Report on Corporate Governance in South Africa*, Johannesburg: Institute of Directors in Southern Africa.

Johannesburg Stock Exchange & Ethical Investment Research and Information Service 2007. *Johannesburg Stock Exchange SRI Index. Background and Selection Criteria*, Johannesburg: publisher.

Johannesburg Stock Exchange n.d., *2009 Results*, viewed 31 May 2010, from http://www.jse.co.za/About-Us/SRI/Downloads/2009_Results.aspx.

Kwenda, C.V. 2003. "Cultural justice: the pathway to reconciliation and social cohesion", in D. Chidester, P. Dexter & J. Wilmot (eds.), *What Holds Us Together: Social Cohesion in South Africa*, pp. 67-80, Cape Town: HSRC Press.

Naudé, P.J. 2007. "In defence of partisan justice – an ethical reflection on 'the preferential option for the poor'", *Verbum et Ecclesia* 28(1), 166-190.

Naudé, P.J. 2008. "What has Accra to do with New York? An analysis of moral discourse in the Accra Confession", *NGTT* December 49(3&4), 206-216.

Naudé, P.J. 2010. "Fair global trade: A perspective from Africa", in G. Moore (ed.), *Fair Global Trade*, pp 99-116, London: Springer.

Rawls, J.1973. *A Theory of Justice*, Oxford: Oxford University Press.

Rawls, J. 1999. *The Law of Peoples*, Cambridge, MA: Harvard University Press.

Roemer, J.E. 1998. *Theories of Distributive Justice*. Cambridge, MA: Harvard University Press.

Seitz, C.R. 2007. *Prophecy and Hermeneutics: Toward a New Introduction to the Prophets*, Grand Rapids, MI: Baker Academic Press.

Sobrino, J. 1984. *The True Church and the Poor*, Maryknoll, NY: Orbis.

Stiglitz, J.E. 2002. *Globalization and its Discontents*, New York: WW Norton.

Stiglitz, J.E. 2006a. *Making Globalisation Work*, WW Norton, New York, NY.

Stiglitz, J.E. 2006b. "Social justice and global trade", *Far Eastern Economic Review*, March 169(2), 18-22.

Tödt, H.E. 1988. *Perspektiven theologischer Ethik*, München: Chr. Kaiser.

Tucker, G.M. 1987. "Prophetic Speech", in J.M. Mays & P.J. Achtemeier (eds.), *Interpreting the Prophets*, pp. 27-34, Philadelphia, PA: Fortress.

United Nations Global Compact 2007. *UN Global Compact Annual Review: 2007 Leaders' Summit*, Geneva: United Nations Global Compact Office.

Vogel, D. 2008. "Is there a market for virtue? The business case for corporate social responsibility", in Crane et al. (eds), *Corporate Social Responsibility: Readings and Cases in a Global Context*, pp. 181-210.

Wilson, R.R. 1980. *Prophecy and Society in Ancient Israel*, Philadelphia, PA: Fortress.

Wittenberg, G. 1993. *Prophecy and Protest: A Contextual Introduction to Israelite Prophecy*, Pietermaritzburg: Institute for the Study of the Bible.

World Alliance of Reformed Churches 2004a. *The Accra Confession: Covenanting for Justice in the Economy and the Earth*, Geneva: WCC.

World Alliance of Reformed Churches 2004b, *Letter from Accra*, viewed 30 May 2010, from http://warc.jalb.de/warcajsp/side.jsp?news_id=1157&navi=45.

World Trade Organisation 2001. *Ministerial Declaration. Ministerial Conference Fourth Session. Doha, 9-14 November 2001*, viewed 2 June 2010, from http://www.wto.org/english/thewto_e/minist_e/min01_e/mindecl_e.htm.

3.3 VIRTUE AND RESPONSIBILITY

Economic-ethical perspectives in the work of Etienne de Villiers

This essay is developed in six statements and attempts to reconstruct the basis for understanding the socio-economic ethics of Etienne de Villiers, its ecclesio-centric nature, and its theoretical formulation in virtue and responsibility ethics. There is reference to De Villiers's shift from an exclusive to an inclusive ethical view as a response to his interpretation of modernity and secularism. Critical questions are raised as to the actual theological character of his ethics and his re-interpretation of Weberian responsibility ethics. The essay concludes with an appreciative consideration of the applied ethics perspectives developed by De Villiers over the past three decades.

First statement: Etienne de Villiers moves from an evangelical to a social-ethical perspective as a result of his acceptance of the Reformed tradition on the basis of which he is able to develop fruitful economic-ethical views on (for example) poverty and economic equality.

Etienne de Villiers grew up in the context of evangelical Christian pietism. This version of the Christian faith places great emphasis on personal faith and holiness, and may at times not be able to fully address the socio-political dimensions of the gospel. It was that pietistic tendency which "often resulted in an almost exclusive concentration on religious matters and an uncritical acceptance of unjust political policies" (De Villiers 2001a:17).

According to De Villiers, he moved toward a more social Christian vision as a consequence of his exposure on a personal level to social philosophy and student politics at Stellenbosch University in the late 1960s,[1] as well as to exposure to people such as Allan Boesak, Hannes Adonis and Johannes Verkuyl whilst studying for a doctorate in The Netherlands. These experiences and discussions "awakened in me the desire to reflect more directly on relevant political and economic issues. The shift to Christian Ethics seemed natural and inevitable" (2001a:18).

This social consciousness then found a theological voice through his overt acceptance of the Reformed faith's perspective on God's rule over all of creation.

De Villiers provides the outline of a specific Reformed social ethics by positioning his work as distinct from two other approaches (De Villiers and De Beer 2009: 110): on the one hand, he refers to the vision of two kingdoms associated with Lutheranism, which might lead to a view that aspects of reality are not to be seen as under the rule of Christ, but governed purely by common sense rationality. On the other hand, he refers to the rise of Pentecostalism, which in most forms propagates a strict division

---

[1] In his own words: "Less a result of theological classes and more the intellectual stimulation that I experienced in philosophy, and linked to my involvement in student politics, this transformation broke my intellectual naivete" (2001a:17). For an illuminating interpretation of De Villiers's biography in relation to his public theology, see Bezuidenhout (2007:164-175).

between "church" and "the world out there", leading in a contradictory way to leaving the world precisely beyond the reach of the Christian faith.

The Reformed vision, however, operates with a theo-logy (view of God) that accepts the rule of God over all of creation and history. This is ethics with an all-embracing vision of God's kingdom[2] which includes all aspects of life – including the economy. A Reformed ethical vision accepts the total corruption of the human person as source of injustice (also in economics), but at the same time professes both full and cosmic reconciliation in Christ and the view that Christ transforms culture (Niebuhr). Another distinct aspect of Reformed ethics is the notion of "calling", i.e. the responsibility of Christians to serve the purposes of God in the transformation of the world (De Villiers 2005: 521-522).

Second statement: One could call De Villiers's ethics an ecclesio-centric ethics because the institutional church – specifically the Dutch Reformed Church – forms the constant institutional basis and reference point of his thought.

De Villiers is a church theologian in the positive sense of the word. He is an ordained pastor and professor in the service of the church, and through the church he is in service of the gospel in the wider society. But the Dutch Reformed Church is the first and foremost "public" he wishes to address. In this regard, it is possible to distil at least five specific conditions for a credible ecclesial ethics as set out by De Villiers in various parts of his work.[3]

   i. The recognition of social-ideological hermeneutics. It is impossible for a church like the DRC (for example) to be self-critical of its own ethical views unless it fully acknowledges the social conditioning of these views and the ideological presuppositions in which its views are undeniably embedded. One could say that de Villiers draws on the so-called Second Enlightenment, the hermeneutics of suspicion emanating from Marx Nietzsche and Freud to instil a critical dimension in a self-satisfied church.

   ii. The development of a comprehensive spirituality. De Villiers is at pains to point out that white, Afrikaans Christians should resist the temptation to withdraw from public life after their relative loss of political power since 1994. He knows the strengths of a pious spirituality, but he also recognises the challenge for the church to foster an outwardly oriented spirituality that would include action in the economic sphere of life.

   iii. The establishment of the church as inclusive community of care (*barmhartigheid*). The DRC has a proud history of caring for the poor and the struggling. But the problem is that this was directed toward its own members and – in a related sense – to far -off communities in the context of mission. An ethics of inclusive care would practise love without seeing the person.

   iv. A radical re-orientation in the new South African situation after 1994. De Villiers spends quite a lot of energy on discussing the impact of Enlightenment ideas on ordinary Christians' perspectives: modernity and liberalisation operate on the basis of a division between church and state. The

---

2   See the defence of the concept "kingdom of God" even in post-modern times by De Villiers (2008:380, specifically footnote 5).

3   For various references to these ecclesiological views, see De Villiers (1995b:567-568; 1999:27-33, and 2008:380-383).

public recognition of "Christian" values can therefore no longer be taken for granted and laws will not necessarily reflect the gospel view. But freedom of religion provides new opportunities and De Villiers is adamant that unless DRC members overcome their fundamental "attitude of victimhood" (*slagoffermentaliteit*) in relation to our democratic dispensation, public ethics will not be possible.

v. The reunification of the DRC Family is seen by De Villiers as a very important marker of Christian credibility. If the churches in the family – divided on racial grounds – cannot find one another in visible unity, their witness on matters of reconciliation and justice will not find fertile public recognition.

Based on these guidelines, De Villiers then challenges the DRC to address the issue of creating a just economic system in South Africa. He believes this church has in its ground-breaking document of 1986 (revised 1990), *Church and Society*,[4] set down useful biblical principles that could assist in this regard. Love of the neighbour (including the enemy!), a biblical sense of justice and of care as well as a strong reliance on the God-given human dignity of each person provide a strong basis from which to address the difficult question of economic justice in a democratic South Africa.

De Villiers does not hesitate to be quite concrete. If these principles are accepted, at least four aspects should be included in any programme to establish a more just economic dispensation[5] (De Villiers 1991:27-29; see also De Villiers 1995b:565-567).

First. Neutrality about economic issues is not an option as this would imply condoning the unjust, historically developed, status quo. There must be a clear commitment to a more just distribution of wealth and affirmative action must be taken seriously as part of restitution in the context of white peoples' unrealistically high life-style.

Second. Social spending by the state should be equalised – for this the church must express support, whilst at the same time serving the poor through the church, irrespective of who the beneficiaries are (*sonder aansien van persoon*).

Third. The DRC must set an example in the way it spends its own resources, keeping in mind that its relative wealth was built on the privileged position of white people over many years. The church must call its own members to adopt a more sober and simple life-style and can only ask the state for equality of remuneration for different race groups if parity in salaries of all ministers in the DRC Family is also propagated.

Fourth. The DRC must convince its own members of the importance to prepare themselves for the sacrifices and life-style adjustments required by a more just economic dispensation for all.

---

[4] See De Villiers (2001c:54) for a discussion of *Kerk en Samelewing* (KS) as part of the DRC's indirect influence on public policy at the time. He is supportive of the 1990 revised version as in this document there is a more critical stance against the socio-political views of the preceding years. For a most recent discussion of the significance of *KS* after 25 years, see Strauss (2011).

[5] On actions to take in the context of growing global inequalities, see De Villiers (2001c, specifically pp. 474-476).

Third statement: Etienne de Villiers approaches social-ethical questions, including economic justice, from two theoretical perspectives, namely an ethics of virtue as set out by Stanley Hauerwas, and – more significantly – an ethics of responsibility derived from Max Weber and subsequent thinkers.[6]

Concerning an ethics of virtue, De Villiers – in line with his ecclesio-centric views – proposes that it is the task of the church to build the character of its members in line with appropriate Christian virtues, leading them in the end to mature moral decision-making. An ethics of virtue has important implications for the economic sphere as it can assist in the character formation of business people by promoting values such as honesty and social responsibility, leading them to take economic decisions on the basis of their Christian morality (De Villiers 1999:33-34 and 2001a: 21).

When De Villiers brings his interpretation of an ethics of responsibility to bear in the economic sphere, he cites four forms of complementarity that should be kept in constant balance (De Villiers and De Beer 2009:112-118)[7]:

i. The complementarity of self-responsibility and co-responsibility for the poor.

Christians are called as individuals to care for the poor as part of the moral dimension of their own lives. But individual action may be totally inadequate in addressing the structural dimensions of poverty. Therefore collective cooperation on the basis of co-responsibility is also required to specifically address both the social and policy dimensions of poverty. Christians should not hold back on participating even with non-religious parts of civil society in taking up their prophetic task to call others to responsible action in this regard.

ii. The complementarity of empirical facts and the reality in Christ.

Assisting the poor must be based on direct cooperation with poor people in order to understand their actual needs, coupled with relevant scientific data to provide a reality check for ethics. Many development aid projects from the West have failed precisely because real needs and cooperation of local communities in designing and executing such projects were not taken into account. But Christians also – at the same time – hold onto the "in Christ" reality and the potential for a new society drawn from the inclusive salvation in Him. One is led by the concrete situation on whether to uphold an ideal morality, or whether to settle for an optimal morality (De Villiers 2003:34).

iii. The complementarity of moral and functional values.

Christians are used to maintain the primacy of moral values based on their specific Christian convictions. It is desirable that in a situation of modernity Christians hold onto the validity of moral values for all spheres of society. But at the same time they should recognise the validity of system-immanent or functional values governing the different spheres of society and linked to specific role responsibilities. Christians

---

6   "In the end, an ethics of virtue and an ethics of responsibility indeed do not exclude one another. They inevitably complement one another" (De Villiers 2001a: 21).

7   These four dimensions of a responsibility ethics are derived from Max Weber and form a common thread in De Villiers's work. See De Villiers (2003: 31-36) and De Villiers (2010b) for a more academic and mature exposition of an ethics of responsibility in dialogue with Max Weber and with Dietrich Bonhoeffer, Hans Jonas, Johannes Fischer and Wolfgang Huber. See specifically 2010b: 269-275, where the same points as above are made more elaborately.

therefore have the difficult task of translating moral values for application in a specific area such as the economy (e.g. what does "love of the neighbour" mean in the case of mergers or acquisitions where job losses are at stake?) in the hope of achieving a significant degree of "overlapping consensus" (Rawls) between moral and functional values.

iv. The complementarity of deontology (principles) and utility (consequences).

Christian ethics normally work with "God-given" or "biblical" principles that should guide action, and in this way they resemble a deontological type of ethics. An ethics of responsibility requires an equally important consideration of the consequences of actions, including the following of principles. These utility considerations should be taken into account in advance of an action so that Christians purposefully deliberate on the effect of their intended actions and take responsibility for that as well. In line with his view on the option for the poor, De Villiers states that actions with the most advantages for poor people should therefore get preference.

Fourth statement: A recurring motif in De Villiers's work is the struggle to ground and defend the uniqueness of Christian morality, a view that he at first defends, but later amends to develop an applied "ethics of compromise" in the light of his interpretation of secularism and modernisation.

What brings De Villiers to a qualified Christian ethics or an ethics of compromise?

There are a number of factors that work in a cumulative fashion to gradually convince him of the necessity to make this shift.

The increasing pluralism of ethical views from within the broad Christian tradition itself makes the claim for a "unique" Christian perspective very difficult if not nigh impossible. This relativity is intensified in a liberal democracy where individual human rights, and not necessarily distinct Christian values, shape the ethics and laws of the country – making room for a great diversity of views.

Furthermore – especially in fields of applied ethics – there is no way that a responsible ethical view can be developed without recourse to insights derived from philosophy and from the science (or whatever field of knowledge) under discussion. One cannot – according to De Villiers – develop a responsible ethics without taking seriously the distinction between specific role and more general moral responsibilities, and neither of these need be specifically "Christian".

There is a definitive apologetic intent (tied to the perennial question in his work on the uniqueness of Christian moral convictions[8]) in De Villiers's call for Christians no longer to proceed from theocratic assumptions, but to live in two value systems: the basically secular value system and Christian values. He adds: "If we, however, want these values to be accepted and applied in our democracy, we will have to use language which non-Christians can understand and arguments which they can accept" (De Villiers 2001c:59).[9]

---

8   See his doctoral dissertation published in 1978, which deals with exactly this question, and his recent self-critical reflection on the narrow moral philosophical view that informed his work at that time (De Villiers 2010a:56-57, 62).
9   There are huge theological and methodological issues behind this statement. The whole struggle between Barth's insistence that apologetics that attempt to answer to the demands of modern man must in the end fail, and the views of those such as

On the basis of these considerations, De Villiers makes a paradigmatic shift in his ethical orientation: the earlier exclusively Reformed view of social transformation with the rule of Christ as reference point is augmented by an inclusive transformation which aims at the humanising of society (anthropocentric dimension) and the optimising of all life on the planet (ecological dimension)[10] with the concomitant prospective responsibilities (Jonas) regarding the future of the whole creation.

This does not mean that De Villiers gives up on his argument for the specificity of a Christian contribution to ethics. He contends that the specific Christian preferential option for the poor is an important contribution to economic ethics. The spiritual content of socio-economic development should also be kept in mind in determining the unique contribution of the Christian faith. De Villiers (1995a) refers to the government's Reconstruction and Development Plan as a specific example of where the church can play a role. He also mentions the fact that moral motivation is an important dimension in determining the moral quality of an action (De Villiers 1995b:567), and that specifically Christian motives such as love and hope can spur people on to do good deeds – including performing actions in the economic sphere.

Despite making room for the enormous impact of secularism and modernism, De Villiers does not relinquish the possibility of a public role for Christian ethics. What is required is to proclaim and enhance "distinctively thick Christian views" as complementary to more generally shared "thin values" (De Villiers 2003:33-34).

Fifth statement: One could ask two sets of critical questions with regard to De Villiers's work: The first relates to the theological quality of his ethics, and the second to his Christian version of Weber's ethics of responsibility.

It is an interesting question whether De Villiers really develops a **theological** ethics. Or is he actually a moral philosopher focusing on meta-ethical questions about the distinctiveness and intelligibility of Christian moral claims? As indicated earlier, he does place himself within the Reformed tradition, but he does not actually build a theological basis for this ethics. One of the marks of the Reformed tradition is the unity between doctrine and life; theo-logy and ethics (Smit 2010), where the former informs and guides the latter. De Villiers does not fully exploit this important mark of being Reformed. Let us take a Trinitarian view as example.

Social ethics is based not only on a vision of the kingdom of God and God's rule over history, but on the very being and character of God who reveals Godself as love and justice, and as standing with the widows, the orphans and the oppressed, as Belhar reminds us.

The reconciliation in Christ does not only reconcile us as totally corrupt people with God. The incarnation and humanity of Jesus Christ – fully divine and fully human – is an exemplar of God's humanising work of salvation. The growth in "Christian

---

Schleiermacher and others who see it as precisely the task of theology to be "rational" and adhere to acceptable scientific criteria (Scholtz) comes to mind. A discussion of this aspect lies beyond the scope of this article. De Villiers does refer to the "later" Barth in his exposition of the humanisation of society in *Christengemeinde und Bürgergemeinde* published in 1946 (see De Villiers 2008: 381). A concise summary of the debates of the science of philosophy with regards to Barth can be found in Van Huyssteen (1986:23-36).

10 This broadening of his views can be read in more detail in De Villiers (2005:525-526) and again in (De Villiers 2008: 381).

humanism" detected by, for example, Chicago ethicist William Schweiker (2004) and South African, John de Gruchy (2006), establishes fruitful dialogue partners. The idea of a Christian humanism may enable one to build a bridge between an exclusively Christian and more general human view of justice, and the integrity of creation claimed as reference points in De Villiers's later work.

I might have missed this, but De Villiers does perhaps not make enough of the social-ethical potential in our understanding of the Spirit of God. The link between pneumatology and ethics – from social justice and equality to ecological perspectives embedded in the cosmic work of the Spirit – is a powerful one and should feature in any theologically inclined ethics.

Apart from the three persons of the Trinity each taken separately, the actual social-ethical interpretation of the Trinity (immanent and economic) has received interesting attention in the work of Miroslav Volf (with some legitimate critique of his too easy analogy between the Trinity and humanity) (see, for example, Volf 1998).

It is probably unfair to expect a stronger and more explicit theological exposition from De Villiers. He may simply respond that this was not what he set out to do. His task was – he could claim – to read the signs of the time, put ethical issues on the table and provide practical guidelines in a sociologically inclined applied ethics. My response is that it is worth exploring whether an ethics of responsibility that claims the label "Christian" would not be open to a richer tapestry of meanings if informed by explicit theological/Trinitarian reflection.

A second set of critical questions may be addressed to the Weberian interpretation which De Villiers puts forward.[11] Weber argues for an ethics of responsibility exactly to escape what he terms a Christian *Gesinnungsethik*. The question is whether De Villiers honours this intention in his retention of a "distinctive Christian version" of this type of ethics, arguing (against Weber) for the primacy of moral (and Christian) values over functional values (De Villiers 2010b:273). On what grounds does De Villiers argue for the system-immanence of functional values whilst maintaining the trans-systemic nature of Christian/moral values? What features do Christian values demonstrate that are so different from functional values that the former can be assumed to transcend the social structure of the church where (one could argue) they are precisely the functional values supporting a religious institution? This is both a theological and a sociological question. Even if one accepts the overarching system-transcendent character of Christian values, in what way are social institutions (such as politics and economics) protected against the often ideological interpretation and practice of these Christian values?

These questions are asked in the spirit of furthering and fine-tuning the solid views that De Villiers advances.

Sixth statement : Etienne de Villiers's significant contribution lies in his ability to interpret contexts and then ask the right ethical question at the right time. What might on the surface of history appear as not so significant topics were in fact each and every time "kairos-type" questions with a significance not only within the narrow confines of the DRC, but for the wider South African society.

---

11   I am not Weber scholar and am open to correction on this point.

De Villiers's question about the Immorality and Mixed Marriages Act[12] around 1984 was in fact a question about racism and the over-stepping of the boundaries of state power into the private lives of citizens. The question about the true Christian meaning of peace[13] and an ethics of peace around 1988/89 was in fact a question about the moral legitimacy of "the war on the border" and the right of individual freedom and conscience to resist conscription into what was considered by some to be an unjust war.

The question in 1990 about values for an inclusive democracy[14] was in fact a question about what kind of morality would inform the building of a new South Africa. The question about modernity, secularism and a liberal constitution was in fact a question of how a public[15] Christian witness would still be possible after liberation, and how specifically white people could use their privileges for the sake of the public good.

The questions in 1996 and beyond of how we could develop a common moral language[16] were an attempt to construct some social cohesion in a situation of growing relativism, moral anomie and pluralism. The questions from 1991 onwards about socio-economic justice and the role of the church in development were in fact questions about how we could embody Christian values in the practice of business and how the church could be a welcoming house of care for the poorest of the poor.

Looking back, then, one sees Etienne's immense ethical contribution. For that we thank him and God who gave him as a gift to church and society. Looking forward, one hopes that Etienne will enjoy good health and still find the time to ask the right questions at the right time, and call us to a Christian ethics of responsibility.

It has been a great honour to participate in this festive occasion.[17]

BIBLIOGRAPHY

Bezuidenhout, Ronell 2007. *Re-imagining life: A reflection on "public theology" in the work of Linell Cady, Denise Ackermann, and Etienne de Villliers.* Unpublished D. Phil. dissertation. Port Elizabeth: Nelson Mandela Metropolitan University.

De Gruchy, John 2006. Christian humanism: reclaiming a tradition, affirming an identity. *Reflections: Centre of Theological Inquiry* 8, 38-65.

De Villiers, Etienne 1978. *Die eiesoortigheid van die Christelike moraal.* Amsterdam: Rodopi.

---

12 See the publication *Op die skaal: Gemengde huwelike en ontug,* edited by De Villiers and Kinghorn in 1984.
13 See De Villiers (1983) on conscientious objection and De Villiers (1989) about conceptions of peace.
14 See *The option for inclusive democracy,* jointly edited by Bernard Lategan, Johann Kinghorn, Lourens du Plessis and Etienne de Villiers (1990).
15 For an exposition of the challenges facing public theology in a democracy as well as an overview of perspectives on public theology in South Africa, see De Villiers (2011). For an analysis of De Villiers as public theologian himself, see the unpublished dissertation by Ronell Bezuidenhout (2007:164-245).
16 De Villiers published three articles with Dirk Smit on the topic of moral judgments. See especially De Villiers and Smit (1996).
17 This lecture was presented at the University of Pretoria at an occasion to honour Etienne de Villiers.

De Villiers, Etienne 1983. Putting the recent debate on conscientious objection into perspective. *Scriptura* 8, 21-33.

De Villiers, Etienne 1989. Peace conceptions in South Africa in the light of the biblical concept of peace. *Scriptura* 28, 24-40.

De Villiers, Etienne 1991. 'n Regverdige ekonomiese stelsel. In Etienne de Villiers en Deon Kitching (reds): *Derdegelui vir more. Die NG kerk voor die uitdagings van 'n nuwe tyd*. Kaapstad: Tafelberg, 18-29.

De Villiers, Etienne 1995a. Die NG Kerk en die Heropbou- en Ontwikkelingsprogram. In: D Kitching and F Linde (reds.): *Geroep om te dien. 'n Huldigingsbundel opgedra aan prof. P.R. van Dyk, rektor van die Hugenote Kollege 1979-1995*. Wellington: Hugenote Kollege, 22-30.

De Villiers, Etienne 1995b. Die Nederduitse Gereformeerde Kerk en die nuwe situasie in die samelewing. *NGTT*, Deel XXXVI (4), 558-569.

De Villiers, Etienne 1999. Challenges to Christian ethics in the present South African society. *Scriptura* 69, 75-91.

De Villiers, Etienne 1999. Die NG Kerk en die oorgang na 'n nuwe Suid-Afrika. *Skrif en Kerk* 20 (1), 15-38.

De Villiers, Etienne 2001a. How my mind has changed. *JTSA* 111, 17-21.

De Villiers, Etienne 2001b. Teologiekroniek – die kerk en ekonomiese globalisering. *Verbum et Ecclesia* 22 (2), 465-477.

De Villiers, Etienne 2001c. The influence of the Dutch Reformed Church (DRC) on public policy during the late 80's and 90's. *Scriptura* 76, 51-61.

De Villiers, Etienne 2003. A Christian ethics of responsibility: Does it provide an adequate theoretical framework for dealing with issues of public morality? *Scriptura* 82, 23-38.

De Villiers, Etienne 2005. The vocation of Reformed ethicist in the present South African society. *Scriptura* 89, 521-535.

De Villiers, Etienne 2008. Kan die NG Kerk nog 'n konstruktiewe rol in die Suid-Afrikaanse samelewing speel? *Verbum et Ecclesia* 29 (2), 368-386.

De Villiers, Etienne 2010a. Defining morality in Christian ethics and the study of New Testament ethics. In: Ruben Zimmerman and Jan G van der Watt (eds.): *Moral language in the New Testament*. Tübingen: Mohr Siebeck, 51-66.

De Villiers, Etienne 2010b. The recognition of human dignity in Africa: A Christian ethics of responsibility perspective. *Scriptura* 104, 263-278.

De Villiers, Etienne 2011. Public theology in the South African context. *International Journal of Public Theology*, Vol. 5, No. 1, 5-22.

De Villiers, Etienne en De Beer, Stephan 2009. Van verhaal tot beleid: die kerk se verantwoordelikheid ten aansien van arm mense in Nederland en Suid-Afrika. 'n verantwoordelikheidsetiese benadering. In: F Gerrit Immink en Cas Vos (reds): *God in 'n kantelende wereld*. Pretoria: Protea Boekehuis, 109-134.

De Villiers, E en Kinghorn J 1984. *Op die skaal: gemengde huwelike en ontug*. Kaapstad: Tafelberg.

De Villiers DE and Smit DJ 1996. Waarom verskil ons so oor wat die wil van God is? Opmerkings oor Chistelike morele oordeelingsvorming. *Skrif en Kerk* 17 (1), 31-47.

Lategan, Bernard, Kinghorn, Johann, Du Plessis, Lourens, and De Villiers, Etienne 1990. *The option for inclusive democracy A theological-ethical study of appropriate social values for South Africa*. Stellenbosch: Centre for Contextual Hermeneutics.

Schweiker, William 2004. We are not our own: On the possibility of a new Christian humanism. In Michael Welker and Cynthia A. Jarvis (eds.): *Loving God with our minds: The pastor as theologian*. Grand Rapids: Eerdmans, 31-49.

Smit, DJ 2010. Trends and directions in Reformed theology. *The Expository Times* 122 (7), 1-14.

Volf, Miroslav 1998. "The Trinity is our social program": The doctrine of the Trinity and the shape of social engagement. *Modern Theology*, 14 (3), 403-423.

Van Huyssteen, Wentzel 1986. *Teologie as kritiese geloofsverantwoording: Teorievorming in die sistematiese teologie*. Pretoria: RGN.

3.4 MODELS OF HOW WE SPEAK ABOUT "HAPPINESS"

A South African perspective[1]

1. INTRODUCTION

The topic of "happiness"[2] is quite complex and can be approached from the perspective of a variety of academic disciplines such as science of religion, philosophy, theology, sociology, psychology, economics and ethics.[3] In each of these fields there is a variety of approaches to the subject, and major developments occurred over a longer or shorter period within the various disciplines. This short presentation adopts a theological and philosophical approach in an attempt to profile different models of happiness as constructed in the (South) Africa context.

Whereas "happiness" is used today in English as a broad humanistic category, referring to a positive state of mind or satisfaction with life, the term "blessedness" (*makarios* in Greek and *welgeluksalig* in Afrikaans) is normally reserved for religious use and is understood in the biblical or Christian way, namely as having a joyful, living relationship with God.

There are different theological approaches to the relation between happiness and blessedness. One can find a dualism or separation between the two, with an emphasis on blessedness as the true, God-given eschatological state to be sought via an active denial of earthly satisfaction and happiness. There is the scholastic division of happiness, sought by humans through their own (i.e. "natural") efforts, and "supernatural" salvation or blessedness, seen as a gift from God. At the other extreme are "prosperity gospels" that conflate happiness (interpreted as physical health/material wealth) and blessedness. The former is seen as a reward for trusting God, while the absence of happiness/prosperity is seen as the result of a lack of faith.

From a broadly Reformed perspective[4] (which I share), "happiness" is not to be separated from blessedness, but also not to be conflated with it. A separation leads to a dichotomy between "ordinary life" and the "life of faith", contrary to the rule of Christ over all of reality. Such separation reduces blessedness to a purely inner and/ or transcendent notion, and reduces happiness to the immanence and vicissitudes of earthly life. A conflation of the two (on the other hand) loses the critical eschatological view that always transcends our best notions of a fulfilled life. *Geluk* (happiness)

---

1 English version of a German paper delivered at the annual meeting of the Gesellschaft für Evangelische Theologie, Erfurt (Germany), 22 February 2011.
2 The official theme of the conference was related to "Glückseligkeit", which is roughly translated as "happiness", though the latter term does not do justice to the breadth of meaning.
3 See the discussion of Glück in *LThK* Band 4, 757-761; and Glück/Glückseligkeit in *RGG* Band 3, 1015-1021. One may discern the rise of a new trans-disciplinary field of study called "happy-ology", in which economics plays a leading role.
4 For an informative discussion on the complexities of what is meant by "Reformed", see the recent essay by Dirkie Smit (2010). He notes that interest in the Christian life in its totality "belongs integrally to the Reformed vision" (p. 13).

stands in the middle of the Afrikaans word *wel-geluk-salig* and establishes an integral link between wellness-happiness-blessedness.

What is a model?[5] In this presentation a "model" is an abstraction of typical features of a given reality in order to represent that reality in more comprehensible terms. Models are by nature abstractions, built on generalisations that are inferred from the most salient features of a perceived reality. Models do not have a direct correspondence to the reality they attempt to capture. They are not useful as empirical descriptions, if such descriptions are understood in the scientist or positivist sense of the word. Models must rather be seen as heuristic tools to assist us making sense of complex realities.[6]

This work-in-progress is written from a (South) African perspective. Four models of constructing notions of happiness/blessedness are described below: the first three are drawn from our recent history, and the last model serves as a critical appraisal from a theological perspective.

2. MODELS OF HAPPINESS

2.1 The apartheid model: "Happy are those who live in blessed segregation"

The theological and philosophical roots of the apartheid model grew from significant late 19th-century European thinking, interpreted from the specific social-political history of the Afrikaner people in South Africa. These roots are the neo-Calvinist theology/philosophy of Abraham Kuyper, the missiological theory of Gustav Warneck and theological Pietism (predominantly of Scottish origin).[7]

The strength of Kuyper's theology was his conviction that Christ's rule extends over all spheres of life, and that politics, education and law should all be reconstructed from a Christian perspective. (This is the reason for the late 20th-century and current attraction of "public theology" in dialogue with Kuyper.) The weakness was his theology of "general grace",[8] which made pluriformity a principle of creation. This pluriformity is seen in different cultures and peoples that develop according to their own innate potential. Pluriformity extends also to the church, where people with different psychological needs have the freedom to form their own churches, because the unity of the church is both a spiritual and an eschatological reality. Peoples of the earth are classified in hierarchical order in accordance with their participation in God's grace, with European peoples at the top of this order because of the particular grace of God.

---

5   For a discussion of "ideal types" (Max Weber) and "models" (Max Black, Ian Ramsey), see Tracy (1978: 22-42, especially footnote 1).
6   Regarding the difference between models as "pictures" and as "disclosures" (Ramsey), I follow the latter conception.
7   For a discussion of these interrelated theologies and their impact on South Africa, see Naudé (2010: 23-44), where extensive references to the original sources and debates on their interpretation are quoted. South African readers will find that this section covers fairly well-known ground.
8   See the three Dutch volumes published as *De gemeene gratie* between 1902-4.

The strength of Warneck's theory of mission[9] was the importance he attached to bringing the gospel into the culture of those who were the objects of mission. He, however, interpreted the great commission (*ta ethne* in Matthew 28:19) in ethnic terms and deduced from the history of missions that *Völkerbekehrung* (conversion of peoples) was more the norm than *Einzelbekehrung* (individual conversion). Mission then became the spreading of the gospel to a specific *Volk* and its culture, with the subsequent formation of ethnically based churches.

The strength of Pietism[10] was its strong focus on a living relationship with God, personal spirituality and a missionary zeal. It was generally a reaction against religious rationalism and the rise of liberal and historical-critical readings of Scripture. In the second half of the 19th century South Africa was under the particular influence of Scottish Pietism (with well-known evangelical preachers such as Andrew Murray). Pietism's weakness was its inability to develop a viable alternative to critical hermeneutics and the tendency to read the Scriptures literally and in an ahistorical way. With its focus on personal devotion, it was not well placed to develop a comprehensive view of the social implications of the gospel, although after 1900 there was a politically naïve identification with the plight of the Afrikaner people.

These three streams found fertile interpretative soil in Afrikaner thinking between 1890 and 1935, especially after the humiliation of Afrikaners in the British war (1899-1902) and subsequent rise of white nationalism (in parallel to black nationalism, which found expression in the founding of the South African Native National Congress in 1912). These theological and philosophical backgrounds collectively provided the moral legitimisation of ecclesial (from 1881) and later political (between 1910 and 1948) segregation between white and black people as the best practical solution to the race question as well as an expression of God's will for the pluriformity of cultures in South Africa.

The result was that white people found their sense of well-being, social identity and fulfilment in their separation from black people. Because this separation could be ideologically founded on the Christian tradition, this social "happiness" was seen as a God-willed and "blessed" segregation. The official political edifice of this happiness was finally dismantled in April 1994, but traces of this notion are still evident in South Africa's private and public life.

It is always easier to change laws than to change hearts.

2.2 The traditional African model: "Happy are those who live in close, interdependent community"

South Africa is a diverse nation. Within kilometres from one another, people live not only in different physical worlds (some of that the remnants of grand apartheid), but also with different worldviews. (There are still many more traditional healers in

---

9   See especially Warneck's *Evangelische Missionslehre* (1897), Volume 3 for an understanding of his theory of mission.
10 See Willie Jonker's (2008) very careful analysis of the complexities of pietism in the history of the church and De Gruchy's (1991:24ff) discussion of pietism as it relates to the South African situation.

Soweto near Johannesburg than so-called "real" medical doctors). An expression of such an indigenous worldview lies in the African philosophy of *"ubuntu"*. This has subsequently been explained as meaning "I am a person through other persons" or "I am because you are".[11] The concept of *ubuntu* has since found wide exploration and application in theology, politics, management theory and ethics.[12]

In highly simplified terms, *ubuntu* can be explained with three related terms:

Holism – understanding reality as one and not in the sense of semi-autonomous social or scientific spheres. In some traditional African languages there is, for example, no word for "religion", as this assumes an abstraction and dissection of life not present in such societies. Because traditional societies are pre-modern (or rather a-modern), the idea of private and public spheres is not as distinctly present as in post-Enlightenment societies.

Vitalism – the whole of reality is filled with life-energy (*mana*) and this surrounds each person (*siriti*) and living object. This has ethical significance: doing good is promotion of this energy, and reducing life-energy is morally negative. Vitalism also partially explains social exchanges such as *lobola* ("payment" for a bride) during marriage, as taking a bride from one family needs to be "balanced" with some reciprocal "life" in exchange.

Communitarianism – life is lived in community and is characterised by abundant benevolence. "Personhood" or "individuality" is primarily a social, relational ideal. Actions are taken in consultation with, and for the welfare of, the community, which extends beyond death to the forebears with whom there is active interaction.

This ideal type of African "happiness" has in recent years been corrupted in (South) Africa in a variety of ways.

When the supposedly universal boundaries of *ubuntu* (humaneness) are drawn along ethnic or party-political lines, they become a vicious philosophy of exclusion and dehumanisation. When life-enhancing social exchange is turned into corrupt buying of favour, public resources are wasted. When the social ideal of community enhancement is replaced by enrichment for powerful individuals or elite groups, poverty and social marginalisation increase.[13] When a communitarian sense of happiness turns into an ideology of communitarianism where dissenting voices and contrasting opinions are seen as treacherous in principle, consultation (open debate), so famous in traditional African *imbizos*, dies.

This traditional African model of *ubuntu* (in a variety of forms) is still very much prevalent in South Africa, although it is not often "voiced" in public as many African people live in a transition between models of life, and many chart meaning by living in two (or more) worlds at the same time.

---

11 An early discussion comes from Mbiti's views of kinship, and reads: "The individual can only say I am, because we are; and since we are, therefore I am. **This is the cardinal point in the understanding of the African view of man**" (1969:108, my emphasis).
12 See the works by Shutte (2001) on *ubuntu* ethics and by Ramose (1999) for a more philosophical analysis.
13 See the discussion by Smit (2007: 84) on the move from *ubuntu* to "narcissistic individualism" in South Africa.

2.3 The modernist model: "Happy is the 'reasonable' man who pursues his own self-interest"

In Western philosophy "modernity" is popularly linked to René Descartes ("I think therefore I am") and the Enlightenment to Immanuel Kant, who famously stated that the *mündiger Mensch* (mature or enlightened person) is someone who has escaped from his self-inflicted *Unmündigkeit* (immaturity). The key to maturity is to have the courage "dich deines eigenen Verstandes ohne Leitung eines anderen zu bedienen".[14]

The "catchwords" describing modernity[15] may therefore be listed as follows: *Reason*, specifically individual reason, is seen as the mark of human distinction. A strong sense of *historicity* emerged with emphasis on the fact that the past can only be unlocked by objective, rational research of the original sources. *Authority* or anti-authority meant that traditional sources of authority (the king, the church, tradition, the Bible) were challenged in the light of personal authority (Kant: "ohne Leitung eines anderen") to make sense of reality through individual and supposedly objective reason. *Freedom*, specifically individual freedom, is understood to be the ability to make one's own choices in all spheres of life from church to politics, ethics and economics.

In this notion of happiness the rational pursuit of self-interest (as broadly developed in modern capitalism) is seen as morally good, because – even without overt intention – this self-interest will in the end contribute to the good of all. Individualism, a distinct understanding of man as "self-made man", is the social ideal (and is still very much constructed in such sexist terms).

Modernity has had ambiguous consequences for the West and for South Africa. No one can deny that modernity brought us huge progress in science and technology, economic growth, educational reform, democracies that entrench freedoms, and human rights as universal guides for political justice.

On the other hand, reason can turn into the reduced anthropology of rationalism and the reduced epistemology of scientism and empiricism. Individuality with some connection to community can turn into self-referential and greedy individualism. The healthy questioning of authority can lead in some cases to anti-authority attitudes in principle, leaving huge gaps in otherwise stable social structures provided by the state and civil society. Freedom can be reduced to rational choice economics and freedom to consume.

The onset of democracy in South Africa in 1994 can be described as a plunge into modernity. The journey into the Enlightenment that took Europe more than a century to achieve, we had and still have to travel in one or two decades. Many people in my country had to make (and are trying to make) the transition from an a-modern/anti-modern to a modern and post-modern world (to employ these not

---

14 Roughly translated this means that to use one's own mind without being led by another person, is the essence of being enlightened. Note Kant's famous essay "Beantwortung der Frage: Was ist Aufklärung?" originally published in *Berlinische Monatsschrift*, December 1784, 481-494. For a recent reprint from which this quotation comes, see Kant 1999: 20.
15 See Smit (1998: 291-296) for a concise description of "Enlightenment".

so useful terms) in a very short space of time and without the required social and educational support processes.

Apartheid was an anti-modern concept. In the same year (1948) that the UN accepted the universal declaration of human rights, the National Party came to power on the platform of a denial of those rights to black people, and continued to intensify these policies until at least the late 1980s. Apartheid was built on the catchphrases of modernity, but all in an inverted sense: limitation of freedom, ideological reason and history, as well as on unquestioned religious/military/political authority.

Traditional African philosophy was/is an a-modern concept: communities are built on the basis of a high regard for tradition and authority figures with limited freedom-in-community; notions of individuality are strongly embedded in community; and forms of "rationality" exist that contrast significantly with the individual, enquiring reason advanced by Descartes, Kant and the experimental reasoning of modern science.

Yes, some embraced the enlightenment ideals and could make the transition fairly smoothly. Others found that their model of happiness, identity and well-being was severely challenged, and in some cases shattered. This led to social bewilderment and *anomie* (Durkheim), exhibited in the excesses of modernity.

Leaders in the struggle for liberation now declare they did not join the struggle to be poor – they have embraced the "self-made" man image and ideal. Anti-colonialists now live with purported political freedom, but with the irony of colonised minds and attitudes. People who wish to reject apartheid and its horrible past need to reconstruct happiness and well-being under the constraints of deconstructing everything that formerly provided social coherence. Some succeed; others take flight into internal or actual physical migration.

The religious results vary and brought intense pluralism to the fore. The two extremes are (on the one hand) those who embrace traditional piety and spirituality in evangelical and Spirit churches, and those (on the other hand) who for the first time in their social context can openly question the rationality of religious beliefs as such, and turn to scepticism or even atheism.

Today "happiness" in South Africa is in flux. Models can in theory be neatly distinguished, but in practice people and communities can and do migrate between models and even live in contrasting models at the same time. What is not uncertain is that the onset of the modern idea of happiness has had a profoundly ambiguous social effect. The big question is whether the negative consequences of a "modern" model can be turned around by recourse to the liberating tradition of modernity itself.

On the other hand, one must understand that South Africa (and most of sub-Saharan Africa) is not a secular society in the European sense of the word. Religion is valued and is publicly displayed and practised in organs of the state, even where a constitutional church-state separation is in place. This opens the possibility that the critical Christian notions of blessedness and happiness have some potential to guide the future of this country and continent.

2.4 A Christian model: "Blessed is the man who finds his joy in the law of the Lord..."[16]

Others at this conference[17] will discuss the complex array of biblical notions of *Glückseligkeit*. For this short paper, a few broad outlines are drawn, knowing that the very notion of a "biblical" or "Christian" understanding is itself a field of strong contestation, and accepting that ideology can lead people to call something "biblical" or "Christian" that is not in line with ecumenical understandings at all.

One could follow a traditional Trinitarian line of thinking and design a notion of blessedness and happiness with reference to human beings in relation to the triune God (leaving aside for the moment the important theme of "happiness" in non-human creation).

In relation to God, the Creator: humans are made in the image of God and live in close union with God (happiness/paradise), but step out of that relation (Genesis 3-11), and are thereafter called to be God's people (Gen 12) who find joy in the law of the Lord (Ps 1) and wisdom/happiness in the knowledge of the Lord (Proverbs 1).

In relation to Christ, the Re-creator: humans are reconciled with God and with one another by the *Heil* that Christ brings to the world. The faithful find joy in the Lord, irrespective of the situation (Philippians 3:1, 4:12-13, 1 Peter) and are blessed in the service of others, especially the weak and the marginalised (Matthew 5; 25).

In relation Holy Spirit/sanctifier: humans are holy in Christ (1 Corinthians, 1 Peter), and they grow in blessedness and happiness as they walk in and bear the fruit of the Spirit, amongst which are love, happiness and peace (Galatians 5), as well as unity amongst diverse peoples (Ephesians 2 and 4).

The theological task is now to interpret and re-interpret these broad theological themes (and the many biblical notions of *Glückseligkeit*) for specific contexts such as South Africa or Germany, with all the complexities prevailing in these countries. It is not possible to give a full account of this task here. In a context dominated by the global catchphrases of modernity, the view must be proclaimed and defended that it is reasonable to believe in God and that rationality itself needs a broader definition; that true freedom[18] is found in Christ and service to others, in particular the weak; that the law and the gospel are inspirational moral codes of happiness and blessedness for individuals and society; and that Scripture and tradition (reinterpreted and subject to historical criticism and ecumenical consensus) remain sources of ecclesial, social, and personal orientation.

In a world seeking happiness, blessed are those who find their joy in the law of the Lord and meditate on the law day and night...

---

16 This refers to Psalm 1 and the gender bias of the original is retained.
17 See footnote 1.
18 For a convincing theological-ethical interpretation of "freedom" in a modern context, see the many contributions by Wolfgang Huber, *inter alia*, Huber (1985, 1990), and note the appropriate title of the Festschrift for his 60th birthday published in 2002 as *Freiheit verantworten*.

BIBLIOGRAPHY

De Gruchy, J 1991. *Liberating reformed theology. A South African contribution to an ecumenical debate.* Grand Rapids: Eerdmans.

Gilhus, I 2000. Glück/Glückseligkeit. In *Religion in Geschichte und Gegenwart,* Band 3,1015-6. Tübingen: Mohr Siebeck.

Huber, W 1985. *Folgen christliche Freiheit: Ethik und Theorie der Kirche im Horizont der Barmer theologischen Erklärung.* Neukirchen-Vluyn: Neukircherner Verlag.

Huber, W 1990. Der Protestanismus und die Ambivalenz der Modernen. In J Moltmann (Hrg.): *Religion der Freiheit. Protestantismus in der Moderne,* 29-65. München: Kaiser Verlag.

Hunold, GW & Glykas, M 1995. Glück. In *Lexikon für Theologie und Kirche,* Band 4, 757-761. Freiburg: Herder Verlag.

Kant, I 1999. *Ausgewahlte kleine Schriften.* Hamburg: Felix Meier.

Kuyper, A 1902. *De gemeene gratie.* Amsterdam: Hoeveker & Wormser.

Mbiti, J 1969. *African religions and philosophy.* Nairobi: East African Educational Publishers.

Naudé, PJ 2010. *Neither calendar nor clock. Perspectives on the Belhar confession.* Grand Rapids: Eerdmans.

Ramosa, MB 1999. *African philosophy through ubuntu.* Harare: Mond Books.

Schutte, Augustine 2001. *Ubuntu: An ethic for the new South Africa.* Pietermaritzburg; Cluster.

Smit, DJ 1998. Biblical hermeneutics: the first 19 centuries. In Simon Maimela & Adrio Konig (eds.) *Initiation into theology. The rich variety of theology and hermeneutics.* Pretoria: Van Schaik, 275-296.

Smit, DJ 2007. *Essays in public theology. Collected essays I.* Stellenbosch: Sun Press.

Smit, DJ 2010. Trends and directions in Reformed theology. *The Expository Times* 122 (7), 1-14.

Tracy, D 1978. *Blessed rage for order. The new pluralism in theology.* New York: The Seabury Press.

Warneck, DG 1897. *Evangelische Missionslehre. Ein missionstheorethische Versuch.* Band 3. Gotha: Berthes.

PART 4 –
ETHICS, BUSINESS AND ECONOMICS

4.1 ETHICS EDUCATION IN ACCOUNTING

An outsider's perspective

"The accounting profession must restore its priceless asset: its reputation."
(Barry Melanchon, AICPA President, 2002)

INTRODUCTION

This essay,[1] written by a South African ethicist from outside the accounting profession, undertakes a close reading of the *International Education Standards for Professional Accountants* (cited as IES 2003) in tandem with the International Federation of Accountants' Information Paper (cited as IP 2006), *Approaches to the Development and Maintenance of Professional Values, Ethics and Attitudes in Accounting Education* (published August 2006). The aim is not to engage with extensive secondary sources, but merely to give a concise overview of these policy documents in relation to four questions:

1. Why teach ethics?
2. Can ethics be taught?
3. What is to be taught?
4. How is ethics to be taught and by whom?

Enough work has been done elsewhere to warrant a full paper on each of these topics. What is presented here is therefore very cryptic and is an attempt to make sense of the current curriculum debate on ethics education for future accountants in South Africa and globally.

At the outset we need to clarify the meaning of both "ethics" and "education" as they are used in the policy documents. **Education** refers to all aspects of developmental activities at pre- and post-qualifying levels to prepare future or equip current accountants to act in a professional manner. This paper does not address continuing professional education and focuses on the pre-qualification level that normally falls within the ambit of a first university degree. **Ethics** is a comprehensive reference to values, ethical principles and attitudes associated with, and considered essential for, distinctive professional behaviour (see Information Paper 2006: 16-17).

Let us now turn to each of the four questions posed above.

1. WHY TEACH ETHICS?

My assessment as an outsider is that the time has never been more opportune to openly and seriously address the issue of ethics in the accounting profession.

---

1 Revised and updated version of a paper delivered at the SAICA international conference held in Durban, South Africa, July 2004.

Without elaborate discussion, it seems as if several negative and positive factors collectively create such an environment conducive to a serious discussion of ethics.

1.1 Negative contextual factors

Foremost in the minds of most lay people are the recent business scandals and financial collapses in which accountants are unfortunately deemed to have played a pivotal role. Examples from all continents make "finger-pointing" inappropriate and unhelpful. The collapse of Arthur Andersen in the wake of the Enron saga was particularly damaging to the image of a "clean, impartial and objective" profession, Unfortunately the events of 2001 in the USA were not "once-off" aberrations, but were followed by a succession of corporate failures or set-backs as a consequence of the unethical conduct of persons in positions of responsibility, including accounting firms that presented audit reports later found wanting, if not misleading. The current South African cases of Mr Brett Kebble and the Fidentia Group, involving hundreds of millions of rands, raise serious questions about both corporate governance and accounting practices.

There is consensus that these and other events resulted in a breach of the public trust[2] so crucial to any profession. The frequency of accounting abuses led to a breakdown in society's belief that the actions of accountants are generally in the public interest. The belief is now that some accountants and accountancy firms bring the traditional values of objectivity, integrity and due care into question (IP 2006:30). The Information Paper is clearly aimed at rebuilding public trust in the profession, starting off with a quotation by Steve Samek, who prophetically announced: "The day Arthur Andersen loses the public trust is the day we go out of business" (IP 2006:105). This is reinforced by the very title of the PricewaterhouseCoopers report on ethics education: *Educating for the public trust* (PWC 2003).

The IES document lists a number of contextual factors that increase "the need for greater accountability", as accountability determines the profession's value to society (IES 2003:29). Mention is made of the pressures of globalisation, transnational trade and commerce, increasing legal action, as well as concern for the environment linked to sustainable development. Writing from an American context, Thomas Piper summarises the contextual factors that provide a rationale for ethics education as follows: "Scandal, evidence of rapidly diminishing trust, heightened environmental concerns, excesses associated with deregulation ... brought issues of leadership, ethics and corporate responsibility back to the fore" (Piper et al. 2003:10).

The ethical problem lies, however, deeper than this. The chief motif behind the policy documents seems to be the restoration of the profession's image and regaining of public trust, not so much for the public's sake but to ensure the pre-eminence of the image of the profession itself. This is ethically acceptable and even laudable. But this view is not in line with the classic view of professions that self-interest is embedded in public values and the seeking of the public good, and not the other way around; and that a profession is chosen not for the lucrative money opportunities it offers, but as a public vocation. One can therefore rightly ask whether the accounting profession has not lost its connections to public values (such as justice and accountability) and

---

2   See the contribution of Neville Bews on "Building trust with ethics", Chapter 13 in Rossouw (2004).

– in its pursuit of narrow self-interest – no longer clearly imagines its own undergirding public purpose (see Parks's discussion in Piper et al. 1993:15).

These contextual factors – negative as they are – do create a unique window of opportunity and must be seen in proper historical perspective. The accounting profession may derive some comfort from the fact that the move from "pure" to "applied" ethics since the early 1970s in fields such as ecology, biomedical research and business studies have all been driven by "crises" resulting in dramatic public questions that required urgent attention.[3]

Ecological ethics rose significantly to the fore after the Club of Rome report in the early 1960s and awareness of the devastating potential of atomic power as a weapon of mass human and environmental destruction.[4] This was given further momentum by the well-known Brundtland report on sustainable development (see Brundtland 1987), the Second King Report on Corporate Governance (Institute of Directors 2002) and the Global Reporting Initiative, which published their sustainability reporting guidelines in 2002.

Bio-medical ethics rose to prominence on the basis of questions related to euthanasia and abortion, and more recently via issues like genetic engineering, cloning, stem-cell research and a socio-economic issue such as the price of drugs for developing countries.[5]

The rise of business ethics[6] as distinct discipline from about 1970 may be related to the macro questions of a fair economic system in the light of the competing paradigms of a free market versus interventionist economies during the height of the Cold War and, after the fall of the Berlin wall, questions related to globalisation and fair trade. The discipline has since mushroomed to address issues such as corporate responsibility, ethical decision-making and ethical risk analyses.[7]

The history of the accounting profession (at least in the USA) tells the same story. Audit failures and congressional investigations were important drivers behind major self-examination that resulted in fairly sweeping changes over the years (see Marquette 1996:233-234; Abdolmohammadi and Nixon 1999:173-176), culminating

---

[3] During a colloquium on ethics in international education at the University of Port Elizabeth in 2004, a colleague in philosophy made the cynical remark that applied ethics normally arrives too late at the scene of the crime! As a variation on a comment by Karl Barth, the great Swiss theologian, one might say: Applied ethics is like covering a well after a few children have already drowned in it. (But rather late than never!)

[4] The important conferences on sustainable development in e.g. Rio de Janeiro and in Johannesburg (2002) put the issue of environmental ethics high on the political and economic agenda, with some specific implications for the accounting profession.

[5] See the publication in July 2005 of *The charter of the public and private health sectors in the Republic of South Africa* for interesting ethical issues related to the provision of public health care.

[6] Norman Bowie (1986:158) argues for the "birth" of business ethics at Kansas University in November 1974 as a joint venture between the Philosophy Department and the College of Business. There is alternative evidence by Piper (1993:8) that initiatives in the late 1950s had already constituted the roots of business ethics as distinct field of study.

[7] See the content pages of Rossouw (2004) or (Bowie) 2002 for a quick glance at the multiple issues related to business ethics, as well as Rossouw (2004a) for a view on business ethics as an academic field.

by 2001 in the Sarbanes-Oxley-Act,[8] which points to a regime of co-regulation rather than self-regulation.

It is now opportune to reconsider applied ethics education in the accounting profession, including raising questions about the nature of the profession itself. Let us turn to a second "negative" factor.

As a highly technical profession attuned to implementing regulations, interpreting empirical data and relying on deductive logic, the issue of ethics has never really been taken seriously in accounting education. The surveys informing the Information Paper clearly demonstrate that "ethics" has been viewed simply as knowledge of the code of conduct of professional bodies (IP 2006:57).

This lack of attention relates to both the epistemological framework of accounting as a discipline and an attitude that relegates ethics to the level of a "soft issue" (read: not serious) in business. "As accounting educators", Professors Gaa and Thorne (2004:1) write, "we continue to upgrade our knowledge base ... to include more and more technical topics. In contrast, there appears to be less emphasis accorded to understanding ethical research and less of a drive to adapt the accounting curriculum to include recent advances in ethical research."

In an academic field where the "goods" of knowledge production have themselves become a commodity, a "cost-benefit" approach apparently leads to a clear result: "Benefits ... are perceived to be insufficient to justify the cost needed to be incurred in the form of time spent to become current in ethics as a field of academic research" (Bernardi 2004:1). In an academic reward system based on short-term outputs, one of the questions asked by academics at Harvard Business School was: "What are the opportunity costs to us turning our attention and time to business ethics?", and how will this be rated by peers and tenure-granting committees? (Cf. Piper et al. 1993: 83, 137.)

There is some statistical evidence worth noting that might explain why accounting actually lags behind other professions and some of the cognate disciplines with regard to a study of ethics:

- Only 2.7% of the approximately 6 200 accounting academics in North America and only 3.1% of journals list ethics as an area of interest (Bernardi 2004:145);
- By the mid-1990s the proportional weighting of ethics in the final qualifying examinations of the UK was between 1 and 4% (IP 2006:87; see reference to original research by Fleming 1996);
- Only 30.3% of participating member bodies of IFAC have a clear policy for ethics in pre-qualification programmes;

---

8   The *New York Times* of 13 March 2007 (page C2) reported that corporate executives and accounting firms are meeting with top government officials "about rolling back post-Enron reforms and limiting liability from government and shareholder lawsuits." This could lead to regulatory changes in the near future. Judge Mervyn King, editor of the King Reports in South Africa, has from the start publicly stated his opposition to the over-regulation of this Act and so have many ethicists in the USA – see the special issue of the *Business and Professional Ethics Journal* Vol. 23, Nos. 1 & 2, 2004 edited by Norman Bowie.

- Ethics makes up less than 10% of pre-qualification programmes for 35.7% of participating IFAC member bodies (IP 2006:56, 57);
- Accounting and auditing text books recommended by member bodies "either avoid consideration of ethical principles, or reduced ethical principles to a mechanistic following of written behavioural guidelines" (IP 2006:119; see reference to original research by Puxty et al. 1994).

1.2 Positive contextual factors

There has been a significant rise in awareness of the issue of ethics and this should not be underestimated as important first step toward a rigorous ethics education. This awareness can easily be observed in the daily newspapers and financial journals (popular public mind) and is highlighted in academic circles by (for example) the very useful recent edition of *Issues in Accounting Education* (Vol. 19, No. 1, Feb 2004), dedicated to ethics.

IFAC is clearly taking its leadership responsibilities seriously and has produced the following important guideline reports: *Rebuilding confidence in financial reporting: An international perspective* (2003), *Proposed revised code of ethics for professional accountants* (2003), *Introduction to international education standards* (2003), of which IES 4 is dedicated to professional values, ethics and attitudes, and has a Compliance Advisory Panel that oversees implementation of the seven SMOs (Statements of Membership Obligations) issued so far (IP 2006:106-107).

Slowly but surely the insight is dawning: ethics is not a public relations addition to a strategic plan, nor a motto on the wall of the CEO, but an actual professional competence on a par with other technical requirements for accountants. Determining ethical risk, managing ethics on strategic, system and operational levels, and more transparency on "triple bottom line" reporting all clearly require a new breed of accountant.

The first and logical reaction to a breach of trust is to tighten self-control. It has in fact become a mark of professions that they have self-appointed bodies that oversee the education and standards of the professions (see e.g. medicine and law). If a situation is reached where this oversight is judged to be inadequate, the political powers of the day (the state) move in with formal requirements and legislation. "While it is clearly preferable for corporate enterprises to control their destiny through proactive self-regulation, governments around the world have demonstrated that they will introduce legislation where necessary if companies fail to do so" (King II Report 2002: 99). This is true of professions as well and (as observed above) we are slowly moving towards co- instead of self-regulation.

A fresh look at professional and government regulations as such is a positive development, as long as one recognises that ethics driven by control or mere technical or tick-box compliance is inadequate to create a culture in which professional values can flourish. The legitimacy of technique can never replace the legitimacy of character. In philosophical terms a blind "principle-driven ethics" (deontology) void of "agency-driven ethics" (virtues) may work in the short term, but it is unable to deal with the unknown or the complexity of real-life moral situations.

If this is the current context in which the issue of ethics education for accountants is set, the next question arises as to whether such education is indeed possible.

2. CAN ETHICS BE TAUGHT?

This question relates not only to accounting, but to a more general suspicion against teaching of ethics, perceived by some as hovering between either indoctrination or nihilistic relativism. I would like to point out the limitations of an affirmative answer to this question, followed by some potential inherent to the teaching of ethics, and close off this section with recent research into the effectiveness of ethics education in accounting.

2.1 Limitations to the teaching of ethics

A first limitation to "teaching ethics" is related to the **complexity of moral formation**.

If one accepts a developmental view of moral formation (as suggested by Piaget and Kohlberg),[9] as well the complexity of the actual process that usually involves a number of informal and formal agents,[10] then the naïve notion that one can "teach someone to be ethical" in a few weeks must be discarded. Moral frameworks and values are inculcated over an extended period through diverse processes involving an equally diverse array of persons, institutions, historical events and culture.

What moral development research does tell us is to discard the naïve notion that "everything is settled in the first six years". Kenneth Keniston recognises young adulthood as a distinct post-adolescent period in human development, when the growth of critical self-awareness and re-imagination of the self in society are crucial tasks. In this process very important decisions are taken that are indeed shaped by mentoring environments such as university education (Piper et al. 1993: 60-61). The assertion that teaching ethics at university comes too late must and has been rejected by most accountants and professional bodies themselves. In the IFAC survey (IP 2006:68) the statement "Moral standards of students are fully developed and can't be changed or improved with education" received the lowest overall mean score (1.7) and "Ethics should be learned as a life-long development" achieved the highest mean score (3.5) of all statements about ethics education.

What is indeed disconcerting evidence is that moral sensitivity actually decreases as students become more senior, and that more senior accountants in practice are less sensitive to moral ambiguities than their junior colleagues! (See IP 2006:31-33.) This may point to a blunting instead of sharpening of moral sensitivity by enculturation into the profession, and might suggest that renewed efforts at ethics education should rather start right at the top with senior partners – an issue beyond the scope of this paper.

A second limitation is the obvious point that there can be **no guarantee that what is learnt in theory will be applied** in the complexity of practice.

---

9   For a brief summary and criticism of the "moral development school", see Parker (1998).
10 See the interesting work by Johannes van der Ven, who develops seven modes of moral education, of which one is moral development (1998:35-42, 181-234).

Unlike purely technical knowledge of taxation or auditing, one cannot "teach someone to be ethical" in the sense that you could provide an antecedent proof of ethical conduct. Ethical reflection on moral ambiguities and conflicts of interest related to and sometimes conflicting with prevailing company ethos are contextually determined. The difference between a "bribe", a "facilitating payment" and a "gift" might vary according to policy and cultural environment. (Un)ethical conduct is the result of many factors such as the psychology of the individual, the culture of the organisation (see Thompson and Strickland 2003:424), coercion by seniors, and the nature of the "temptation" to deviate from accepted norms (see Rossouw 2004: 169-162). Responses to these factors may be influenced by prior ethics education, but they do not fall completely under its control.

2.2. The potential inherent in the teaching of ethics

The limitations above do not, however, warrant total scepticism or a stance of ethical agnosticism. It must be noted that to explicitly avoid ethics education (for whatever reason, from curricula that are too full to personal uneasiness) would in fact have severe ethical implications. There is no such a thing as a neutral education. What implicit values have students of accounting absorbed in previous generations?

In an ascending order, the dimensions of ethics outlined below are indeed within the reach of ethics education.

The first dimension is teaching **about ethics** in the sense that classical and modern theories[11] are espoused and examples of their application are provided. The philosophical and historical contents are made available and knowledge can be assessed as in any other discipline of a historical or conceptual nature.

Teaching "about ethics" may lead to the development of an **ethical sensitivity** or awareness, so that learners are able to perceive the moral dimensions of a situation. It is a process of conscientisation that heightens the ethical "antennae" of learners to acknowledge "ethical" information. The very first step in ethics is to perceive an apparently "ethically neutral" or "a-moral" situation as a "moral" one. (If you do not see the problem, you will also not seek a resolution!)

Teaching ethics is, as argued above, in itself a **shaping and formative force** in the overall moral formation of learners. In many cases students explicate, question and re-state their ethical stance for the first time during a course in ethics. There are many effective delivery modes and teaching aids (see below) to ensure maximum formative influence, although this will obviously vary from learner to learner.

Teaching **ethical decision-making skills** is open to all – from total agnostics to the most moral or religious. There are many examples of such decision-making models such as, for example the six-stage process outlined by the American Accounting Association (IP 2006:115-116; see reference to original research by Langenfelder and Rockiness 1989). Common to all is a rational process of discernment (see Rossouw 2004) that can indeed be taught through case studies as a testable skill that is subject to external assessment.

---

11 Two of the best recent examples of such overviews are the new edition of Alasdair MacIntyre's *A short history of ethics* (1998) and Harry Gensler (ed.): *Ethics. Contemporary readings* (2004).

Ethics education is also highly suitable for **experiential learning**. Armed with theoretical knowledge and decision-making skills, trainee accountants or students can return to a discussion of actual work-based experiences, and consequently progress in both their knowledge and skills to be better equipped for dealing with future situations of potential moral compromise.

The following illustration explains the levels of ethical teaching that can be accomplished. Note that the triangle suggests an increasing complexity as one moves "up" the graph.

Is there any evidence of the effectiveness of ethics education in Accountancy?

The question arises as to what "effectiveness" means and how to measure it – if possible at all. If effectiveness means that students have greater knowledge about ethics, are more ethically aware, and are able to successfully resolve ambiguous case studies through ethical decision-making models, any proper assessment will tell you that it is and can be "effective".

Some empirical work has indeed been done on this issue. Using Thorne's *Accounting Ethical Dilemma Instrument* (AEDI) and Rest's *Defining Issues Test* (DIT), Professors Earley and Kelly report on an ethics intervention in a undergraduate accounting course in a pre-Enron (2001) and post-Enron (2002) situation. They make the interesting finding of "a significant increase in moral reasoning scores using an accounting context-specific instrument" for both groups (i.e. pre- and post-Enron), thereby "supporting the effectiveness of educational interventions." However, in line with other studies, there was not "a corresponding increase in general moral reasoning scores" (Earley and Kelly 2004:54).

In their survey of previous research, Earley and Kelly find supporting evidence that interventions at undergraduate level seem to be most promising, and the introduction of a generalist course in ethics could in fact contribute to non-contextual moral reasoning (see Early and Kelly 2004:55). Armstrong's study was published in 1993 – one of a few focusing on accounting students only – and found that a course in ethics affected students' moral development beyond what could be expected to occur naturally. Many other studies have been done with mixed results (see Information Report 2006:31-32, 92), but the generalisation value of such studies needs to be questioned in the light of cultural and contextual contingencies.

It is clear that the hype of a post-scandal period should not lead accounting professors to think ethics is the answer "to make all future accountants moral". There are also material limitations to the teaching of ethics, though there is no reason to believe that this is more so than in other subjects of the same social scientific nature. There is, however, a strong enough basis – philosophically, morally and empirically – to support an educational intervention. This raises the questions of what should be included in such a curriculum.

3. WHAT SHOULD BE TAUGHT?

I have already referred to the IFAC documents pertaining to education generally and mentioned that the *International Education Standards for Professional Accountants* has a specific section on *Professional Values, Ethics and Attitudes* which provides guidelines for professional ethics education (IFAC 2003).

The Education Committee EDCO of SAICA (South African Institute of Chartered Accountants), which participated in the IFAC surveys, will introduce a syllabus on ethics by 2006 with the aim of making it examinable in Part I of the Qualifying Examination in 2008. The first delivery of the undergraduate modules is scheduled for second-year university students in 2007.

There are two implicit questions facing IFAC as a global organisation in the prescription of a model curriculum.

The first is whether an input or output approach to global education will be followed. Here IFAC's methods wisely point toward a double approach of wide consultation with member bodies (input) on which the global proposals are then based (output).

The second is whether ethics should be standardised in the same way as accounting or auditing standards, and whether they should then be issued as member obligations with strict rules of compliance. This raises the vexing issue – well-known in philosophical, theological and anthropological circles – of the relation between "universalism" and "cultural relativism". The policy documents show an awareness of this, and make remarkably many references to cultural diversity and the adaptation of guidelines for local situations (IES 2003:55-56, 60, 62- 63; IP 2006:89-90)

However, and as to be expected from its nature as a regulatory body, IFAC clearly leans in the direction of universally accepted professional values and attitudes seen as globally accepted standards.[12] This is an idealistic approach not to be discarded as it maintains a certain inspirational value. In real life, however, the challenge to global standards does not come from open questions about the standards or values themselves – who wants to argue (for example) against avoiding a conflict

---

12   See the provocative book by Prof. DR Myddelton (2004), who argues very strongly against global harmonisation of accounting standards. See specifically his arguments in Chapter 5 that reinforce the title of his book: *Unshackling Accountants* (!). This is in line with Karim Jamal's view that the audit profession is "in such a mess" exactly because of regulations (Jamal 2004:67ff.).

of interests? Who will object to signing the international code of conduct? No, the real challenge comes from actual business practices that point to a different cultural **interpretation** of "conflict of interests" not premised on a post-Enlightenment notion of individuality and objectivity but, for instance, on the kinship or communitarian understandings of responsibility prevalent in Eastern and African societies.

Let us now turn to the curriculum itself and discuss it under three items: (i) the required knowledge domains; (ii) the required professional skills; and (iii) the actual content of ethics education.

i. Knowledge domains

The IES states clearly that professional accounting education consists of three knowledge domains: **accounting, finance and related knowledge** constitute the core of the technical competencies. This is complemented by **organisational and business knowledge**, and (thirdly) **information technology knowledge** and competencies. Ethics is integrated into the first two domains as "professional values" under the first domain, and as "corporate governance" and "business ethics" under the second domain (IES 2003:46, 47). There is no explicit reference to ethics in the information technology component. This is regrettable, as many "old" ethical challenges acquire a completely new character in our digital economy. Think, for example, of issues such as privacy, copyright, insider trading and commercial espionage, as well as the global ethical questions arising from the digital divide between North and South.

ii. Professional skills

In its discussion of professional skills, IES 3 lists five sets of skills that individuals aspiring to become professional accountants should acquire: **intellectual, technical, personal, interpersonal and organisational skills** (IES 2003:54). Where does ethics fit in?

Although not specifically mentioned, it is implied that ethics – as part of general education – makes an important contribution to intellectual skills as it requires analysis, critical understanding and good judgment. Ethics fosters personal skills as it shapes the attitudes and decision-making of the individual. Ethics contributes to interpersonal and communication skills as it heightens awareness of and sensitivity to cultural and intellectually diverse settings. Ethics promotes organisational and business management skills as it assists in "professional judgment and discernment" (IES 2003: 55, 56)

It is noteworthy that the only skills component where ethics is absent is the technical and functional skills, which focus on items such as numeracy, reporting, decision modelling and risk analysis, as well as IT proficiency. The IES document obviously assumes that ethics will "permeate" all areas of accounting education, but to an outsider the dichotomies between "professional" and "non-professional" as well as between "technical" and "ethical" remain unfortunate, as they implicitly (and unknowingly) reinforce the separation of ethics from the professional/technical with the former clearly a "soft" issue not belonging to the core, but only brought to bear "afterwards".

iii. Ethics education

It is in this instance helpful to link the IES and the IP to get an overall picture of ethics content and educational goals. In what the Information Paper calls the "Ethics

Education Framework" (EEF) there is a four-stage learning continuum based on the broad objectives of ethics education. These four objectives resemble what was noted under the "triangle" in 2 above and are explained as:

- establishing the intellectual background to understand ethical positions;
- developing ethical sensitivity;
- developing ethical competence and skills; and
- translating knowledge into actual ethical behaviour (see IP 2006:77-78).

It is now possible to place the specific curriculum items listed by the International Education Standard (particularly IES 4, see pages 62-63) into one of these four stages. The result is a grid that looks as follows (adapted from IP 2006:99), with stage four probably falling just beyond pre-qualification education, unless some workplace learning is included prior to formal qualification.

Stage one

Ethics knowledge – traditional theories of ethics, virtues and moral development.

IES items: the nature of ethics; differences between rules-based and framework approaches with their respective advantages and drawbacks; compliance with fundamental ethical principles of integrity, objectivity, professional competence and confidentiality.

Stage two

Ethical sensitivity – common issues and dilemmas facing accountants in practice.

IES items: professional behaviour; application of concepts such as independence, scepticism, accountability and public expectations.

Stage three

Ethical judgment – application of theories, codes of conduct and decision-making models.

IES items: ethics and the profession: social responsibility; ethics and law; ethics in relation to business and good governance.

Stage four

Ethical behaviour – concrete workplace factors affecting ethical behaviour.

IES items: ethics and the individual professional accountant: whistle-blowing, conflict of interests, ethical dilemmas and their resolution; consequences of unethical behaviour to the individual, to the profession and to society at large.

It is clear from the above discussion of the curriculum that the IFAC documents have really taken ethics education very seriously and have set up both a framework and suggested content that can be adapted to local contexts, whilst maintaining a tie to a broad global consensus. It is now the responsibility of member bodies to implement these guidelines.

4. HOW IS ETHICS TO BE TAUGHT?

Under this rubric I wish to discuss the format of the ethics component in a pre-qualification curriculum, followed by short notes on teaching staff, teaching methods and aids, and possible assessment methods.

In their interesting discussion of the processes underlying the introduction of business ethics into the Harvard Business School curriculum, Piper and colleagues (1993) had to grapple with both the initial scepticism of staff and the "format" issue. Transferred to the accounting curriculum, basically **three options are available**: a stand-alone optional ethics module; a stand-alone compulsory module (known as the discrete approach); or integration into several existing modules (the pervasive approach).

It is clear from the analyses above that an optional module as the only form of ethics education will not satisfy the intentions and material content of what has been proposed. It will also send a clear message that "ethics is an optional extra" to the "real accounting content". An optional module may be an interesting complementary choice if, for example, students have limited elective choices in putting together their curriculum. This would yield the opportunity for more advanced study or for specialisation in one or two aspects of accounting ethics, e.g. corporate governance, sustainability reporting, or the sociology and psychology of fraudulent actions.

The participating member bodies in the IFAC survey prefer the integration approach to the tune of 87% (see Table 4.7, IP 2006:57). If "integration" means a small ethics component in the auditing or law course in which ethics receives about 8 hours per year (IP 2006:53), then it is obviously inadequate. But if integration means that all accounting educators undergo a basic orientation in ethics and adjust their respective curricula to integrate ethical issues as part of their core teaching, then it seems to be a viable option. The gains are obvious: no isolation of ethics as a "separate issue" and high legitimacy amongst staff and students. The potential negative factors – if integration is the only form of ethics education – are fragmentation and inadequate covering of basic ethical knowledge, and little or no dedicated assessment of ethical skills.

This is why a dedicated ethics module seems an attractive option. It is – according to Piper (1993:130) – easy to administer, ensures focus that allows teaching of ethical reasoning, and sends a strong signal to students that ethics is taken seriously. If, however, a compulsory module is in the only form of ethics education, it may have negative consequences: it is seen as "the ethics course" and lacks integration into the rest of the curriculum.

From my own experience in faculty management and the painful processes of curriculum reform, it seems wise to suggest a phased approach.

A compulsory module introduced not later than the fourth semester (second half of second academic year in a three-year degree) is an immediate possibility. This should be implemented through consultation and conscientisation of all accounting staff members in preparation for the next phase, where integration into the rest of the curriculum should commence and be completed in first draft over a period not exceeding three years. Once ethics has "settled" into these two formats, the optional module (as part of the elective list, if any) can be introduced for third- or fourth-year students with a pass mark in the core ethics module as a prerequisite.

The format will obviously determine the staff requirements to offer ethics education. **Who should teach ethics?** There is a strong case to be made that the compulsory module be delivered through team-teaching by a professional ethicist (in the initial phases probably someone from philosophy, religion or theology) in tandem with a respected senior member of the accounting staff. Division of work is fairly simple as it is based on the respective academic competencies, and may shift as staff members acquire confidence in new knowledge areas. (A good social scientist can attain adequate knowledge of corporate governance and professional codes, and accounting staff might find ethical theories equally interesting!).

The integration of ethics into the overall curriculum would – in the end – require all accounting staff members to have a basic understanding of what is taught in the core module, and would require them to link ethical insights to their areas of expertise. The staff needs for an optional module will obviously depend on the level and area of specialisation, and might in some cases require input from different disciplines such as law, taxation, IT or auditing.

What about **teaching methods and teaching aids**? This is an important question, because curriculum content and outcomes should determine delivery modes. If we return for a moment to the triangle sketch under point 2 above, one senses immediately that "teaching about ethics" (the nature of ethics, history, theories, main representatives) may be facilitated through older-style transfer of knowledge. The moment one moves to ethical awareness and decision-making, other modes are required, for example, case studies (real or imaginary), role playing, ethical games and small group discussions. Experiential and workplace learning is best done through individual journals/diaries and project reports.

One of the most useful aspects of the Information Paper is its list of sample programmes (pp. 119-121), the offer of the IFAC Ethics Education Toolkit (p. 121); resources such as a wide array of websites (Appendix 8) from where material can be accessed (either for free or for payment); various decision-making models (Appendix 9) and an excellent bibliography on ethics education in accounting (pp. 176-184). In the South African context the publication of *Ethics for accountants and auditors* (Rossouw et al. 2006) is an important step toward a contextualised approach to ethics.

What are the implications for **assessment**?

We know that students (unfortunately) only take seriously what is formally assessed. This is not the most important motivation behind an assessment policy, though. If we accept that assessment is constructed in such a way that it gives credence to the curriculum outcomes, and if we accept the four broad goals for ethics education as set out above, no one form of assessment would be adequate. Old-style examination questions ("Write a short essay on virtue ethics and its implication for the professional accountant") are to be complemented by decision-making exercises (individual assignments) and group tasks ("Collect business ethics issues from the public media and provide them with the group's informed comment").

An examination situation is also suitable for case study analysis and resolution as long as adequate time is allowed. Journals – based on work or practical experience – might be an interesting reflective component of an overall assessment portfolio. Needless to say, ethics is eventually a must for official qualifying examinations on a par with any other section of the work, and should be made a compulsory component of CPD programmes. (These last two areas fall beyond the scope of this paper).

CONCLUSION

It is clear that the accounting profession stands at the threshold of very important innovations with regard to ethics education. The context requires urgent action at the level of policy and implementation, and the response from IFAC has been decisive.

The debate about the necessity of ethics has been driven by protection of the profession's image, but lacks a focus on the public good and professional vocation. The question of whether ethics can indeed be taught has been answered with reference to moral development theory as well as the overwhelming support of participating member bodies. Although empirical evidence as to the efficacy of ethics interventions has so far yielded mixed results, there is a limited amount of research on accounting students specifically that points to positive conclusions.

The content of ethics teaching, including programme outlines and teaching aids, has been sufficiently addressed in the IES and IP documents. It has been suggested that a three-phase approach to the format of ethics teaching at pre-qualification level be followed, starting off with a dedicated compulsory module. Team teaching is the ideal, as is the involvement of all staff in the growth of an ethical awareness in the overall accounting programme. Assessment should take on various creative forms and should ensure that curriculum outcomes are indeed met in terms of skills, attitudes and values.

As an outsider I am – despite some critical remarks – impressed by the various initiatives. I hope that this very essay is a small contribution toward successful implementation of wider ethics education in the accounting profession.

REFERENCES

Abdolmuhammadi Mohammad J and Nixon, Mark R 1999. Ethics in the public accounting profession. In Frederick, Robert E (ed.): *A companion to business ethics*. Oxford: Blackwell, 164-177.

Armstrong, MB 1993. Ethics and professionalism in accounting education: A sample course. *Journal of Accounting Education*, Vol. 11:77-92.

Bernardi, Richard A 2004. *Issues in Accounting Education*, Vol. 19, No. 1: 145-146.

Bowie, Norman E 1986. Business ethics. In Joseph P DeMarco and Richard M Fox (eds.): *New directions in ethics*. New York: Routledge & Kegan Paul, 158-172.

Bowie, NE (ed.) 2002. *The Blackwell guide to business ethics*. Oxford: Blackwell Publishers.

Bowie, Norman (ed.) 2004. Ethics in the financial services after Sarbanes-Oxley. *Business and Professional Ethics Journal*, Vol. 23, Nos. 1 & 2.

Brundtland, G (ed.) 1987. *Our common future: The world commission on environment and development.* Oxford: Oxford University Press.

Earley, Christine E and Kelly, Patrick T 2004. A note on ethics educational interventions in an undergraduate auditing course: Is there an "Enron Effect"? *Issues in Accounting Education*, Vol. 19, No.1: 53-72.

Gaa, James C and Thorne Linda 2004. An introduction to the special issue on professionalism and ethics in Accounting education, *Issues in Accounting Education* Vol. 19, No.1:1-6.

Gensler, Harry J (ed.) 2004. *Ethics. Contemporary readings.* London: Routledge.

Institute of Directors 2002. *Second King Report on corporate governance for South Africa.* Johannesburg: Institute of Directors.

International Accounting Education Standards 2006. *Approaches to the development and maintenance of professional values, ethics and attitudes in accounting education programs.* (Information Paper). New York: IFAC.

International Federation of Accountants 2003. *International education standards for professional accountants.* New York: IFAC.

Jamal, Karim 2004. After seven decades of regulation, why is the audit profession in such a mess? *Business and Professional Ethics Journal*, Vol. 23, Nos. 1 & 2, 65-92.

MacIntyre, Alisdair 1998. *A short history of ethics.* London: Routledge.

Marquette, Penny R 1996. Ethics, Professional. In Chatfield, Michael and Vangermeersch, Richard (eds.): *The history of accounting. An international encyclopedia.* New York: Garland Publishing, 233-234.

Myddelton, DR 2004. *Unshackling accountants.* London: The Institute of Economic Affairs.

Parker, Michael 1998. Moral development. *Encyclopedia of Applied Ethics,* Volume 3. Amsterdam: Elsevier, 267-273.

Piper, Thomas R; Gentile, Mary C; Parks, Sharon Daloz 1993. *Can ethics be taught? Perspectives, challenges, and approaches at Harvard Business School.* Boston, Massachusetts: Harvard Business School.

PricewaterhouseCoopers 2003. *Educating for the public trust: The PricewaterhouseCoopers position on accounting education.* PWC http://www.pwc.com/images/us/eng/careers/car-inecp/EducatingPublicTrust.pdf.

Rossouw, Deon 2004. *Business Ethics.* Oxford: Oxford University Press.

Rossouw, Deon 2004a. *Developing business ethics as an academic field.* Johannesburg: BEN-Africa.

Rossouw, Deon; Prozesky, Martin; Van Heerden, Bernard & Van Zyl, Mine 2006. *Ethics for accountants and auditors.* Cape Town: OUP.

Thompson A and Strickland P 2003. *Strategic management: Concepts and cases* (13th edition). New York: McGraw-Hill.

Van der Ven, Johannes 1998. *Formation of the moral self.* Grand Rapids: Eerdmans

4.2 TRANSPARENCY AND CORPORATE SOCIAL RESPONSIBILITY

A South African perspective[1]

1. INTRODUCTION

This essay will discuss the link between transparency and corporate social responsibility from a South African perspective. Transparency can be understood as the reliability, relevance, clarity, timelessness and verifiability of information, although it does not entail the disclosure of competitive or sensitive information detrimental to a company's legitimate interests. In terms of business, transparency can therefore be understood as "the ease with which an outsider is able to make a meaningful analysis of a company's actions, its economic fundamentals, and the non-financial aspects pertinent to that business" (Institute of Directors of Southern Africa 2002: 10).

The role of transparency continues to be of great relevance, especially in developing markets. Of the 47 African countries reviewed for Transparency International's 2009 Corruption Perceptions Index (CPI) 31 countries scored less than 3 out of 10 (indicating that corruption is perceived as rampant) and 13 scored between 3 and 5 (indication that these countries' experts and businesspeople perceive corruption as a serious challenge) (Transparency International 2009a: 1). Based on the eight surveys used, South Africa is ranked fifth on the continent and 55th out of the 180 countries surveyed (Transparency International 2009a: 2). Although scoring only 4.7 out of 10, South Africa achieved a higher rating than countries such as Slovakia (4.5), Italy (4.3), Turkey (4.4), Greece (3.8), Romania (3.8), Brazil (3.7), China (3.6), India (3.4), Thailand (3.4), Mexico (3.3), Argentina (2.9) and Indonesia (2.8) (Transparency International 2009b).

Understanding corporate social responsibility is a somewhat more complex endeavour than describing transparency. The traditional view of corporate social responsibility is that entails voluntary philanthropic action done for the public good. According to the traditional view, it is not required by law and is not aimed at maximising profits. Alongside this traditional view, an extended view of corporate social responsibility is developing. It is increasingly being integrated into core business operations and understood as encompassing the economic, social and ecological conduct of a business. In some countries – such as South Africa – certain elements of a business enterprise's conduct in the socially responsible investment environment may even be legally required.

A narrower view of corporate responsibility is that it involves a link between investment decisions and social responsiveness. It is meaningful to note that on this topic an authoritative South African textbook on corporate governance outlines three understandings of socially responsible investment (Wixley & Everingham 2005:130-131). Firstly, from the perspective of investors, socially responsible investment can

---

1 This essay was written in close cooperation with Willem Fourie, currently from the Faculty of Theology at the University of Preotria.

be used as a tool to screen an enterprise to ensure that its (investment) activities are socially responsible. It can also be understood, secondly, as the investments of enterprises themselves in the communities in which they operate. Lastly, it can refer to shareholder influence being used to bring about corporate, social and environmental change – primarily by influencing the company directly.

As the extended understanding of corporate social responsibility is well established in South Africa, the role of transparency will be investigated with this understanding as basis. The first section will investigate the legislative framework to promote and uphold transparency. The second section will outline some important instruments that promote and protect transparency in the corporate sphere. The third section will discuss broad-based black economic empowerment (BBBEE) as an example of the interplay between political and corporate dimensions of corporate social responsibility in South Africa.

2. CREATING A LEGISLATIVE FRAMEWORK FOR CORPORATE SOCIAL RESPONSIBILITY IN SOUTH AFRICA: TRANSPARENCY AS POLITICAL VALUE

Transparency as political value is enshrined in the South African Constitution and protected and promoted by a number of important pieces of legislation.[2]

Already in the Preamble of the country's Constitution it is stated that the Constitution is adopted so as to "[l]ay the foundations for a democratic and *open society* in which government is based on the will of the people and every citizen is equally protected by law" (emphasis added). This is expressly formulated in sharp contrast to the "secretive and unresponsive culture in public and private bodies which often led to an abuse of power and human rights violations" (Preamble, Act 2 of 2000) during the previous political regime. In the Constitution's first chapter the political importance of transparency is further emphasised when the values of "accountability, responsiveness and openness" are identified as primary goals of the South African system of constitutional multi-party democracy. These values are expressed by a number of fundamental rights, notably every South African's right to any information held by the state and any information that is held by another person and is required for the exercise and protection of any rights (Article 32(1)(a-c), Constitution of the Republic of South Africa).

In 2000 transparency was further embedded into the political fibre of South African society when the Promotion of Access to Information Act (Act 2 of 2000) was promulgated in the *Government Gazette* in order to flesh out Article 32(1)(a-c) of the Constitution. This far-reaching Act is aimed at "fostering a culture of transparency and accountability in public and private bodies" and to "actively promote a society in which the people of South Africa have effective access to information to enable

---

2   The relation between the legislative framework and business concerns is, of course, of fundamental importance for transparent business practices. Cf. e.g. the OECD's Principles of Governance on this relationship: "Increasingly, the OECD and its member governments have recognised the synergy between macroeconomic and structural policies in achieving fundamental policy goals. ... Corporate governance is only part of the larger economic context in which firms operate that includes, for example, macroeconomic policies and the degree of competition in product and factor markets" (Organisation for Economic Co-operation and Development 2004: 11-2).

them to more fully exercise and protect all of their rights" (Preamble, Act 2 of 2000). This is done by creating a detailed and practical statutory framework within which five objectives can be reached, namely (a) to give effect to all citizens' constitutional right to information; (b) to consider and apply limitations to these rights that are in accordance with the Constitution; (c) to enact the state's obligation to promote a human rights culture and social justice; (d) to establish procedures to translate Article 32 into practice and – importantly for this chapter – "to promote transparency, accountability and effective governance of all public and private bodies" (Article 9(a-e), Act 2 of 2000). Since its enactment the Promotion of Access to Information Act has proved influential in a number of important court cases and public debates.

The political importance of transparency and its implications for responsible business practices in South Africa is illustrated by the promulgation of another act, also in 2000. On 1 August 2000 the Protected Disclosures Act (Act 26 of 2000) was published in the *Government Gazette* in terms of which employees in both the public and private sectors who disclose corrupt conduct are protected from occupational detriment.

To understand the importance of the Act, one should take note of three basic definitions. In this Act "disclosure" is defined as any disclosure of information regarding the conduct of an employer made by any employee who has reason to believe that the information concerned shows or tends to show (a) a criminal offence, (b) failure to comply with any legal obligation, (c) the miscarriage of justice, (d) that the health or safety of an individual has been or is likely to be endangered, (e) that the environment has been or is likely to be damaged, (f) unfair discrimination (Article 1(i)(a-g), Act 26 of 2000).

"Protected disclosure" is defined as "any disclosure made in good faith by an employee who believes that the information disclosed … [is] substantially true, and who does not make the disclosure for purposes of personal gain, excluding reward payable in terms of any law" (Article 9(1)(a-b), Act 26 of 2000). The occupational detriment from which the Act protects employees who make protected disclosures is very widely defined and includes harassment, intimidation, dismissal, transfer against the employee's will, non-promotion or denial of an appointment, or any way in which an employee is adversely affected (Article 1(vi)(a-i), Act 26 of 2000).

Although not expressly aimed at promoting transparency, the Financial Intelligence Centre Act 38 of 2001 (FICA) is playing a significant role in promoting transparency in both the political and corporate spheres. The Act was promulgated in order to "combat money laundering activities and the financing of terrorist and related activities" (Preamble, Act 38 of 2001). In order to do so, especially financial institutions are required by law to adhere to very high standards of transparency. In terms of the law, no financial institution may "establish a business relationship or conclude a single transaction with a client" if the identity of the client cannot be established and verified (Article 21, Act 38 of 2001) and if record of both the client's identity and the transaction cannot be kept for at least five years (Articles 22 and 23, Act 38 of 2001). In order to combat terrorism and money laundering an authorised representative of the Financial Intelligence Centre, which this Act establishes, has access to these records. Any person with knowledge of "suspicious and unusual transactions" is required by this Act to report these transactions to the Centre – even when only "reasonably suspecting" such transactions (Article 29, Act 38 of 2001). The subsequent Financial Intelligence Centre Amendment Act (Act 11 of 2008) instituted even clearer and even stricter measures for inspecting the recordkeeping systems of financial and related institutions.

3. FOSTERING SOCIALLY RESPONSIBLE INVESTMENT AND RESPONSIBLE CORPORATE GOVERNANCE: TRANSPARENCY AS CORPORATE VALUE

In the South African corporate sphere, the value of transparency is closely connected with socially responsibility and corporate governance, and in both these areas practices and measures are continuously developed, implemented and reviewed.[3] The Socially Responsible Investment Index (SRI Index) of the Johannesburg Stock Exchange (JSE) and the third King Report on Corporate Governance (King III) serve as two of the most influential expressions of these practices and measures.

The JSE launched its SRI Index in 2004 in order to reach at least four key objectives, namely to identify companies that integrate the principles of good governance in their business practices, to provide a tool for a holistic assessment of companies based on local realities and international standards, to enable responsible investment by providing non-financial risk variables and to contribute to responsible business practices in South Africa (JSE & EIRIS 2007: 2).

To achieve these objectives the index is structured in terms of three themes as criteria, namely Environment, Society and Governance.[4] To be included in the

---

3   Many analyses of the state of these practices and measures in South Africa have been undertaken. Two reports by EIRIS illustrate the state of socially responsible investment and corporate governance in South Africa well. In its analysis of responsible investment in emerging markets South Africa is identified (after Brazil) as "[a] country leading the way towards improved ESG [environmental, social, governance] disclosure" and as "the [emerging market] making the most positive steps towards ESG disclosure" (EIRIS 2009b: 13). These results correspond with those of other studies that show that South Africa has "a strong background of domestic responsible investment as well as important guidelines for disclosure" (EIRIS 2009b: 13). In a report investigating ESG practices in developing markets in more detail it was found that "South Africa appears to be ahead of other emerging markets in disclosing corporate responsibility activities which seems to reflect the impact of ... codes ... [requiring] the annual use of the Global Reporting Initiative (GRI) guidelines for disclosing social and environmental performance for companies listed on the Johannesburg Stock Exchange (JSE) as well as addressing core corporate governance issues" (GRI 2009a: 31).

4   The broad themes for the Environment category are "working to reduce and control [the company's] direct negative environmental impacts; promoting awareness of [the company's] significant direct and indirect impacts; working to use natural resources in a sustainable manner; and committing to risk reduction, reporting and auditing". For the Society category the themes are the following: "Treating all stakeholders with dignity, fairness and respect, recognising their rights to life and security and free association, and their rights to freedom from discrimination; actively promoting the development and empowerment of [the company's] employees and the community; ensuring that core labour standards are met and good employee relations maintained; and working to promote the health and safety of [the company's] employees". For the Governance category the broad themes are to "uphold and support good corporate governance practices as the foundation for [the company's] business policies and practices, through strategies to achieve and maintain internationally recognised corporate governance

index companies are assessed by means of stringent industry-specific criteria relating to each of these categories. Although the criteria are industry-specific, some overarching themes are covered in each of these categories. Transparent practices and reporting are fundamental to each of these themes (JSE & EIRIS 2007: 4-5). On a first level the policy and strategies of the company are measured. On a second level the management systems that implement the company's policies and strategies are measured, as well as the way in which the company monitors its own performance in this regard. On a last level the way in which a company reports on its own policies and strategies, the related management systems and their implementation are reported. Indeed, the basic principle is "to provide stakeholders with access to information about aspects of the company's business activities within a reasonable time period, ensuring that relevant information is available on a reasonably regular basis" (JSE & EIRIS 2007: 5).

Since its inception the SRI Index has grown to become one the JSE's most prestigious products, with 34 of its top 40 companies on the Index in 2009 (JSE 2009). The Index also continues to conform to international best practices through its alignment to the FTSE4Good Index Series (JSE & EIRIS 2007: 2) and integrates this Series' focus on continuing to evolve selection criteria "to reflect changes in globally accepted corporate responsibility standards and codes of conduct" (FTSE 2006: 1).

The King Reports on Corporate Governance in South Africa, and in particular the third report (which comes into effect in March 2010 and is referred to as King III from here on) is a second significant expression of the importance of transparency in South Africa's corporate sphere. The King Committee on Corporate Governance in South Africa was formed by the Institute of Directors of Southern Africa in 1992 to investigate the role of boards of directors and was chaired by former judge Mervin E. King. This Committee wrote the first King Report in 1994 and it set an internationally recognised industry standard for comprehensive board practice.

The Reports were expressly written to be in line with global trends, such as those set by the United Nations' Global Compact, the Global Reporting Initiative's G3 guidelines and the OECD's Principles of Corporate Governance, whilst at the same time augmenting these trends by addressing South African realities (Institute of Directors of Southern Africa 2009: 9-10). King III specifically identifies "social transformation" and "redress from apartheid" as South African realities that should be integrated into South African codes of governance (Institute of Directors of Southern Africa 2009: 12).

Distinct from, for example, the United States of America's Sarbanes-Oxley Act and the statutory framework of "comply or else", King III adopts an "apply or explain" approach (Institute of Directors of Southern Africa 2009: 6). Rather than forcing a diverse array of enterprises to comply with the same rules, King III chooses an approach also applied in the 56 countries of the Commonwealth and the 27 countries

---

standards and implementing sound ethical practices; work towards long-term growth and sustainability by assessing and managing the risks to sustaining [the company's] business while adapting to changing demands, trends and macro-economic driving forces; identify and manage the broader impact of the company within the company's sphere of influence or where the company operates from a social, environmental, ethical and economic perspective, directly as well as indirectly" (JSE & EIRIS 2007: 4).

of the European Union (Institute of Directors of Southern Africa 2009: 5). King III explains this approach as follows:

> It is the legal duty of directors to act in the best interests of the company. In following the "apply or explain" approach, the board of directors, in its collective decision-making, could conclude that to follow a recommendation would not, in the particular circumstances, be in the best interests of the company. The board could decide to apply the recommendation differently or apply another practice and still achieve the objective of the overarching corporate governance principles of fairness, accountability, responsibility and transparency. Explaining how the principles and recommendations were applied, or if not applied, the reasons, results in compliance. *In reality, the ultimate compliance officer is not the company's compliance officer or a bureaucrat ensuring compliance with statutory provisions, but the stakeholders.* (Institute of Directors of Southern Africa 2009: 6, emphasis added).

It is important to note that there is a reciprocal relationship between the King Reports and the related statutory environment. Although the King Reports opt for the "apply or explain" approach, they have led to practices that were later on taken up in law, whilst at the same time being significantly influenced by changes in the law. King II influenced subsequent laws relating to business, whereas the Companies' Act of 2008 again played a role in the writing of King III (Institute of Directors of Southern Africa 2009: 4).

Transparency is of central importance to the corporate governance framework suggested in King III. Its importance is especially clear when one considers the three premises on which the Report is based. The Report's first premise is that "[g]ood governance is essentially about effective leadership" and that the board has the responsibility the enact the ethical values of fairness, accountability, responsibility and transparency in its governance (Institute of Directors of Southern Africa 2009: 9). Chapter 1 of the Report is consequently devoted to the type of "ethical leadership" required by the Board and the ways its ethical foundation should be made transparent by practising and disclosing it (Institute of Directors of Southern Africa 2009: 16-22, esp. 22).

The second premise on which the Report is based is that "[s]ustainability is the primary moral and economic imperative of the 21st century" (Institute of Directors of Southern Africa 2009: 9).[5] Throughout the Report the importance of responsible business practices and transparent integrated reporting are identified as key elements in reaching the goal of sustainability. The whole of Chapter 9, for example, is devoted to describing the framework for "integrated reporting and disclosure",

---

5   The central importance of sustainability and transparency is a central theme in virtually all recent corporate governance codes. Cf. e.g. the Global Reporting Initiative's Preface: "The urgency and magnitude of the risks and threats to our collective sustainability, alongside increasing choice will make transparency about economic, environmental, and social impacts a fundamental component in effective stakeholder relations, investment decisions, and other market relations. ... Transparency about the sustainability of organisational activities is of interest to a diverse range of stakeholders ..." (GRI 2006: 2).

with transparency and accountability as its basic values (Institute of Directors of Southern Africa 2009: 86). The Report unambiguously states:

> Integrated reporting should be focused on substance over form and should disclose information that is complete, timely, relevant, accurate, honest and accessible and comparable with past performance of the company. It should also contain forward-looking information (Institute of Directors of Southern Africa 2009: 86).

It then continues:

> Reporting should be integrated across all areas of performance, reflecting the choices made in the strategic decisions adopted by the board, and should include reporting in the triple context of economic, social and environmental issues. ... Companies should recognise that the principle of transparency in reporting sustainability (commonly but incorrectly referred to as "non-financial") information is a critical element of effective reporting. The key consideration is whether the information provided has allowed stakeholders to understand the key issues affecting the company as well as the effect the company's operation has had on the economic, social and environmental wellbeing of the community, both positive and negative (Institute of Directors of Southern Africa 2009: 87).

The third premise on which the Report is based is that "[c]orporate citizenship is central to the business enterprise" (Institute of Directors of Southern Africa 2009: 9). The King Committee chooses to work with the "inclusive stakeholder approach" instead of the "enlightened shareholder approach" (Institute of Directors of Southern Africa 2009: 9).[6] This means that the legitimate interests and expectations of stakeholders do not simply have instrumental value in considering the interests of shareholders, but that these legitimate interests and expectations influence the (long-term) wellbeing of the company directly and should therefore be taken seriously (Institute of Directors of Southern Africa 2009: 11).

The Report therefore speaks of "the new constitution of commerce" and motivates its stance as follows:

> The company is integral to society, particularly as a creator of wealth and employment. In the world today, companies have the greatest pools of human and monetary capital. These are applied enterprisingly in the expectation of a return greater than a risk-free investment. ... Although the board is accountable to the company itself, the board should not

---

[6] This approach is also evident, for example, in the UN's Global Compact. In the GC's 2007 Annual Review this perspective is formulated as follows: "The involvement of civil society, labour, government, the United Nations and academia serves many important purposes, as each group brings different strengths and focus to the corporate citizenship agenda. In many cases, these stakeholders can provide expertise on issues, hold businesses accountable for their commitments and deficiencies, offer incentives and rewards for responsible actions, provide knowledge that facilitates implementation, and serve as excellent partners on a variety of issues, such as education, health, infrastructure and water" (United Nations Global Compact 2007: 13).

ignore the legitimate interests and expectations of its stakeholders. In the board's decision-making process, the inclusive approach to governance … dictates that the board should take account of the legitimate interests and expectations of the company's stakeholders in making decisions in the best interests of the company (Institute of Directors of Southern Africa 2009: 8).

The section on governing stakeholder relationships identifies the transparent and effective communication with all stakeholders as essential in ascertaining who these groups are in order to understand the interests and expectations they represent; it also identifies those whose interests and expectations may be regarded as legitimate, and stresses the need for building and maintaining their trust and confidence (Institute of Directors of Southern Africa 2009: 79-85).

4. COORDINATING THE POLITICAL AND THE CORPORATE: THE EXAMPLE OF BROAD-BASED BLACK ECONOMIC EMPOWERMENT

The sections above illustrated the extended understanding of corporate social responsibility current in South Africa by means of examining the role of transparency in the broader socially responsible investment environment. Of fundamental importance to this extended understanding of corporate social responsibility in South Africa is the reciprocal relationship between the political and corporate spheres. One of the clearest examples of this coordination between the political and corporate, which is also intimately connected the country's history, is the policy of broad-based black economic empowerment (BBBEE).

The policy of BBBEE is a unique feature of corporate social responsibility in South Africa and illustrates how it can be extended to be an ethical, business and legislative imperative. After the country's first fully democratic election in 1994 there was consensus amongst the most important role-players in the different spheres of South African society that a process of restorative justice should be initiated in order to include the majority of the country's inhabitants into the mainstream economy. This required from business a comprehensive understanding of its role in society.

In order to initiate and guide this process of restorative justice in the corporate sector, a number of pieces of legislation were promulgated, of which the important Employment Equity Act and Skills Development Act came into affect already in 1998. The significant Broad-Based Black Empowerment Act came into effect in 2003 and is accompanied by a Code of Good Practice from the Department of Trade and Industry, which guides businesses in their implementation of legislation and in voluntarily deepening their corporate citizenship. The core aim of the Act is to provide state intervention to address the systematic exclusion of black South Africans from participating fully in the economy. This Act consists of industry-specific charters and specific targets aimed at broadening black participation in South Africa's economic sphere.

In order to aid businesses in achieving the prescribed targets and to foster good practices, the Act is linked to a "scorecard" to determine the "empowerment status" of any company operating in South Africa. This scorecard is based on the basic elements of BBBEE, namely the participation of black South Africans in terms of ownership, their representation on management level, they way that employment equity is practiced, the company's contribution to and participation in skills development (especially by means of learnerships), preferential procurement, enterprise development (how the business enterprise achieves sustainable growth in order to create more employment) and how it contributes towards socio-economic development, especially by targeting disadvantaged areas.

These Acts and related material mean that business enterprises are required by law to extend their social responsibility far beyond the confines of voluntary philanthropic actions. Indeed, BBBEE illustrates the far-reaching influence business people can exert in restoring justice in South Africa and in this way ensuring the long-term stability of both the country and their own interests.

5. CONCLUSION

This essay started with a definition of transparency and an extended view of corporate social responsibility. Transparency as a political value was then explained with reference to the South African Constitution and core pieces of legislation to ensure the embodiment of the constitutional ideals in the actual practices of the public and private sectors.

It was then explained that the Johannesburg Securities Exchange promotes the link between transparency and corporate responsibility through its SRI Index. The important contribution of the Third King report on transparency as corporate value was then set out in the light of the fact that these guidelines are effective as from 1 March 2010 and influence both the public and private sectors, as well as broader civil society structures.

The short discussion of black economic empowerment is an interesting illustration of how transparency and social responsibility intersect: companies governed by this act are subject to public scrutiny via their scorecards (transparency) and are compelled by legislation to contribute to redressing the injustices of the past and ensuring the integration of the majority of the population into the mainstream economy.

South Africa is indeed an interesting case study of global policies that address issues of transparency and corporate responsibility.

BIBLIOGRAPHY

EIRIS (Ethical Investment Research and Information Service) 2009a. *A Review of ESG Practices in Large Emerging Market Companies.* London: EIRIS.

EIRIS (Ethical Investment Research and Information Service) 2009b. *Emerging Markets Investor Survey Report. An Analysis of Responsible Investment in Emerging Markets,* London: EIRIS.

FTSE (Financial Times Stock Exchange) 2006. *FTSE4Good Index Series Inclusion Criteria,* London: FTSE.

GRI (Global Reporting Initiative) 2006. *Sustainability Reporting Guidelines,* Amsterdam: GRI.

Institute of Directors in Southern Africa 2009. *Third King Report on Corporate Governance in South Africa,* Johannesburg: IOD.

Institute of Directors in Southern Africa 2002. *Second King Report on Corporate Governance in South Africa*, Johannesburg: IOD.

JSE & EIRIS (Johannesburg Stock Exchange and Ethical Investment Research and Information Service) 2007 *Johannesburg Stock Exchange SRI Index. Background and Selection Criteria*, Johannesburg: Johannesburg Stock Exchange.

JSE (Johannesburg Stock Exchange) 2009. 2009 Results. http://www.jse.co.za/About-Us/SRI/2009Results.aspx (Accessed 5.2.2010)

Organisation for Economic Co-operation and Development 2004. *OECD Principles of Corporate Governance*, Paris: OECD.

South Africa 1996. *Constitution of the Republic of South Africa*. Preamble, Pretoria: Government Printer.

South Africa 1998. *Employment Equity Act* (Act 55 of 1998), Cape Town: Government Printer.

South Africa 1998. *Skills Development Act* (Act 97 of 1998), Cape Town: Government Printer.

South Africa 2000. *Promotion of Access to Information Act* (Act 2 of 2000), Cape Town: Government Printer.

South Africa 2000. *Protected Disclosures Act* (Act 26 of 2000), Cape Town: Government Printer.

South Africa 2001. *Financial Intelligence Centre Act* (Act 38 of 2001), Cape Town: Government Printer.

South Africa 2003. *Broad-Based Black Economic Empowerment Act* (Act 53 of 2003), Cape Town: Government Printer.

South Africa 2008. *Financial Intelligence Centre Amendment Act* (Act 11 of 2008), Cape Town: Government Printer.

The Department of Trade and Industry 2005. *Codes of Good Practice for Broad-Based Black Economic Empowerment*. Second Phase, Pretoria: Government Printer.

Transparency International 2009a. *Corruption Perceptions Index 2009*. Regional Highlights: Sub-Saharan Africa. http://www.transparency.org/policy_research/surveys_indices/cpi/2009/regional_highlights (Accessed 9.2.2010)

Transparency International 2009b. CPI 2009 Table http://www.transparency.org/policy_research/surveys_indices/cpi/2009/cpi_2009_table (Accessed 9.2.2010)

United Nations Global Compact 2007. *UN Global Compact Annual Review*. 2007 Leaders' Summit, Geneva: UN.

Wixley, T & Everingham, G 2005. *Corporate Governance*, 2nd ed., Cape Town: UCT Press.

4.3 FAIR GLOBAL TRADE

A perspective from Africa

In this essay section one (the introduction) consists of (1.1) a brief statement on the limitations of the exposition below, followed by (1.2) a short explanation of what is meant by "Africa", the African Union and the urgent socio-economic development needs of the continent.

Section two focuses on the historical background to Africa's current position in the global economy with reference to (2.1) the slave trade; (2.2) colonialism and post-colonial misrule; and (2.3) the shaping of the monetary system within which current trade negotiations occur.

The third section (3) is an outline of the core expectations that Africa has of the WTO and the current "Development Round" of trade negotiations, followed by section 4, a discussion of "special and differential treatment", and section 5, consisting of concluding remarks on the value of *ubuntu* for life in a global village.

1. INTRODUCTION

I consider it a great honour to be part of the global panel[1] on fair trade and thank my colleagues for their constructive comments and co-operation. I am proud to be an African and wish to present the view of my continent in an open and objective way.

1.1 Personal and hermeneutical limitation

My academic background was shaped by the disciplines of philosophy and Christian theology, and I have only recently ventured into exploring the relationship between ethics, on the one hand, and economics and business, on the other. My knowledge of economics and the financial world is therefore extremely limited and this restricts my ability to make informed judgments on technical data, or intra-disciplinary arguments and counter-arguments. However, issues related to fair global trade require an open inter-disciplinary approach such as the one attempted in this essay. A possible weakness in this chapter is a lack of depth and specific detail in certain instances. However, the strengths are – hopefully – the breadth of scope and the presentation of new questions that extend beyond the boundaries of the traditional disciplines that usually engage in any consideration of global economics.

Debates concerning fair global trade and analyses of globalisation are notoriously emotive.[2] There are ideological positions over a wide spectrum and data (both historical and current) are interpreted differently according to the economic

---

1 Paper presented as part of an international panel discussion during the Business Ethics Network of Africa conference in Cape Town, 2008.
2 No wonder books by Joseph Stiglitz (2002, 2006) and Jagdish Bhagwati (2004) on globalisation have become international bestsellers! There is a growing mountain of literature on the subject from all different perspectives. See the excellent overview of contrasting views by Held and colleagues (1999).

or social development assumptions of the proponents of a particular view, for example, the neoliberal, structuralist, "left", "right" or Marxist viewpoints. Perhaps a debate about assumptions and presuppositions would aid the hermeneutics of dialogue. Unfortunately, this essay does not have room for an extensive debate on historiography, the benefits or not of the free market, and the contradictory impacts of globalisation. At certain points in the chapter convictions will merely be stated without the requisite ground-work argumentation.

1.2 The complex notion of "Africa" and its dire socio-economic development needs

If one wishes to bring historical and contemporary perspectives into the debate on fair global trade, one is struck by the complexities of what we call "Africa". There is no single history for Africa, only a multitude of regional histories. "Sub-Saharan Africa" is mostly used as a geographical demarcation[3] of the "southern" half of the continent, but even in this region the histories of slavery, colonialism, post-colonial politics and current socio-economic development are widely divergent, in most cases defying any unifying terms. Therefore, for the purposes of an overview such as this, we have to accept generalisations beyond what would make serious historians, economists or political scientists feel comfortable. There are always exceptions to whatever claims are made in the name of "Africa".

This essay is not an attempt to speak "on behalf of" Africa. This I cannot do, as I have neither the necessary knowledge nor the mandate to do so. What is presented here, though, is a perspective on fair trade and related issues from Africa, based on the work of the African Union, and developed through my own views and auxiliary literature.

The African Union (AU) was established as an inter-governmental organisation in July 2001 as an amalgamation of the former African Economic Community (AEC) and the Organisation of African Unity (OAU). Its headquarters are in Addis Ababa, Ethiopia, where the African Union Commission (AUC) co-ordinates the work on behalf of the 53 member states. The AU has ambitious goals to achieve greater unity among African countries through the creation of a free trade area, a central African bank, a common currency and the creation of a single customs union. The AU aims "to promote and defend common African positions on issues of interest to the continent and its peoples" (www.african-union.org). The main sources for this chapter are the *Strategic Plan of the African Union Commission* (3 volumes, cited as AUC [Vol. No.] 2004) and the *Economic Report on Africa 2007: Accelerating Africa's Development through Diversification (ERA)* drafted by the Economic Commission for Africa.

Africa is in serious need of socio-economic development, but the continent is currently under threat of marginalisation in an increasingly globalised economy. Unlike Asia and Latin America, which have succeeded in taking advantage of the global economy, Africa has failed to become an important member of the international economic community. The consequences are a cause for deep concern

---

3   The African Union insists that one of Africa's greatest challenges is precisely to overcome divisions based on so many differences, for example, culture, language, religion, economic status and political systems (AUC 3 2004:4-22).

and the source of a general Afro-pessimism within and beyond Africa itself. Here is some basic information.[4]

- Africa's population of 832 million represents 13% of the world population, but Africa accounts for only 1% of foreign direct investment, and about 2% of world trade.[5]

- Of the 48 least developed countries in the world, 35 are in Africa and African countries are mainly in the lowest 20% of the UN Human Development Index.

- Over 40% of the sub-Saharan population live below the international threshold of $1 a day.

- Nearly 80% of the continent's labour force "remains mired in manual and archaic agricultural practices" (AUC 1 2004:6) compounded by hostile climatic conditions and persistent animal diseases that threaten food security. Per capita food production fell in 31 of the 53 African countries in the period 2000-2005.

- Diseases such as malaria and AIDS (a deadly combination in many cases) are taking their daily toll on life expectancy (2 million AIDS deaths in 2005) and the economy: 60% of HIV-positive people worldwide live in Africa and on average adult HIV prevalence is 6.1% of the population (UNAIDS 2006).

- Africa's isolation, marginalisation and even exclusion (Hoogvelt 2002) is increasing as a result of the continued widening of the digital divide (AUC 1 2004:13) with huge backlogs regarding intra-African communication and the inability to "log into" the digital global economy.

This list can be extended, but is adequate to highlight the dire socio-economic development needs of Africa and the danger of its remaining a marginalised continent. From an African perspective, a fair global trade regime must contribute to the continent's development and enhance Africa's ability to participate in the processes of global decision-making, overcoming its marginalised position and weak negotiating power, and ensuring that benefits accruing from global economic interaction are sustainable.

2. HISTORICAL BACKGROUND TO THE CURRENT DEBATES ABOUT FAIR GLOBAL TRADE

As Africans we argue that our current marginal position must be viewed from a historical perspective. According to paleo-anthropological studies, Africa is the motherland of *Homo sapiens*. It was a major force in world affairs over the centuries with its various empires and kingdoms from long before the Christian era up to the fifteenth century (AUC 1 2004:4-5). An understanding of the marginalisation and exploitation of Africa and Africans between the fifteenth century and the present time illustrates the reason for the asymmetrical trade situation in which Africa finds

---

4 This information is mostly available in AUC 1 2004:9ff.
5 If one accepts that a very high percentage of international trade is "virtual" (shares, futures), Africa's share of real commodity trading – minerals and, increasingly, oil – would be considerably higher. The lack of participation in all forms of trade is a sign of Africa's marginalisation as it points to weak financial institutions and a lack of connectivity in a widening digital divide.

itself today. This disproportionate economic and technological situation arose over many centuries and is the cumulative result of at least three factors: 1) the Atlantic slave trade (1440-1870); 2) the colonisation of Africa (1884-1961) and post-colonial misrule in Africa (1950-present day); and 3) the creation of a global monetary system (1878-1990).

Hundreds of books have been written on each of these topics. For the purpose of this chapter I will spend more time on the emerging monetary system (as this is the current context in which the fair trade debates occur) and offer only very brief comments on the other two factors.

An important prior observation is necessary: this chapter does not attempt to apportion "blame" for Africa's current weak position in international trade. The aim of the historical material is to provide a context in which the current situation may be interpreted. This will provide credence to the moral and material claims made by Africa and other developing regions, in order to support such concepts as "special and differential treatment" (see below) with a view to establishing a new trade order for the global economy. History is not to be used as a cheap tool for moral propaganda. However, there is mounting empirical evidence to support the argument that there is an implicit causal link between history and the current economic performance of Africa, and indeed this could be credibly demonstrated.[6]

2.1 The slave trade[7]

The Atlantic slave trade developed over a period of just more than 400 years (1440-1870). There is no scholarly consensus as to the origin, extent and effects of the slave trade on Africa and slave-importing nations. A middle position would probably agree on the encapsulation of the African slave trade outlined below.

Slave trading was an integral part of African societies long before the actual Atlantic slave trade started. In the absence of clear rights to property, slaves (cheap labour) were an important means of production and slaves were taken from African tribes themselves in the normal course of inter-tribal conflicts.[8] However, it must be stated, that the rising demand for slave labour in the Americas led to an enormous expansion of intra-African trade in human resources , with competitive co-operation amongst European slave merchants and the African elite. Only in rare cases were slave raids undertaken by Europeans, which normally occurred during the course of war on the African continent.[9] However, this does not imply that Europeans played a passive role, as they entered into agreements with their African counterparts to ravage the lives and social structures of ordinary Africans.

---

6 For an empirical argument, see Nathan Nunn (2007) and his many references to literature from development economists defending the link between Africa's current state of underdevelopment and historical legacies.
7 For this section I rely on Hugh Thomas (1997). *The slave trade. The history of the Atlantic slave trade 1440-1870* and John Thornton (1998) *Africa and Africans in the making of the Atlantic world, 1400-1800*.
8 See Thornton's persuasive argument on the link between slavery and African social structures (1998:72-97).
9 See Thornton's discussion of early slave raids in Angola by the Portuguese army (1998:115), as well as his sober conclusions on the link between European war-making abilities and enslavement (1998:116ff).

The outcomes for Africa were mixed. On the one hand, the barter trade in goods such as iron, textiles and liquor, and the opportunity to access more advanced arms brought about many positive economic effects, including a diversification of the local economies. On the other hand, there were devastating demographic[10] and social impacts on African societies that were built primarily on kinship ties and patriarchy. The increasing power of African rulers as a result of the slave trade led to them selling even more people into slavery, thus aggravating and perpetuating the social crisis.

The effects on the Americas and Europe were more uniformly positive. Africa provided a market for goods produced and was a source of labour that made possible the agricultural revolution in what is now known as Latin America and parts of North America (then under European colonial rule). Contrary to Eric Williams's argument,[11] it is not feasible to claim that there was a linear causal relationship between the slave trade and the subsequent emergence of industrialisation. However, there is no doubt that industries such as ship-building, marine insurance and rope-making were stimulated by the slave trade and that the capital acquired from trading humans and agricultural products produced by (virtually free!) slave labour made a variety of industrial projects possible (Thomas 1997:795).

The thesis by Walter Rodney that the Atlantic slave trade was a first step towards the under-development of Africa is no longer supported by mainstream academics. However, one has to state clearly that between 10 and 13 million slaves were exported from Africa[12] and this played an indispensable role in the economic and cultural[13] development of Europe and the Americas. In fact, the rapid progress in agriculture in these regions would have been very difficult – if not impossible – without enslaved African human capital.

2.2 Colonialism[14] and post-colonial Africa

The abolition of the slave trade eventually led to a markedly different economic and political relationship between Africa and Europe. What slowly emerged was

---

10 The AUC refers to this as a "demographic haemorrhage occasioned by the paroxysm of the slave trade" (AUC 1 2004:5).
11 Williams was the prime minister of Trinidad and wrote the controversial book *Capitalism and slavery* (1944) in which he argues for a link between slavery and industrialisation.
12 See the estimated statistics of the slave trade as cited by Thomas (1997:805-806) in terms of carrier countries (Portugal 4.6 m; Britain 2.6 m); destinations (Brazil 4 m); origins (Congo/Angola 3 m) and type of labour (sugar plantations 5 m).
13 See Thornton's very interesting chapters (5-9) on the impact of slaves on the cultures of the so-called New World and how reciprocal transformations occurred.
14 For this section I rely heavily on J.D. Fage (1988), *A history of Africa*. He commences his study with early African societies (part 1), the impact of Islam (part 2) and, more importantly for this chapter, he discusses European expansion and colonial power in parts 3 and 4. The well-known book by Thomas Pakenham (1991), *The scramble for Africa* reads like a novel and focuses more closely on the colonial period and actual territorial invasions of Africa between 1870 and 1906. Each region is discussed in detail and makes clear how complex the process of colonisation was. A more journalistic book with a fairly critical view of Africa is Robert Guest's (2004), *The Shackled Continent*. He starts off by arguing that Africa's basic problem is not its past, but its lack of leadership in the post-colonial period (see pp. 12, 23).

that Europe no longer needed to control human resources, but rather that it needed economic and political control over actual African territories. This was necessary to secure trade in goods such as gold, ivory, timber and palm oil, and the drive for such control was also influenced by the competitive intra-European rivalries over the period 1870-1945.

Trade in pre-colonial times was essentially co-determined by Africans and their European counterparts, when Africans (although mostly rulers and the trading elite) had a direct influence on events. However, we now enter a phase where asymmetrical power relations are playing themselves out on the African continent. Commenting on the nineteenth century, Fage observed: "In any clash between European and African interests or beliefs, Europe now possessed both the material means – steam power, firepower, medical power – to impose its will upon Africa, and the moral strength – the certainty that European civilisation would prevail, and also that it was in the interest of the African peoples to do so" (Fage 1988:333; see also p. 352).

Starting in West Africa and spreading over into South, East and North Africa, the major European countries increased their administrative, economic and eventually military-political control over Africa. By 1914 Africa – with rare exceptions in cases such as Liberia – was under foreign control[15] (see map in Fage 1998:402), and lost the ability to compete equally in the commercial exploitation of its own natural resources.

Both the process leading up to, and the "reasons" for, colonisation are too complex when examined over various regions to summarise in one sentence.[16] Colonisation occurred in phases and whereas the initial phases of partial control were motivated by factors as diverse as securing the abolition of the slave trade and expanding commercial trade in products such as palm oil, the later phases were more directly linked to European political events (the two World Wars and the depression of the 1930s). As Europe's industrialisation reached its fulfilment, greater emphasis was placed on the direct economic benefits that the colonies could provide in the form of raw materials (rubber, iron ore) and precious goods such as oil, gold and diamonds.

Not all the colonies brought immediate profit and wealth to the colonisers and the idea that colonies ought to be invested in only emerged much later in the colonisation process. The colonies were considered to be indispensable political building blocks in the intra-European conflicts among countries such as Britain, France, Belgium, Italy, Germany and Spain (see Pakenham 1991:xxii). The proverbial "scramble for Africa"[17] was driven by a powerful combination of economic and political forces, and was based on the emerging assumption that European civilisation was superior to Africa's and that the latter needed to develop towards a societal model based

---

15   Fage remarked that "Europe and the world had accepted by 1902 that the whole of Africa was the property of one or other of the European colonial powers" (1988:391).
16   See Pakenham's (1991) fairly detailed accounts of the various regions, starting with King Leopold II of Belgium's dealings with the Congo.
17   *The scramble for Africa* is – as indicated above – the title of the magnificent account of colonisation by Thomas Pakenham (1991), but this expression probably originated as early as 1884.

upon European religion and values.[18] The first comprehensive development plans for the socio-economic upliftment of Africa occurred only after the Second World War (Fage 1988:422-423).

The rapid de-colonisation of Africa started in the late 1940s and occurred *inter alia* as a result of the rising tide of nationalist liberation movements, political instability and the acceptance of the Universal Declaration of Human Rights by the newly established United Nations. Post-colonial Africa was ill prepared by its colonial and cultural histories to accept responsibility for its own affairs. A number of factors contributed to a somewhat sombre picture of Africa after independence. Colonial powers neglected to invest in general education and in training in political-administrative rule. Power transitions were poorly managed and the new rulers devised economic policies that could not be sustained and which lead to indebtedness. Dictatorships emerged because of weak civil societal structures, and corruption and misrule became widespread. Tribal wars escalated and multi-party democracies proved to be not sustainable because of inadequate levels of preparation for governments of this nature.

There is just no way in which we as Africans can escape the failures of leadership in many parts of post-colonial Africa and which have contributed to a general Afro-pessimism. The AUC mentions slavery and imperialism only in passing. It notes that we should not forget, but "we must learn to put things behind us" and focus on Africa's own responsibilities (AUC 1 2004:7). The self-judgment is fierce and candid: "Distrust of constituted authority, corruption and impunity, coupled with human rights abuses have kept Africa in a situation of conflict, thereby undermining all initiatives towards sustainable development" (AUC 1 2004:14). Coupled to this is the deep and enduring socio-psychological impact of a colonised self-perception and a mindset that leads to cultural diffidence and a notion that "foreign" must be "better".

Although Africa eventually regained her political independence, an important factor – crucial to the overall argument of this chapter – must be kept in mind. Between 1935 and 1950 there were dramatic increases in foreign trade in areas such as the Belgian Congo, French West Africa, Uganda and Northern Rhodesia (see Table 5 in Fage 1988:423), and by the mid-1950s "African colonies were participating in the world economy as never before" (Fage 1988:423). The question then arises: How was this world economy in which Africa was participating structured? The answer to this important question lies in the monetary system that emerged from approximately 1870 to the present day.

---

18   The link between Christian mission and colonial power is an ambiguous one. Pakenham states unequivocally that the scramble for Africa was led by "the empire-building alliance of God and Mammon" (1991:673), introduced as "Christianity, commerce and civilization" by British explorer, David Livingstone. For us in Africa, a fourth "c" is added: conquest.

2.3 The evolution of the contemporary monetary and trade regime

The growing economic integration of the world[19] implies that decisions taken by one actor in the economic sphere affect other actors much more directly and intensely than ever before in history. This necessitates forms of co-operation to ensure orderly trade, generally accepted rules and regulations for the stabilisation of the various monetary systems *inter alia* through the "standardising" of exchange rates.

Economic historians[20] generally agree that three such attempts at "standardised monetarisation" (SM) developed between 1870 to our present time: the gold standard, the Bretton Woods system, and the current emerging system of free capital flow that is subject to negotiated trade rules.

The gold standard (GS), formalised in 1878, remained in force until the advent of the First World War.[21] In simple terms, the monetarisation at work here was to link the value of major currencies to a fixed price of gold, setting up a system of regulated exchange rates. The initial key currency areas committed themselves to a free flow of gold and to converting national currencies at a fixed rate into gold, when requested to do so.[22] This created a system of standardised monetarisation, facilitating international transactions and protecting participants against currency volatility.[23]

However, the collapse of the GS did not remove the need for international monetary cooperation. Already during the Second World War negotiations commenced that eventually led to a monetary agreement amongst the forty-four nations at a conference in Bretton Woods, New Hampshire, July 1944. This became known as the Bretton Woods System (BWS) and entailed the declaration of fixed exchange rate parities by a substantial group of countries (Held 1999:199-201).

In contrast to the GS, the BWS was a managed multilateral system that left individual countries with considerable autonomy to pursue national economic goals, whilst they subjected their exchange rates and international trade practices to international agreements. The BWS consisted of two important institutions: the International Monetary Fund (IMF) focused on monetary cooperation and an orderly exchange rate system, whereas the World Bank (WB) financed economic reconstruction and development (Isard 2005:27-29; 69-118).

---

19   Madison (2001) shows how this integration has grown by indicating that for the world as a whole the ratio of merchandise exports to GDP rose from 5.5% in 1950 to 17.2% in 1995.
20   I am not an expert in economics or monetary policy and for this section rely heavily on the exposition by Peter Isard (2005), the author of *Exchange rate economics* (1995), who was for many years a senior adviser at the IMF.
21   There was still fractional support for the GS up until 1933 – see Isard (2005:15, footnote 5).
22   For a simple explanation of the orthodox account of the gold standard, see Held et al. (1999:196).
23   In theory at least, this is the first example of a system embodying globally integrated financial markets, where domestic or national economies were subject to international financial discipline, to which they were required to adjust. One might refer to the gold standard as the origin of what has become known as economic globalisation, i.e. "the increasing flow of goods and services, financial resources, workers, and technologies across national borders" (Isard 2005:4).

Gold still played a role, although a considerably different international gold standard was established in this new exchange rate system. The USA was the only country that actually pegged its currency to gold (at a par value of $35 per ounce), but other countries in turn pegged their currencies to the dollar. The BWS was thus a monetary system based on the dollar. In this system private financial flows were restricted and to diminish market volatility the US undertook to sell gold only to foreign central banks and governments, and to licensed private users (Isard 2005:29).

According to Held (1999:201-202), the BWS, which operated formally between 1946-1971, broke down under precisely the three forces that shaped the current situation of financial globalisation. Firstly, the dramatic increase in highly mobile private capital placed the control systems of the BWS under severe stress. Secondly, the emerging Eurocurrency markets (dollar deposits in European banks from multinational companies and the Soviet Union) were also not easily subjected to national capital controls. Thirdly, the OPEC crisis of 1973 resulted in a huge flow of funds from oil-exporting to oil-importing countries. This increased the liquidity of international banks with an even greater flow of capital across national boundaries and higher speculative trading. In short, the intensity and increasing diversity of global financial flows broke the back of the BWS and its intended stable monetary system. In place of the fixed system, where the value of gold, or the dollar acted as a "standardisation measure", a floating exchange rate system emerged where the only remaining "standard" was the value assigned to a particular currency by the day-to-day trading on foreign exchange markets (Held 1999:209). Needless to say, in such a system volatility is higher and the power to determine market perceptions is a crucial factor in determining who will gain or lose. The "hot money" of private speculators moves with great velocity and intensity. This has a significant impact on financial markets, in some cases leading to currency crises that threatened national and regional economies as a result of the contagion effect on emerging market economies (Held 1999:209, 213).[24]

This third, and still evolving, international monetary system has retained the major institutions of the BWS (the IMF and WB), although their roles have been redefined on the basis of lessons learnt about currency instability and development economics. To ensure some coherence in the increasing volume and extent of trade, the WTO replaced the failed GATT and has become the only global organisation dealing with the rules of trade between nations, acting as tribunal in the case of disputes. General trade agreements reached at the WTO are ratified in the parliaments of participating nations, of which there were 146 in 2003 (Bhagwati 2004:270).

In the first era from around 1870 the gold standard was fairly tightly controlled with restricted national autonomy. In the BWS there was more freedom to pursue national economic goals, but the stability was provided by the gold-dollar price and restrictions on private capital flow. In the current era there is such a high degree of interconnectedness, and such a rapid flow of (speculative) capital that national autonomies are severely restricted – especially in weaker nations.

Consequently, there has been a structural shift in the balance of power between public and private authority in the global financial system. This is a matter of fierce

---

24 For a discussion of the different currency crises between 1994 and 1999 in Mexico, the Asian countries and Russia, see Isard (2005:119-151).

debate and one could cite examples and counter-examples, but without being a "hyperglobalist", one must admit that "there is much compelling evidence to suggest that contemporary financial globalisation is a market-driven rather than a state-driven phenomenon" (Held 1999:234). The nation-state, according to Stiglitz, is squeezed between political demands at local level and the economic demands of a global system. The problem is that economic globalisation has outpaced political globalisation, resulting in uncoordinated systems of global governance, which is particularly evident in issues of global health and the environment (Stiglitz 2006:21). The power vacuum has been filled by the most powerful proponents of unlimited trade liberalisation and by staunch believers in "trickle-down" economics (which has proven to be only partially successful) (Stiglitz 2006:23).

For the purposes of this chapter, I wish to point out a common element in all three monetary systems. **From the beginning they created a fundamental differentiation between the "centre" and the "periphery".** The gold standard was managed by the Bank of England in London; the BWS was dependent on dollar policies in Washington; the current emerging financial system is determined by the triad of New York, London and Tokyo. Today's poorer countries were for the most part still colonised when these monetary systems took shape and they played only a marginal role in their origin and current direction. The consequence is that a hierarchical, uneven and asymmetrical system has emerged (Held 1999:213, 224) with clear democratic deficits in decision-making power, and trade agreements that leave the poorest countries worse off (Stiglitz 2006:58). This forms the background to the establishment of the WTO, the current trade negotiations, and the expectations that Africa has of these initiatives.

3. AFRICA'S EXPECTATIONS OF THE WTO AND DOHA TRADE NEGOTIATIONS

The Doha Development Round of the WTO trade negotiations commenced in 2001 and ended in July 2006, but continue on an informal and bi-lateral level. As the promise of multilateral trade negotiations continues to disappoint, Africa is clearly seeking to develop closer ties with the rising giants of China, India[25] and to a lesser extent Latin America in the form of South-South partnerships. The movement toward a truly "Development Round" of trade negotiations raised Africa's expectations and brought the following salient factors to the fore.

3.1 Values[26]

Despite experiments in "African socialism" in early post-colonial times, Africa accepts the principles of a market economy to maximise its potential. But contrary to a narrow mercantilist view of trade negotiations, based on the principle of self-interested bargaining, "economic efficacy and solidarity, efficiency and equity, growth and sustainable development, short-term gains and long-term prospects"

---

25 At the first major bilateral meeting between Africa and India in New Delhi (8 April 2008), it was announced that India would grant priority trade access to the least developed countries of the world.
26 See the discussion of *ubuntu* as a value expression under section 5. See also the passionate arguments for embedding fairness and social justice in the WTO by Stiglitz and Charlton (2005).

must be combined (AUC 1 2004:10) to inform trade negotiations and judge their outcomes.

3.2 Participation

Like many other developing regions, Africa has low negotiation capacities both in terms of human resources[27] and technical knowledge. "Africa could in effect remain in a 'spoke' situation while richer countries with more negotiating capacities are able to place themselves at the centre – the hub – of a network of trade agreements" (ECA 2007: 90). Africa is in the process of self-developing its trade negotiation capacities, but would need the assistance of the WTO to participate effectively.

3.3 Agenda

An explicitly pro-development agenda holds the potential to overcome the imbalances of earlier trade negotiations (e.g. the Uruguay Round) by actually reforming the multilateral trading system to ensure a more equitable share in the gains of global trade (ECA 2007:76). Africa has a particular interest in negotiations concerning agriculture and services. Although the outcomes have not been finalised, there is at least agreement in principle that the distorted subsidies in the North and market access for the South should be realised by 2013, though intermediate deadlines have yet to be achieved.

3.4 Trade liberalisation and "Aid for Trade"

Africa accepts trade liberalisation as the general aim of trade negotiations, but has been at the receiving end of failed development interventions in the form of enforced structural adjustment programmes (AUC 1 2004:9). Therefore, allowance must be made for trade liberalisation according to the development needs and adjustment capacities of a particular country or region, because a "one size fits all" strategy generates huge adaptation costs and actually retards development (ECA 2007:87). In this regard Africa supports the notion of aid specifically aimed at meeting the adjustment cost of trade liberalisation. However, it is important that this aid is not misused as a political weapon in the negotiation process, or as a replacement for current aid commitments (0.7% of Gross National Income) (Stiglitz & Charlton 2006).

3.5 African Union initiatives and the question of identity

The underlying question facing the AU is how to regain relative autonomy and initiative for a continent that has lost its sense of self-worth over the past 500 years? This is extremely difficult for a continent that is emerging from colonial rule and finds itself on the margins of a global system from which it cannot and does not want to escape, but where the power to shape that system towards justice and equity

---

27 There are hundreds of meetings and informal negotiations to be conducted, but some developing countries can scarcely afford a permanent trade representative in Geneva and are outnumbered by other countries and the special interest groups that represent them.

is clearly lacking. This fundamental question of identity underlies initiatives like NEPAD and the African Renaissance. In a courageous paragraph the AUC writes:

> Therefore, as far as Africans are concerned, it is no longer a question of catching up with anything; it is no longer a question of trailing behind any one or being relegated to the sidelines by anyone; rather, it is a question of being at the centre of their own affairs. Africans should devise for themselves watchwords, namely self-development, self-reliance, self-reliance for recognition and development... Having thus clarified the direction of its endeavors for full development, Africa can seek to integrate itself into the globalization process without losing its soul (AUC 1 2004:10).

One could translate the above as implying the following: Without reconstructing African identity, socio-economic reconstruction will be extremely difficult. This brings trade negotiations into the ethical arena of cultural justice and the rights of indigenous peoples. Only then can the hard economic policies outlined by the AU follow, namely: modernisation of agriculture; acceleration of industrialisation; beneficiation of Africa's enormous mineral wealth; integration of the sub-regions of Africa; and a decisive drive towards the diversification[28] of African economies.

4. DIFFERENTIAL TREATMENT AND PRIORITARIAN JUSTICE[29]

Africa has high expectations concerning the principle of "special and differential treatment" (part of GATT and accepted by the WTO) and especially the hope that it will be mainstreamed into all trade negotiations and enforced in practice. For example, there are 34 African countries in the Least Developed Countries (LDC) group, and initiatives such as the Generalised System of Preferences and the EU's "Everything but Arms" have brought additional benefits to them. Although not directly related to WTO negotiations, special actions like debt relief[30] and collective efforts to reach the Millennium Development Goals are important to many African countries.

The notion of "special and differential treatment" introduces **new kinds of justice** that were previously absent or under-represented. One thinks, for example, of emerging debates about ecological justice, inter-generational justice, cultural justice[31] and participative justice.[32] Africa understands that it will never reach a point

---

28 Note the sub-title of the Economic Report on Africa: "Accelerating Africa's development through diversification" and the discussion of diversification in the report itself (ECA 2007:113ff).
29 For an elaborate discussion of this notion, see chapter 1.2 of this book.
30 Of the 19 countries that reached completion point in the HIPC debt relief process, 15 were from Africa.
31 This is a form of justice not widely discussed in the literature yet. I have found the essay by Kwenda (2003) very helpful in this regard. He argues that cultural justice is established when people are allowed unselfconscious living, i.e. they live in acceptance and appreciation of their own identity. For an analysis of the link between cultural justice, identity and globalisation, see Naudé (2005) and chapter 1.1 above.
32 Bedford-Strohm makes the astute observation that both material and socio-cultural poverty find their origin in "fehlende Teilhabe" (1993:169). People are poor because of a lack of participation in the (in)formal economy and a lack of power to influence

of higher integration into the global economy unless a **redefinition of distributive justice** in the context of an integrated global monetary system is accepted.

Distributive justice[33] is a form of socio-economic justice that regulates the distribution of goods and services amongst the people of a specific society, or amongst societies in a regional or global arrangement. The result of such a distribution will obviously depend on the notion of justice and the specific theory of justice adopted. Egalitarian understandings of justice will, for example, seek to spread benefits more equally than entitlement notions of justice.[34]

There is now a growing consensus that to make the emerging global monetary system moral and sustainable, special focus on disadvantaged nations and people is needed. The notion of "preferential" treatment has over the last few decades been expressed in different terms by theologians, philosophers and economists.

In the 1960s and 1970s Latin American liberation theologians[35] – followed later by African liberation theologians[36] – developed "the preferential option for the poor" as a prophetic critique against failed development and structural adjustment policies in Latin America and Africa.

John Rawls developed his ideas about "justice as fairness" and the priority of the least advantaged person in his remarkable book, *A theory of justice* (1971). He based this on his judgment that utilitarian ethics that simply maximises happiness will not create just societies, and later (1999) stated that burdened societies need – at least for a specified period – special assistance in a new global order.

Joseph Stiglitz (2006) recently made a strong economic argument to replace "reciprocity for all" with the dictum of "special and differential treatment" for the poor nations of the world. In what he calls "fair trade for the poor", he suggests a reform of international trade. This reform entails that the principle of "reciprocity for and among all countries – regardless of circumstances" should be replaced by the principle of **"reciprocity among equals, but differentiation between those in markedly different circumstances"** (Stiglitz 2006:83, my emphasis).

In practice, Stiglitz proposes a three-tier system of rich, middle-income and poor countries – a classification based on agreed empirical norms. The rich countries open up their markets to others in their own group, but also to the middle-income and poor countries without reciprocity or political conditionality expected from the latter two groups. The middle-income group opens trade to all in its own group and to the poor countries without conditionality, but is not required to extend such preferences to the rich countries. In such a system, developing nations will receive "special and

---

decisions. This is one of the most urgent issues in discussions of global economic justice today.

33   For a definition and wide-ranging discussion of different theories of distributive justice, see Roemer (1998).
34   This difference is illustrated in, for example, the debate between John Rawls (egalitarian view) and Robert Nozick (entitlement view).
35   The most famous proponent of this radical challenge to traditional Catholic social thought is Gustavo Gutierrez, whose classic Spanish exposition was published in English as *A theology of liberation* (1973).
36   Well-known names are Manas Buthelezi, Desmond Tutu, Itumeleng Mosala and Allan Boesak, and womanists like Mercy Oduyoye and Isabel Phiri.

differential treatment", as has already happened in some bilateral trade agreements (see examples in the EU as from 2001 onward; Stiglitz 2006:83). However, such preferential treatment should not be voluntary, but become part and parcel of WTO negotiations and enforced in fields such as agriculture, tariffs and non-tariff barriers.

The clear WTO Ministerial Declaration adopted on 14 November 2001 gave Africa at least theoretical hope:

> We agree that special and differential treatment for developing countries shall be an integral part of all elements of negotiations and shall be embodied in the schedules and concession and commitments and as appropriate in the rules and disciplines to be negotiated, so as to be operationally effective and to enable developing countries to effectively take account of their development needs, including food security and rural development (paragraph 13 accessible from www.wto.org/english/thewto_e/minist_e/mindecl_e.htm).

We as Africans view this as a sincere commitment to, and as a yardstick for, the processes and outcomes of trade negotiations.

5. *UBUNTU* AS GUIDING PHILOSOPHY FOR A NEW TRADE REGIME?

The ancient value system of traditional African societies is condensed in the notion of *ubuntu*.[37] Whereas the Enlightenment view of the human person – powerfully expressed by, for example, René Descartes and Immanuel Kant – focuses on individuality and an assumed universal rationality, African philosophy rests on the assumption of communality: *Cogito ergo sum* stands in contrast to *ubuntu* as explained by African philosopher, John Mbiti (1969, pp. 108-109): "I am, because we are; and since we are, therefore I am." In short: I am a person through other persons. The "other" does not stand in an accidental or *a posteriori* or pragmatic relation to me, but is in fact a constitutive ontological part of my identity. My success is invariably tied up with the promotion of communal wellbeing, and the criterion of "success" is not in the first place material wealth accumulation, but the promotion and restoration of vital force, the life-giving spirit that permeates our existence and the cosmos of which we are a part.

If one translates this ethic from its tribal and local roots to the emerging global order, one realises that what the ecological crisis and global warming recently brought to our attention – namely that we share this finite world and we are literally dependent upon one another and cannot "go it alone" – was already embedded in ancient African wisdom. A trade negotiating system, primarily imbued by self-gain in the power game of win-lose scenarios, may lead to short-term "victories", but will not yield the required social goods for sustainable economic growth in the medium to long term.

---

37 *Ubuntu* has been widely discussed by African and other international scholars. Mbiti (1969) is considered to be the *locus classicus* in academic literature in this regard. Recent contributions are by Gyekye (1996), Ramosa (1999) and Shutte (2001). Like all good notions, *ubuntu* has also been misused and must obviously be subject to critical analysis. *Ubuntu* has in recent years also been translated into business management and leadership literature. See, for example, Broodryk (2005) and Mbigi (2005).

If all countries enter trade negotiations on the premise to build one human community, they will understand that building such a community requires sacrifices and at times altruism instead of strict reciprocity. Furthermore, if burdened societies (Rawls) that are in transition are treated in a special and differential way, Africa might at one point in history also be in a position to reciprocate materially to a greater extent than is possible at the moment.

Despite the shortcomings of the WTO,[38] ranging from member access to asymmetrical enforcement, the Ministerial Declaration does reflect this spirit of a single world community:

> We recognize the need of **all our people** to benefit from the increased opportunities and welfare gains that the multilateral trading system generates... We shall continue to make positive efforts designed to ensure that developing countries, and especially the least developed among them, secure a share in the growth of world trade commensurate with the needs of their economic development (paragraph 2, my emphasis).

As far as we keep one another to this vision, there is indeed hope.

Nkosi sikelel' iAfrika![39]

BIBLIOGRAPHY

AUC (African Union Commission). 2004. *Strategic Plan of the African Union Commission* (3 volumes). Addis Ababa: AUC.

Bedford-Strohm, H. 1993. *Vorrang für die Armen. Auf dem Weg zu einer theologischen Theorie der Gerechtighkeit*. Gütersloh: Chr. Kaiser Verlag.

Bhagwati, J. 2004. *In defense of globalization*. Oxford: Oxford University Press.

Broodryk, J. 2005. *Ubuntu management philosophy*. Randburg: Knowres.

Dunkley, G. 2004. *Free trade. Myth, reality and alternatives*. Cape Town: David Philip.

ECA (Economic Commission for Africa) 2007. *Economic report on Africa 2007*. Addis Ababa: African Union.

Fage, J.D. 1988. *A History of Africa*. 2nd edition. London: Unwin Hyman.

Guest, R. 2004. *The shackled continent. Africa's past, present and future*. London: Macmillan.

Gutierrez, G. 1973. *A theology of liberation*. London: SCM.

Gyekye, K. 1996. *The unexamined life: Philosophy and the African experience*. Accra: Sankofa.

Held, D., McGrew, A., Goldblatt, D. & Perraton, J. 1999) *Global Transformations. Politics, economics and culture*. Stanford: Stanford University Press.

---

38 See the incisive critique of both the assumptions and actual functioning of the WTO by Australian economist Graham Dunkley (2004, especially Chapter 8).

39 "God bless Africa" is the first line of a pan-African hymn and is also the first line of the official anthem of the Republic of South Africa.

Hoogvelt, A. 2002. Globalization, Imperialism and exclusion: The case of Sub-Saharan Africa. In Zack-Williams, T., Frost, D. & Thomson, A. (Eds.), *Africa in crisis. Challenges and possibilities* (pp. 15-28). London: Pluto Press.

Isard, P. 2005. *Globalization and the international financial system.* Cambridge: Cambridge University Press.

Kwenda, C.V. 2003. Cultural justice: the pathway to reconciliation and social cohesion. In Chidester, D., Dexter, P. and Wilmot, J. (Eds.). *What holds us together? Social cohesion in South Africa* (pp. 67-80). Cape Town: HSRC Press.

Madison, A. 2001. *The world economy: A millennium perspective.* Paris: OECD

Mbigi, L. 2005. *The spirit of African leadership.* Randburg: Knowres.

Mbiti, J. 1969. *African religions and philosophy.* Nairobi: East African Educational Publishers.

Naudé, P. 2005. The ethical challenge of identity formation and cultural justice in a globalizing world. *Scriptura* 89, 536-549.

Nunn, N. 2007. Historical legacies: A model linking Africa's past to its current underdevelopment. *Journal of Development Economics* 83, 157-175.

Packenham, T. 1991. *The scramble for Africa.1876-1912.* London: Abacus.

Ramosa, M.B. 1999. *African philosophy through ubuntu.* Harare: Mond Books.

Rawls, J. 1971. *A theory of justice.* Oxford: Oxford University Press.

Rawls, J. 1999. *The law of peoples.* Cambridge, Massachusetts: Harvard University Press.

Roemer, J.E. 1998. *Theories of distributive justice.* Cambridge, Massachusetts: Harvard University Press.

Shutte, A. 2001. *Ubuntu: An ethic for the new South Africa.* Pietermaritzburg: Cluster.

Stiglitz, J.E. 2002. *Globalization and its discontents.* London: Penguin.

Stiglitz, J.E. 2006. *Making globalization work.* New York: WW Norton.

Stiglitz, J.E. & Charlton, A. 2005. *Fair trade for all. How trade can promote development.* Oxford: Oxford University Press.

Stiglitz, J.E. & Charlton, A. 2006. "Aid for trade." *International Journal of Development Studies,* Vol. 5, No. 2, 1-41

Thomas, H. 1997. *The slave trade. The history of the Atlantic slave trade 1440-1870.* London: Macmillan.

Thornton, J. 1998. *Africa and Africans in the making of the Atlantic world, 1400-1800* 2nd edition. Cambridge: Cambridge University Press.

UNAIDS. 2006. *Report on the global AIDS epidemic.* Geneva: UNAIDS.

4.4 ECONOMIC POLICY AND THEOLOGICAL REFLECTION IN SOUTH AFRICA

An overview and assessment after 20 years of democracy

Given the limited space of this essay, it is only possible to write on the relation of "the economy" and "theology" over a 20-year period in South Africa if a decision on strong demarcations is taken at the outset.

Part one of this essay gives an overview of major economic policy developments in South Africa in the period following the transition to democracy in 1994 up to the most recent times. This entails that, of the many possible angles one could take to discuss "the economy", the one on policy is the preferred focus. The outcomes of the policies are then quantitatively measured against the explicit and most consistently recurring three aims of this period, namely poverty reduction, job creation and establishing a more equal society.

Part two, on theology, carries through this demarcation to focus on economic policy. In the light of the well-known threefold ethical approach "to see", "to judge" and "to act" as guideline, it must be noted that the focus of this essay will not fall on an "ethics of seeing" or making theoretical assessments of the situation. (What forms of economic justice are required? Which is the most appropriate economic system for South Africa? What does globalisation mean? How can theology and development be linked?) Nor will the focus be on an "ethics of being" which enables us to make ethical judgements. (What virtues do caring faith communities or sharing moral individuals display? How can we form a moral society? What are the roots of corruption? How does Christian worship motivate charity?).

The focus is rather on an "ethics of doing", "to act", insofar as economic policy directives are viewed as guidelines and prescriptions to put into action and real-world practice the underlying decisions about justice and building a good society. (What should we do about this or that specific economic issue such as poverty reduction or job employment? What specific directive would "just action" require in this specific case?).[1]

Part two thus gives an overview of various attempts to construct public theologies in post-apartheid South Africa in which moral policy discourses related to the economy could be adequately addressed.[2]

---

1. See the elaborate discussion and examples provided by Dirk Smit (1996/2007 and 2004) on this threefold ethical approach. About the problem of acting after due process (discussing Tödt's well-known six aspects of ethical discernment), Smit notes: "Too often we only see, and analyse, and talk, and consult... Too often we stay with theoretical discussions and deliberations and we do not practice what we said, we do not go back from our consultations and implement what we have decided" (1996/2007: 395). Below I will attempt a partial explanation for theology's seeming inability to engage at policy level.
2. It is also beyond the scope of this essay to discuss the widespread local and national initiatives of churches involved in many sectors of South African society, from pre-school care centres to support for Aids patients, the feeding of hungry people and providing basic skills training. These interventions are not conceived as related to "economic

A short concluding **third part** highlights the difficulties of theological discourse pertaining to economic matters, followed by a few broad guidelines that might assist in forging closer ties between theological reflection and economic policy formation/ execution up to 2030, the termination date of the National Development Plan, the latest major policy initiative in South Africa.

PART ONE: ECONOMIC POLICY FORMATION SINCE 1994

1.1 The Reconstruction and Development Plan (RDP)

The first major policy statement on the future economic dispensation of a democratic South Africa was produced just before the elections of April 1994. The year before, Cosatu (Congress of South African Trade Unions) – a major partner of the ANC – developed a Reconstruction Accord, which was finally accepted after six drafts as the Reconstruction and Development Plan (RDP): "The RDP is an integrated, coherent socio-economic policy framework. It seeks to mobilise all our people and our country's resources toward the final eradication of apartheid and the building of a democratic, non-racial and non-sexist future" (*The reconstruction and development plan* 1994: 4).

In the preface Nelson Mandela writes that the document is built on the tradition of the Freedom Charter of 1955, but recognises that to assume actual government responsibilities they would have to "go beyond the Charter to an actual programme of government" (RDP 1994:3).

Observers from both outside and inside the ANC noted that the liberation movement had a clear political vision, but that there had been insufficient preparation to actually run an economy. The situation was aggravated by the fact that the former regime left the economy in a bad shape with huge balance of payment problems, low foreign investment as a result of sanctions, high inflation and interest rates on top of apartheid-based spatial and educational development that excluded black people from meaningful participation in the economy.[3]

The RDP set the core agenda for all successive policies, namely addressing the interlinked challenges of **poverty, inequality and unemployment.**

As is to be expected from a document at that point in time, the RDP places a huge emphasis on the political basis of poverty and inequality. The history of "colonialism, racism, apartheid, sexism and repressive labour policies" was the root cause that had to be addressed. The imminent first inclusive elections were to be held in April of that year and "a victory for democratic forces" was the basis for reconstruction, development and peace.

---

policy", but are expressions of the care and love of God for those who suffer and are need of being confirmed as full human persons created in God's image.
3 See references to these views as expressed by Hein Marais (*South Africa pushed to the limit: The political economy of change*, 2011), Ben Turok (*The evolution of ANC economic policy: from the Freedom Charter to Polokwane*, 2008) and Max du Preez (*A rumour of spring. South Africa after 20 years of democracy*, 2013:78-79, 84).

But even at that point – with the political dimension of liberation at the forefront – the RDP understood the integral link between political and economic freedoms: "No political democracy can survive and flourish if the mass of our people remain in poverty, without land, without tangible prospects for a better life. Attacking poverty and deprivation must therefore be the first priority of a democratic government" (*The reconstruction and development plan* 1994: 7).

The RDP did reflect the fragile social situation at that point and included as part of its six basic principles the promotion of peace and security, with specific reference to the National Peace Initiative and establishment of non-partisan and professional security forces. It also accepted nation-building as "the basis on which to build a South Africa that can support the development of our Southern African region" (*The reconstruction and development plan* 1994: 9).

One of the most enlightened aspects of the RDP was its purposeful and decisive break with the blind commitment to "economic growth" *per se* as the answer to all socio-economic ills, and to the notion that development stands in contradiction to redistribution. The RDP states clearly: "If growth is defined as an increase in output, then it is of course a basic goal. However, where that growth occurs, how sustainable it is, how it is distributed, the degree to which it contributes to building long-term productive capacity and human resource development and what impact it has on the environment, are crucial questions when considering reconstruction and development" (*The reconstruction and development plan* 1994: 9).

In summary, the six basic principles of the RDP were "(i) an integrated programme, (ii) based on people, (iii) that provides peace and security for all and (iv) builds the nation, (v) links reconstruction and development and (vi) deepens democracy" (RDP 1994:10).

The RDP was enthusiastically embraced, with a special minister without portfolio, Jay Naidoo, as driver, and the first budget was seen as an "RDP fund". But faced with huge structural economic problems, and under immense pressure from the IMF and local business, the RDP's provincial structures were disbanded, and it was integrated into the line function of the Finance ministry. Only a year later – by March 1995 – Naidoo was removed and the RDP lost its traction as a major policy directive (Du Preez 2013: 83).

1.2 Growth, Employment and Redistribution Plan (GEAR)

Into this vacuum was inserted the 1996 Growth, Employment and Redistribution (GEAR) plan, the result of a smaller expert group, led politically by Trevor Manuel (later Finance Minister) and Thabo Mbeki (Deputy President and a trained economist). It is clear that this plan moved government policy ideologically to the right. Economic growth took precedence and the RDP integration of growth, development and redistribution is lost, despite GEAR's references later in the plan to social policies (15-16) and the move "towards a national social agreement" (21).

Typical measures to ensure economic growth were proposed and imposed on an underdeveloped economy such as South Africa's some of the following policies: accelerated tariff liberalisation, gradual relaxation of exchange controls, sharper budget deficit reduction ("fiscal containment"), a tight monetary policy ("responsible monetary policies"), creating conditions favourable for foreign investments, and – interesting for a time of intense labour relations reform – calls for wage moderation, productivity-linked wage increases and greater labour market flexibility (18-19), with the role of government for the greater part restricted to policy coordination (22).

The reasons for this policy trajectory – described as "one of the most decisive ideological turning points in the ANCs approach to economic issues" (Terreblanche 2002:98) – are manifold and complex. Two points might provide some illumination.

First is the point made by Sampie Terreblanche, Stellenbosch professor of economics, who notes that when the ANC borrowed $850 m from the IMF just before the 1994 elections, the Transitional Executive Committee (8 members of the ANC and NP each) also signed a "Statement on Economic Policy". This was the seedbed for "pure neoliberal" thinking and set the trajectory for policies beyond 1994, and was "a curtain raiser" for the GEAR strategy of 1996 (Terreblanche 2002: 96-98).

Second is the sobering point that the ANC found itself confronted with a large domestic debt, a collapsed Soviet bloc, and in the ambit of the triumphant-looking capitalist West (where investments were sought), the power of globalism, plus a private sector within the country which had to be placated to retain a credible tax base and preserve major aspects of the economy (Du Preez 2013:80-83; Terreblanche 2002: 100).

1.3 Accelerated and Shared Growth Initiative – South Africa (ASGISA)

A decade after GEAR, the ANC government published a new policy in 2006 called Accelerated and Shared Growth Initiative – South Africa (ASGISA). One is struck by the up-beat tone of the document, which is based on mostly positive economic data. Whereas economic growth had averaged around 3% in the first 10 years of democracy, there was an upward trend to 4% in 2004 and 5% in 2005 with a higher inflow of foreign capital, a drop in the unemployment rate from 32% to 26%, and a high business confidence index (ASGISA 2006:2).

ASGISA follows in the footsteps of the immediately preceding policies in emphasising the need for high GDP growth (above 6%) through macro-economic measures such as reducing currency volatility, inflation targeting and improved budgeting and expenditure measures (ASGISA 2006:14) complemented by investment in infrastructure, reducing the burden on small and medium businesses, and the promotion of skills development.

Special measures to ensure sharing in the fruits of higher growth are included in ASGISA: the extension of black economic empowerment (BEE) from benefiting only a few elite and politically connected business people to the more inclusive broad-based BEE; the Joint Initiative for Priority Skills Acquisition (JIPSA) to address the dire shortage of skills and bringing back retirees and expatriates to assist in building the economy; increasing the role of the state in creating short-term employment through the Expanded Public Works Programme (EPWP) and – through Project Consolidate – addressing the project and financial management capabilities in local government, where failures were setting in.

The document ends on a high note: "Our second decade of freedom will be the decade in which we radically reduce inequality and virtually eliminate poverty. We know now that we can do it, working together around an initiative which has the support of the nation" (ASGISA 2006:16).

Looking back, we now know that at that point the international financial crisis of 2008 – with its dire consequences also for South Africa – was not on the horizon. The ideal of halving poverty and unemployment by 2014 would simply no longer be possible to achieve.

1.4 The New Growth Path (NGP)

In the second half of 2009 – just after the 2008 global financial crisis started – the government started work on a re-assessment of the economy and published the NGP in November 2011. It paints a sober picture of an abrupt fall of roughly 3% in GDP growth from the third quarter of 2008 to mid-2009. It notes that over a million jobs were lost between 2008 and 2010 and "the employment ratio fell back from a high of 45% in 2008 to 41% in 2010 – virtually the same level as in 2002, before the economic boom started" (*The new growth path* 2011:15). President Jacob Zuma writes in his foreword: "The New Growth path is our vision to place jobs and decent work (see ILO definition on page 11) at the centre of economic policy. It sets a target of five million new jobs to be created by 2020" (*The new growth path* 2011:2).

The NGP is therefore focused on employment creation and identifies five job drivers, namely public infrastructure investment; targeting more labour-absorbing activities in mining, services and agriculture; taking advantage of the green and IT economies; leveraging social capital; and fostering rural development (*The new growth path* 2011: 24; 27-36; 71-76).

Because of the global constraints and the realisation that governments are not able to address employment by themselves, the NGP gives due credence to institutional drivers of job creation outside the state, namely private business, organised labour and civil society actors such as NGOs and co-operatives (*The new growth path* 2011: 62-64).

This narrow focus on job creation is understandable as a response to the global economic crisis as well as the internal pressures that were building up through service delivery protests, often led by frustrated unemployed youths who had dropped out of the education system with little or no hope of entering gainful employment.

But in the meantime the government realised that a bolder, integrated and more long-term vision was required to possibly address the triple challenges of poverty, inequality and unemployment.

1.5 National Development Plan

This is the backdrop to the most recent policy initiative, namely the National Development Plan. The National Development Plan 2030 (NDP), published with the subtitle, *Our future – make it work*, is without doubt the most ambitious policy document produced in the post-apartheid era.

The National Planning Commission of 26 members from across South African society was appointed in May 2011. They produced a Diagnostic Report in June 2011 and the draft plan itself was produced by November 2011 and finally accepted by the ANC national conference in Mangaung in December 2012.

The NDP follows through on the key focus areas addressed in earlier policy documents, but shifts the time horizon significantly forward: "The National Development Plan aims to eliminate poverty and reduce inequality by 2030" is the very first sentence of the introduction (National Planning Commission 2012: 24). These aims are expressed in quantitative terms, namely the total elimination of income poverty by reducing people living on a monthly income of less than R419 (in 2009 terms) from 39% to zero by 2030. Inequality should be reduced in terms of the Gini coefficient from 0.69 to 0.6, with the share of national income of the bottom 40% of the population increasing from 6 to 10% (NDP 2012:34). And employment should increase from 13 million employed people in 2010 to 24 million in 2030.

The NDP's diagnostic report is a frank, less ideological and research-based mirror of South African society after two decades of democracy. The report states no uncertain terms that, inter alia, "too few people work, the quality of school education for black people is poor, spatial divides hobble inclusive development, corruptions levels are high, and SA remains a divided society" (National Planning Commission 2012: 25).

To address the issues raised in this diagnosis, six inter-linked priorities are set: (i) uniting South Africans around a common programme; (ii) promoting an active citizenry; (iii) increasing economic growth; (iv) developing key capabilities of people; (v) building a capable and developmental state; and (vi) encouraging strong leadership in all spheres of society to commonly solve problems (National Planning Commission 2012: 26).

The NDP approaches the same problems of poverty, inequality and unemployment from a more inclusive and multidimensional perspective and makes it abundantly clear that "social cohesion needs to anchor the strategy" (27). It still links higher economic growth to employment, but links this strategy within an insistence that if the quality of education does not improve and if the state does not increase its capabilities, then there can be no progress in reducing poverty, inequality and unemployment.

This integrated strategy to "attack poverty" is demonstrated through the proposals that highlight the links between nutrition programmes for pregnant women and young children, access to primary health care, early childhood education, spatial planning and housing, public transport provision, social wages and then the more obvious matters such as public employment programmes and labour market incentives for youth employment (National Planning Commission 2012: 28).

The NDP acknowledges that a holistic and longer-term integrated strategy is required to address poverty and that the "economistic" approaches that tend to focus only on GDP growth – evident in the policies following the RDP – will not yield the desired results by 2030. However, the NDP itself follows the NGP view that growth needs to exceed 5% per annum to create the financial base for policy implementation (National Planning Commission 2012:39-40).

The proposals regarding education must be seen in the context of the overall objectives. One could interpret the NDP as saying – in simple terms – that if unemployment is one of the root causes of poverty, education and skills development are crucial measures to move people out of the poverty cycle by increasing earning potential and social mobility (National Planning Commission 2012:48). Despite huge overall improvements in enrolments and extension of free basic education, the under-performance and in some cases dysfunctionality of South Africa's school and post-school system after 1994 must be recognised as a huge stumbling block to address unemployment, poverty and inequality (National Planning Commission 2012:49-50).

Because the NDP buys into the notion of a "developmental state" as crucial in the fight against poverty and in leading economic growth, it has to address the concerns about public service incapabilities, governance and parliamentary oversight, the role of independent bodies (e.g. the Public Protector and Special Investigating Unit) and fighting corruption through deterrence, prevention and education, whilst addressing the societal factors that contribute to corruption (54-57).

The NDP ends by stating that the successful implementation of the plan requires strong leadership and partnerships among government business and civil society. It is of the view that "at present, South Africa has high levels of mistrust between major social partners. A virtuous cycle of building trust and engaging in discussion to confront the most pressing challenges is needed – one that takes a long-term view" (57).

1.6 Material outcome of policy developments?

The natural question is: What are the actual results after 20 years of intense policy and law making in relation to the core issues of poverty, inequality and unemployment?[4]

These are not simple matters as economists themselves differ on how quantitative data are constructed (who counts as "unemployed"?) and interpreted (does the official figure tell us the whole story, or must one take the informal sector into account as well?). The integrated context in which one should place these core issues – as ably demonstrated by the NDP – also requires more than simple number crunching.

---

4   Whereas the new policies were aimed at enhancing distributive justice, a large number of legislative and other initiatives were introduced apart from these policies to address matters of restorative justice.

One could mention the Truth and Reconciliation Commission (1995), which attempted to deal with difficult questions of amnesty for gross human rights violations and reparation to victims; the Employment Equity Act (1997) that prioritises previously disadvantaged groups, including disabled persons, in employment practices; the black economic empowerment (BEE) and later "broad-based" BEE initiatives that attempted to provide black people with a direct share in the ownership of listed companies; the establishment of the Land Claims Court, which dealt with land claims of people forcibly removed under the infamous 1913 Land Act and the later Group Areas Acts that literally enforced the racial separation amongst whites, Indians, coloureds and blacks in every South African city and town, leading ultimately to the creation of so-called independent black homeland areas; and the introduction and rapid expansion of social grant payments (almost equivalent to a basic income grant) to provide a safety net to just over 15 million people by 2014.

However, the information outlined below does provide some comparative data.

1.6.1 Poverty

The proportion of people living below the national poverty line first increased from 31% (1995) to 38% (2000) and then dropped to 23% in 2006.

It is clear that the government's significant expansion of the social security grants (or "social wage") has had a positive effect on alleviation of poverty in South Africa. There are eight forms of social grants: from temporary social relief of distressed persons to grants for child support, foster care, war veterans and disabled persons (www.sassa.gove.za/index.php/socialgrants). Grant recipients increased from 13.1 m in 2009 to 15.8 m in 2014 and the figure is projected to reach 16.5 m people by 2016, with the greater majority being child support grants (R310 pm in April 2014) (Gordhan 2014:11). This implies that close to 32% of South Africa's total population is dependent on the state for its basic economic survival, consuming 57% of consolidated budget spending in 2014 (Gordhan 2014:23). There are questions as to the sustainability of this programme, but the real effect has been a markedly positive one.

1.6.2 Inequality

In terms of the Gini coefficient, inequality first decreased from 0.59 in 1993 to 0.57 in 2000 and then increased again to 0.67 in 2006 with an improvement to 0.63 in 2009.

In 1995 the poorest 20% of the population earned 3.6% of the total income, whilst the richest 20% earned 61.8%. When one compares the 2009 with the 1995 figures, it emerges that the richest 20% of the population increased its share of income to 68.2%, whilst the share of the poorest 20% dropped to 2.7%. In fact, all people outside the top 20% were worse off in 2009 when compared to 1995 (the 4th quintile dropped from 18.4 to 16.3 and the 3rd quintile dropped from 6.1 to 4.6%).

These comparative figures show that South Africa is a more unequal society now than at the advent of democracy, and – like many countries – struggles to restructure the economy so that poor and middle-class people increase their proportion of the income. In line with global trends, the rich are becoming richer.[5]

1.6.3 Unemployment

The unemployment rate increased from 16.9% in 1995 to peak at a high point of 31.2% in 2003 and then improved to 24.1% in January 2014, a figure still unacceptably high (Gordhan 2014:12). The trend since the financial crisis in 2008 and the recent labour unrest in the mining sector has led to a situation where government has grown employment, whilst the private sector has reduced employment. With tougher economic conditions looming, the government itself has declared the growth in its wage bill as too high, and there are no ground to forecast a significant reduction in the unemployment rate to below 24% (Gordhan 2014:27-28).

---

5   The question of explaining growing inequality in terms of economic history has been Sampie Terreblanche's life-long passion. His most recent book (Terreblanche 2014) reinforces his view that the ANC has become a shadow image of the old National Party by enriching themselves and creating a new elite, whilst inequality worsens and may lead to serious social disruptions by 2030.

Despite all the policy initiatives, and spending in excess of R100 bn in the period 2009-2014 (Gordhan 2014:10), South Africa is currently worse off than in 1994 as far as employment creation is concerned.

One could thus conclude that as far as **poverty** goes, there has been an improvement in some areas, mainly as a result of direct government social spending, whereas – despite significant policy work and related initiatives – the situation regarding **inequality** and **unemployment** have actually worsened over the last 20 years.

PART TWO: THEOLOGY AND (ECONOMIC) POLICY DISCOURSE

To understand the relation between theology and the economic (policy) sphere of South African society after 1994, one first has to understand what actually happened in South Africa during the transition and what effect this had on theology itself.

2.1 An immersion into modernity and the struggle around the public nature of theology

One way to come to grips with the quite deep-seated changes in South Africa around 1994 is to describe the transition as a rapid immersion into modernity with its concomitant transformation of the public spheres of society.

Dirk Smit – following the trajectories of Habermas's thought – has written an informative overview of how the concept and reality of a "public life" distinct from the intertwined relation of politics (throne) and religion (altar) developed in Western Europe during the 17th and 18th centuries (Smit 2007). This led to the emergence of a "civil society" and a distinct "public opinion", informed by a public press and enhanced by a wide range of civil society institutions that eventually became the basis for democratic nation-states. Whereas the public sphere in pre-modern Western societies was dominated by religion and politics, a modern society is shaped by civil society, independent public opinion and economics as well.

For the purposes of this essay one could point out that economics itself played a crucial role in this very transformation of the public spheres: the seeds to disrupt the politics/religion monism of pre-modern societies were sown – according to Habermas – by forms of early commercial capital in the 13th century (Smit 2007:13). The market-place slowly became a sphere of power independent from the palace and the cathedral, and by the time late capitalism has established itself in the 19th century, it became impossible to ignore economics as a dominant force shaping public life. With the onset of economic globalisation and digital capitalism in the 20th century, there is no sphere of society not affected by economic forces.

Apartheid can be described as pre-modern totalitarianism in which the dominant religious/Christian sphere provided moral and theological legitimacy to the ruling political sphere, from which it could hardly be distinguished at times, and in which the development of a distinct public opinion and civil society was resisted by legal and military means. When the majority of the world moved toward open democracies and human rights in 1948, South Africa – in the very same year – moved in the opposite direction towards becoming a closed, oppressive society in which human rights and civil space were denied. South Africa became a pre-modern bubble, for the most part cut off from the impact of modernity.

The consequences of apartheid society on theology were immense. In broad terms, Christian theology was forced into becoming either a defence or a critique of apartheid (with various positions in between). What is crucial to note, however, is that both neo-Calvinist supporters of apartheid and the variety of liberation theologies opposing the system shared the fundamental pre-modern assumption that religion had an automatic and natural public significance. Yes, one could argue that opponents of apartheid struggled precisely to open up public space and use the emerging and even underground civil society structures (including churches) to work toward democracy. But the implied position was always: religion is a powerful force to transform society and there is no question as to its public relevance.

Then came the tsunami of modernity, perhaps most significantly expressed in the Constitution (Act 108 of 1996), which included a Bill of Human Rights: "What would take centuries in other societies, including the structural transformations that would make a more democratic formation of public opinion both necessary and possible, happened overnight in South Africa…" (Smit 2007:38).

The secularisation of public life; the growth of independent public opinion and a free press; the break between Christianity and official politics; the legitimacy and moral power of the new political leadership under Nelson Mandela; the rule of law and law-making as public moral consensus-building and the rise of economics as an independent force shaping society and asking serious questions about transferring economic power to the previously excluded majority – all of these together required a rethinking of theology and its apartheid modes of discourse.[6]

Whereas theologies of all convictions during the apartheid era were "public" in the general sense of dealing with public – mostly political – issues, post-apartheid theologies had to learn a different discourse. They had to become public theologies in the narrower, more specific sense, namely public theology understood as a "normative concept, designating an ideal that developed together with typically Western democratic culture", where theology, theologians and the church are but one set of players affecting public life with no assumed or "natural" influence. Public theology in this sense "refers to a specific sphere of human life together distinct from politics, the economy and civil life, namely a deliberate formation of public opinion which has the common good at heart and promotes human dignity and justice" (Smit 2007:39; see also Smit 1996).

In his essay "From political to public theologies" John de Gruchy states clearly that "the transition to democracy has thus introduced the need for a new approach to doing theology in the public arena" (2004:53). Two temptations were to be avoided: the belief that liberation has arrived and therefore theology could return to private

---

[6] For analyses of these "modern" trends as applied specifically to those previously advantaged people and churches, see Du Rand (2002) and the many essay by Etienne de Villiers on the "new situation" in South Africa and the implications for ethics and the church (for example, De Villiers 1995, 1999 and 2005). For De Villiers's contribution to economic ethics, see Naudé (2012). For a short argument on why a transition to a post-modern paradigm is required, see Petersen (1995).

piety and "ecclesiological ghettos", or trying to "replicate the days of struggle back in Egypt when at least the issues were clear..." (De Gruchy 2004:52).

For the purposes of this essay on the economic dimension of the transition to democracy, one could infer two fundamental challenges for theology: the challenge of a new way of doing theology (questions of methodology), and the extension of the narrow political agenda by the overt inclusion of economics and issues of economic policy in theological reflections (questions of agenda).[7]

The methodological challenge for post-apartheid theologies finds its expression in two themes: the definition and profiling of theology as pubic theology in a narrower, technical sense (briefly referred to above), and the question of whether prophetic theology – the dominant form of anti-apartheid theologies – would still be the most appropriate mode of discourse to address matters of public concern, including questions related to economic justice.

2.2 The potential and limitation of prophetic discourse

Can prophetic theology still serve us well in addressing matters of economic justice?[8]

One response to this question is that the strength of prophetic discourse – the ability to state a radical alternative vision for justice in the name of the Lord – might be its greatest weakness as well. And this for two reasons.

First. Prophets are enthusiastic about matters like justice, but in order to function well, they need a well-defined enemy to speak against and, because they are not strong on technical analysis, they sketch a picture of this enemy that the enemy itself may not recognise. When Stan du Plessis, an economist, comments on the Accra Declaration (for example), he refers to the ideological construction of "neoliberalism" and states that "it is not at all clear that a coherent ideology by that name exits, and when it appears, it does so almost exclusively on the pages of those who proceed to reject it" (Du Plessis 2010:63).[9] Because Accra takes an ideological position within the social sciences as point of departure to analyse the economy, the result is itself an ideological product predicated upon an "elaborate conspiracy" that does not exist.

---

[7] See Nürnberger's remark that "the political settlement may collapse if it's not **matched by a similar feat in the economic realm**" (1994:3; original emphasis). See also Koopman (2003:16-17).

[8] This was the theme of a conference held at the University of Pretoria in 2009; the papers were published in 2010 in *Hervormde Teologiese Studies* (HTS) 66 (1). This is an excellent collection of essays addressing the complexities, limitations and potential of prophetic theology and prophetic moral discourse.

[9] Du Plessis – inter alia – refers to the fact that no entry for "neoliberalism" is found in any standard economic dictionary, whilst this has become an ethically derogatory term in church documents on globalisation. Terreblanche – an economist who published a paper in *Reformed World* – would differ from this and actually provides a description of the rise of neoliberalism under Reagan and Thatcher with policies such as "privatization, deregulation and the retrenchment of the welfare state...". He views neoliberalism as an expression of the ideology of market fundamentalism or laissez-faire capitalism (Terreblanche 2009: 5-6).

Second. Prophets – by their very nature – pronounce the truth as they believe they received it from God. This may make prophets weak dialogue partners[10] and in fact "precludes [their] participation in the piecemeal policy debate, which is most consistent with a modest assessment of what economists know about the economy" (Du Plessis 2010: 65). Du Plessis, whilst highly critical of prophetic discourse in this particular case, does provide some pointers to answer the question in the title of his article: "How can you can be a Christian and an economist?"

Various theologians have addressed the continued significance of prophetic theology, and the consensus may be summarised as follows.

The eschatological infusion into society of an alternative vision of justice and equality should be endorsed and maintained. Political liberation is but a part of our liberation journey. And against all odds, the critical element of Christian prophecy, its upholding of a "concrete utopia"[11] (De Gruchy 1995: 274), is one of the key contributions it makes in debates around economic issues such as poverty, redistribution, restitution and inequality. Theology in this mode keeps the language of hope alive. "It reminds everyone of justice not yet real and fulfilled". This eschatological orientation also strengthens critical and self-critical thought, always reminding us of the provisional historical realisation of justice (Smit 2005/2007: 348-349).

But there is also consensus that – as Gustafson (1988) taught us – matters of economic justice will not be adequately addressed by prophetic discourse alone, and we shall have to be skilled in a variety of moral discourses, including not only the narrative and ethical, but also – crucially important for this essay – the policy discourse.

Why do South African theologians find it so hard to engage in economic policy debates if in fact those policies are the most realistic expression (or not) of the prophetic ideals of justice, dignity and equality?

The methodological answer to this question may lie in the following: we struggle to construct a new public theology under modern conditions, and we are used to prophetic and narrative discourses, but less able to engage in the technical aspects of ethical discourse and the practical specificity of policy discourse.

There are further answers to this question of inadequate engagement between theologians and economists.

South African theologians are well versed in engaging in inter-disciplinary discussions with practitioners of linguistics, hermeneutics, philosophy and social theory in general, but – apart from the pioneering early works by Klaus Nürnberger (1987, 1988, 1994) – we have never established an adequate dialogue between

---

10 This weakness is the focus of an interesting article by Verhoef and Rathbone (2013), two young philosophers, who propose a *dialogical* mode of discourse beyond an ideological rejection of neoliberal capitalism as also found reflected in *The Oikos Journey* (2013:93), a church statement on global justice. They illustrate this mode of discourse through an ethical engagement with the underlying concepts of justice in the work of Adam Smith, JM Keynes and John Rawls.

11 Russel Botman, speaking as chair of the SACC in 1994, says clearly: "I also believe that politicians are those trained in the art of what is possible and what is affordable. We are trained in the art of utopia. We believe that the best is really possible" (Botman 1995: 251).

economics and theology.¹² Very few – if any – theologians display the same expertise in matters of the economy as we do in matters of politics and philosophy. This leads to "meddling and easy answers ... that warrant dismissal by economists who often share the passion and vision of these theologians, while being forced to grapple with realities that undercut the easy solutions which theologians seek to promote" (Villa-Vicencio 1992: 207).

There are obviously economists who profess to share the convictions and vision of the Christian faith. But unlike (for example) the Catholic and Lutheran Churches, South African churches do not normally produce discussion and policy documents on the economy that draw on the expertise of Christian economists in the way one finds in, for example, Evangelische Kirche Deutschlands or Lutheran World Federation texts on various matters related to economic justice, from global justice and poverty to the question of minimum wages or a stance on the financial crisis of 2008.¹³

Because of the broad generalisations that necessarily inform prophetic-type theology, theologians are good at formulating (biblical) "principles", but weak at proposing and supporting specific economic proposals that might fit a specific situation as it is judged at that point in time. In doing so, theology and the church might make serious mistakes. But, as Charles Villa-Vicencio reminded just before 1994, "the most serious failure which the church can commit is not to be wrong in deciding which social initiative supports the common good, but to fail to support any initiative out of fear of being wrong. Such action suggests social indifference ... It might further suggest an archaic (medieval) residual sense of dogmatic pride ... out of fear of being seen as less than a divine creation!" (1992:283-284).

There is thus a mixture of methodological inadequacies, lack of expertise in cross-disciplinary dialogue, and even the psychology of fear (infused by our ideological past) at play in the relative weakness of theology to influence economic policy after 1994.

2.3 From prophetic theology to liberative practices?

In the light of the exposition above, the question arises: How can one translate prophetic zeal into actual practical, liberative practices? If one reads the creative responses to this question by South African public theologian, Nico Koopman, in relation to earlier work by others in this regard, at least three guidelines emerge.

First. Following Gary Simpson,¹⁴ Koopman reinterprets Gustafson by extending traditional "prophetic speaking" to include all four varieties of moral discourse, so that policy discourse becomes an integral form of prophetic speaking. He

---

12 Nürnberger, probably the only South African theologian with a formal qualification in economics, states in a passionate plea for Christians and the church to become involved in matters of the economy that "this implies that they build up the same level of analytical, prophetic and constructive competence that they have built up concerning ethnicity, race, oppression and human rights" (1994:3).
13 For the Lutheran World Federation's view on globalisation, see Bloomquist (2004), and see the EKD publications in 2006 and 2009 on distributive justice and the global financial crisis respectively. Also see De Villiers and Smit (1995) for an extensive discussion on the nature of church documents with respect to public issues.
14 Koopman has drawn on Simpson's book (2002): *Critical social theory. Prophetic reason, civil society, and Christian imagination* (Minneapolis: Fortress Press).

describes "prophetic speaking as policy-making" (Koopman 2010:42) and refers to Gustafson's description of policy discourse as seen from the internal perspective of the policymakers who are the agents responsible for making decisions under complex circumstance, often having to settle not for what is desirable, but for what is possible (Gustafson 1988:47; Koopman 2010:43).[15] This extension or reinterpretation of prophecy is already present in the remarkable booklet by Klaus Nürnberger on the task of the church in the post-apartheid economy in which he calls on the church to "be prophetic in practical terms", because "our words **should be effectual**" in the realities of economic life (1994:52, original emphasis).

Second. Koopman draws on the earlier work of Villa-Vicencio (1992:280-284), who utilises the ecumenical debate on "middle axioms"[16] to bridge the perceived gap between general statements and pronouncements on specific and more detailed policies. "The middle axiom debate", says Villa-Vicencio, "can be seen as an attempt to state what the gospel requires at a given time in a given place, without ignoring its ultimate ethical demands on humankind" (1992:282). He places his own theology "at this encounter between theory and practice" (283).

The following marks of middle axioms may, according to Koopman, assist theology and the church to actually engage in policy making processes. They are developed through interdisciplinary means to include both an empirical dimension (derived from economics and so forth) and a Christian-ethical dimension so as retain their uniquely Christian aspect; they ideally include not only experts, but the local and indigenous knowledge of people affected by policies; and the church could over time "develop minimal levels of sophistication about public issues", without pretending to be experts in everything (Koopman 2010: 53).

Third. The translation of prophetic insights into the realities of (economic) life may be facilitated through Christian, ecclesial or congregational "practices". Koopman refers to Craig Dykstra and Dorothy Bass, who propose the term "Christian practices" as "things Christian people do together over time to address fundamental human needs in response to and in the light of God's active presence for the life of this world" (Dykstra and Bass 2002:18,[17] as cited by Koopman 2004: 447).

This discussion ties in with the very practical advice given by Nürnberger for the church's involvement in the post-apartheid economy. What he calls the "practical tasks" for the church include simple but effectual involvement in matters like "dethroning the gods" of greed and selfishness; assisting in family budgeting and

---

15 Examples of theology in this more practical sphere are churches with offices in the democratic parliament involving themselves in policy processes, as well as the SACC's annual "people's budget", which assesses the budget as put forward by the Finance Minister (Koopman 2010:43).
16 The idea stems from JD Oldham's address to the 1937 Life and Work conference in Oxford, and has been critically adopted by Gustafson and especially Forrester, who is not entirely convinced that such an approach is workable in a pluralistic society (see Villa-Vicencio 1992:282).
17 The full details of this publication are: A theological understanding of Christian practices. In: M. Volf and D.C. Bass (eds) 2002. *Practicing theology. Beliefs and practices in Christian life*. Grand Rapids: Eerdmans, 13-32. Dykstra and Bass propose twelve distinct Christian practices (Koopman 2004:446) that assist the transition from visionary declarations to actual interventions in the realities of life.

family planning; warning against indebtedness as a result of questionable hire purchase deals or excessive marriage and funeral events; and standing for "old-fashioned values of self-discipline, hard work and frugality" (1994:56).

These seemingly unimpressive "Christian practices" – within the realm of the institutional church and through Christians who live out their calling in the secular sphere of business – are perhaps the most important aspect of the relation between "theology" and "economics", because they translate into the reality of economic life the insights of the gospel. But they are also the most difficult to capture in academic writing, as this would require empirical work beyond the scope of this essay.

2.4 Theological criteria for judging the economy?

Despite the relative weakness of theological work relating to economic policy, and the lack of concrete examples related to (for example) "middle axioms", a broad consensus has grown around some definitive criteria that the Christian tradition brings to the discourse around the economy.[18]

There is the Christian understanding of **human dignity** (all people created in the image of God) which should translate into political rights such as freedom of speech and socio-economic rights such as the right to food security, shelter, health care, education and employment. It does imply economic democracy as well, because 'democracy dies when inequality grows', and "an economic system which systematically excludes people from sharing fully in the shaping of economic … life must inevitably face theological censure" (Villa-Vicencio 1992: 239-240)

There is also a strong Christian tradition of a taking the **perspective of the poor and the suffering** as point of departure. "From the perspective of the gospel, the care for, and the empowerment, of the poor and other social victims is the chief criterion by which to evaluate social structures and to become involved in them" (De Gruchy 1995: 268) Christian theologies and churches therefore insist that special economic measures be instituted to care for those who suffer from marginalisation, injustice and abuse. This implies forms of redistributive justice that would provide first for the basic necessities of people before it allows exorbitant accumulation of wealth.[19]

If economics is about the "laws of the household", this household includes the whole of the earth. Christian theology rightly claims much greater ecological responsibility from the economy to protect and enhance the **integrity of creation** – especially in the light of a globalised economy.

The concern remains that these theological criteria or pointers are still one step away from actual policy making. It is one thing to say that "the option for the poor should guide the economy", but quite another thing to explain what this means for progressive tax policies or priorities regarding spending on infrastructure, or whether this implies automatic support for the payment of basic income grants in a situation of scarce pubic resources that always requires trade-offs between what is morally desirable and what is practically feasible.

---

18 See Smit and Koopman (2008) for a broader discussion and literature.
19 See Naudé (2007) and chapter 1.2 above for an elaborate discussion of "the option for the poor" and prioritarian justice.

2.5 Theology meets economic policy: What happened?

The foregoing discussion hopefully gives a partial explanation for the rather weak relation between theology (and the churches), on the one hand, and economic policy making, on the other. In his assessment of the impact of the church ten years after democracy, Dirkie Smit wrote: "In the economic sphere the absence of Christian language and commitment in the real corridors of power is even more painful. The free market in the form of global capitalism seems to be the reigning idol, proclaimed and celebrated through popular culture and eagerly worshipped by many, even in many churches" (Smit 2004/2007:73).

The extensive and intense policy making of the last 20 years attracted active interaction only at the beginning during the time of the RDP, and – as a result of some of the factors outlined below – almost disappeared in the subsequent years.

Although written before the actual adoption of the RDP, Villa-Vicencio's attempt at a "theology of reconstruction" (1992), focusing on nation-building, human rights, the law and political economy, was a major (and much criticised) effort to reframe political and liberation theologies stemming from the anti-apartheid era. The same could be said about De Gruchy's book on the fundamental link between the Christian tradition and the development of democracy (1995) and his later work on reconciliation, providing the contours to reconstruct the former apartheid society into a just and equitable democratic order, and addressing our past through the means of restorative justice (De Gruchy 2002: 201-209). Some churches – such as the URCSA – affirmed and supported the RDP in spite of minor points of criticism and questions about its spiritual dimension (Smit 1995/2007:383-385).

A landmark publication – in terms of economic policy and not yet surpassed over the last 20 years – appeared in 1995. Edited by Renier Koegelenberg from EFSA (Ecumenical Foundation of South Africa) under the title *The reconstruction and development programme (RDP): The role of the Church, civil society and NGOs*, this anthology contains papers and discussions around the RDP held from 5-7 October 1994. This publication demonstrates some key requirements for fruitful exchange on economic policy: participation was broad-based and included theologians, development specialists, gender activists, economists, grassroots civil society structures, representatives from credible ecumenical bodies, and politicians involved in the constructing and implementation of the RDP itself. The agenda was equally wide-ranging (from biblical exegesis to descriptions of community development and the outlining of changing state priorities) and ensured multidisciplinary perspectives on matters of economic reconstruction and development.

A quite specific encounter with economic policy as expressed in the RDP was written by ethicist, Etienne de Villiers, in 1995.

He first tells his readers (chiefly persons in the Afrikaans DRC) about the broad contents of the RDP (De Villiers 1995: 22-23). He then addresses possible concerns that Christians might have in a call to the church to make its own contribution to or cooperate in the RDP – especially in the light of the DRCs close political ties with policy formation during the apartheid years (24). He renounces the views of both Kuitert and Hauerwas, and then states that the church should judge any policy, including the RDP, not from a party-political view, but on the basis of biblical principles, and then give it qualified support (or not) (25).

In an interesting rhetorical strategy, De Villiers proceeds to demonstrate the close similarities between DRC church polity (Church and Society 1986) and the RDPs concern for the plight of poor people; its addressing of economic inequalities; restoring of human dignity; and emphasis on the creation of employment. He reminds Afrikaner Christians of their own struggle against poverty and how the DRC then played a major role in uplifting them (26).

On this basis, he subsequently calls on the local churches in the (white) DRC to actively participate and support concrete RDP initiatives and to align already existing initiatives related to pastoral support programmes with the RDP so that any person in need would be assisted (27-28).

He concludes: "We in the DR Church have always believed that God placed us at the southern tip of Africa for a purpose ... May God inspire us to accept the new challenges awaiting us with conviction, this time not alone, but together with others who were also placed by God here at the southern tip of Africa" (29, my translation).

Looking back, it is a pity that these promising and almost paradigmatic interactions between theology and public policy could not have been integrated into the intense policy-making processes after the RDP. The initial policy interactions with the RDP were well intentioned and did in fact make an intellectual contribution to the link between theology and the church (on the one hand) and economic policy (on the other).

One of the intellectual weaknesses in post-apartheid theology has been the low level of engagement with the new science of public policy which arose after the Second World War as a tool to design rational means to assist policy makers – under constraints of resources and political pressures – to take the best decisions and to measure the outcomes of those decisions. The interesting work done by James Cochrane[20] around 1997 was never taken further to establish a proper basis from which theologians and church leaders could direct the content and implementation of economic policies beyond the RDP.

Because the government itself quite quickly lost its commitment to the plan (see above) and "replaced" the RDP with a myriad of successive economic policies and laws, as a consequence of the re-direction of donor funding after 1994, and because of the relatively slow adaptations to a secular democracy and public policy processes, it was very difficult for theologians and churches to actually influence policy directives apart from the broad criteria listed above – the influence of which one will probably never be able to fully estimate.

Perhaps one could agree with Smit's sobering conclusion that the impact of post-apartheid developments on the church was greater than the impact of the church on

---

20 See Cochrane's theological interactions with the history of policy studies and current paradigms in his articles "The church and the reconstruction of South African society", "Conceptual issues in the making of public policy actuality: Limits to a social vision" and "Public challenges to Christianity in Africa" published as part of special *JTSA* editions on "Theological reflection on public policy" in March, July and November 1997 (numbers 97-99).

those developments – especially as far as the local and global economy are concerned (Smit 2004/2007: 72).

PART THREE: LOOKING BACK AND CHARTING A WAY FORWARD...

The analyses above tell us that, during the 20 years after democracy, South Africa developed a myriad of policies to address the threefold challenges of inequality, unemployment and poverty. From the economic data it seems that we are a more unequal society than in 1994 and adequate responses to unemployment have not yet been found. South Africa did make significant progress to halt extreme poverty, mainly through an extensive network of social grants.

It is also clear that there were initial attempts by theologians to engage in policy discourse – specifically around the RDP in 1994 – but that the impact of theology on economic policy *per se* is difficult to determine for practical reasons related to rapidly shifting policy directives and reasons internal to theology itself – *inter alia* relating to questions of methodology, lack of economic expertise, and the huge energy spent on finding some orientation in a fast-changing, modern society.

It also emerges that on the level of a critical and prophetic "vision" for an alternative society, theology's eschatological orientation played a useful guiding role over the last 20 years. Theology has been able to translate this vision into core criteria against which any economic system or policy could be measured. But – despite (limited) theoretical work on middle axioms and on public policy – very little evidence has emerged of actual theological contributions to shape economic policy directives in their specificity.

Concerning the way forward, the following points may be noted.

1. Post-apartheid theology's preoccupation with methodology – including its emergent understanding of "public theology" – remains important to orient reflection in a secular democracy, but must be complemented by more work on economic ethics and policy.

2. A concerted effort must be made to establish and strengthen the link between theology and economics, so that the discussion on empirical realities and moral criteria is conducted at a higher level of complexity than what is apparent in "prophetic" theologies. Churches would do well to draw on economists from their own ranks to assist in building consensus-seeking dialogues, where the limitations from and divergent views on both sides are opened up and taken seriously.

3. An understanding of public policy as a discipline, as well as the inherent tensions, compromises[21] and ambiguities involved in both policy decisions and their implementation, is a requirement if theologians and churches wish to participate fruitfully in economic policy debates.

4. Theology should not give up on its proven strength of providing a critical vision of society – affirming where signs of God's kingdom appear in the economic

---

21 "The challenge of possibility (thus) finds its dialectic counterpart in the actuality of constraint" (Cochrane 1997a:2).

field, and providing self- and other critique in the knowledge that no historical reality can ever fully encompass God's reign. Providing a social vision might be the prime Christian contribution to shaping policy.

5. Armed with greater knowledge on the intricacies of economic policies, coupled with a contextual understanding of the gospel – even in ambiguous policy discussions – theologians can humbly assert themselves as legitimate partners in influencing public policy. Theologians, Christian economists and churches should learn to speak via the powerful (social) media and make use of the space for free speech provided by our democracy.

6. The NDP seems to be the most stable and long-term policy accepted by the government since 1994. Despite internal political and ideological differences within government circles, it seems like a solid policy directive worthy of theological analysis and worthy of notice and participation by the churches. Theologians – as far as could be established – have not participated in shaping the actual content of the NDP.[22] But there are now opportunities to engage in the spirit of critical solidarity, so that the worthy ideals of an inclusive democracy with greater equality, higher employment and zero poverty be realised over the next 16 years toward 2030.

BIBLIOGRAPHY

ASGISA (*Accelerated and shared growth initiative – South Africa*) 2006. Pretoria: The Presidency.

Bloomquist, Karen L (ed.) 2004. *Communion, responsibility, accountability. Responding as a Lutheran communion to neoliberal globalization.* Geneva: Lutheran World Federation.

Botman, Russel 1995. Church and community service. In Renier Koegelenberg (ed.), 250-254.

Cochrane, James R 1997a. The church and the reconstruction of South African society. *JTSA* 97 (March), 1-15.

Cochrane, James R 1997b. Conceptual issues in the making of public policy "actuality": Limits to a social vision. *JTSA* 98 (July), 89-94.

Cochrane, James R 1997c. Public challenges to Christianity in Africa. *JTSA* 99 (November), 130-139.

De Gruchy, John 1995. *Christianity and democracy. A theology for a just world order.* Cape Town: David Philip.

De Gruchy, John 2002. *Reconciliation. Restoring justice.* Cape Town: David Philip.

De Gruchy, John 2004. From political to public theologies: The role of theology in public life in South Africa. In Wiliam F. Storrar and Andrew R. Morton (eds.): *Public theology for the 21st century. Essays in honour of Duncan B. Forrester.* London: T & T Clark, 45-62.

De Villiers, DE and Smit, DJ 1995. Met watter gesag sê u hierdie dinge? Opmerkings oor kerklike dokumente oor die openbare lewe. *Skrif en Kerk* 16/1, 39-56.

---

22 There was, for example, not a single theologian appointed as commission member for writing the massive NDP policy document. The only instances where the church is implicitly mentioned is under the possible role that NGOs can play in building social cohesion in society.

De Villiers, Etienne 1995. Die NG Kerk en die Heropbou- en Ontwikkelingsprogram. In D. Kitching and F. Linde (eds.): *Geroep om te dien. 'n Huldigingsbundel opgedra aan Prof PR van Dyk, rektor van die Hugenote-Kollege 1979-1995.* Wellington: Hugenote Kollege, 22-30.

De Villiers, Etienne 1999. Challenges to Christian ethics in the present South African society. *Scriptura* 69, 75-91.

De Villiers, Etienne 2005. The vocation of a Reformed ethicist in the present South African society. *Scriptura* 89 (2), 521-535.

Du Plessis, Stan 2010. How can you be a Christian and an economist? The meaning of the Accra declaration today. *NGTT*, 51 (1 & 2), 62-71.

Du Preez, Max 2013. *A rumour of spring. South Africa after 20 years of democracy.* Cape Town: Zebra Press.

Du Rand, Jaap 2002. *Ontluisterde wêreld: Die Afrikaner en sy kerk in 'n veranderende Suid-Afrika.* Wellington: Lux Verbi.BM.

Evangelische Kirche Deutschland 2006. *Gerechte Teilhabe. Befähigung zu Eigenverantwortung und Solidarität.* Gütersloh: Gütersloher Verlagshaus.

Evangelische Kirche Deutschland 2009. *Wie ein Riss in einer hohen Mauer. Wort des Rates der EKD zur globalen Finanzmarkt- und Wirtschaftskrise.* Hannover: Kirchenamt der EKD.

Gordhan, Pravin 2014. *2014 Budget speech.* Pretoria: National Treasury.

Growth, employment and redistribution. A macroeconomic strategy. 1996. Pretoria: Department of Finance.

Gustafson, James 1988. *Varieties of moral discourse: Prophetic, narrative, ethical and policy.* Grand Rapids: Calvin College.

Koegelenberg, Renier (ed.) 1995. *The reconstruction and development programme (RDP): The role of the Church, civil society and NGOs.* Bellville: EFSA.

Koopman, Nico 2002. Christian ethics in post-apartheid South Africa – a reformed perspective. *NGTT*, 43 (3&4), 443-454.

Koopman, Nico 2004. Let the plight of the voiceless be heard. Prophetic speaking about poverty today. *NGTT* 45/2 (supplementum), 440-451.

Koopman, Nico 2003. Some comments on public theology today. *JTSA* 117, 3-19.

Koopman, Nico 2009. Public theology as prophetic theology: More than utopia and criticism? *JTSA* 134: page numbers not visible in copy

Koopman, Nico 2010. Churches and public policy discourses in South Africa. *JTSA* 136:41-56.

National Planning Commission. 2012. *National Development Plan 2030. Our future – make it work.* Pretoria: The Presidency.

Naudé, Piet 2007. In defence of partisan justice? An ethical reflection on "the preferential option for the poor". *Verbum et Ecclesia* 28/1, 166-190.

Naudé, Piet 2011. Is prophetic discourse adequate to address global economic justice? *HTS Teologiese Studies/Theological Studies* 67 (1) Art. #1014, 8 pages. DOI:10.4102/hts.v67i1.1014.

Naudé, Piet 2012. Virtue and responsibility: Economic-ethical perspectives in the work of Etienne de Villiers. *Verbum et Ecclesia* 33 (2), Art. #737, 6 pages.

Nürnberger, Klaus (ed.) 1979. *Ideologies of change. Capitalism, socialism, Marxism and the gospel.* Durban: Lutheran Publishing House.

Nürnberger, Klaus 1987. *Ethik des Nord-Süd-Konflikts. Das globale Machtgefälle als theologisches Problem.* Gütersloh: Gütersloher Verlagshaus.

Nürnberger, Klaus 1988. *Power and beliefs in South Africa.* Pretoria: Unisa.

Nürnberger, Klaus 1994. *An economic vision for South Africa. The task of the church in the post-apartheid economy.* Pietermaritzburg: Encounter Publications.

Peterson, Robin 1995. Theological reflection on public policy. *JTSA* (July), 76-82.

Smit, Dirkie and Koopman, Nico 2008. Human dignity and human rights as guiding principles for the economy? In Clint le Bruyns and Gotlind Ulshöfer (eds.): *The humanization of globalization: South African and German perspectives.* Frankfurt: Haag & Herchen Verlag, 59-70.

Smit, DJ 1996. Oor die kerk as 'n unieke samelewingsverband. *Tydskrif vir Geesteswetenskappe* 36/3, 190-198.

Smit, DJ 1996/2007. Reformed ethics and economic justice? In *Essays in public theology. Collected essays I.* Stellenbosch: Sun Press, 379-398.

Smit, DJ 2004. Sien, nadink, doen? Oor teologie en armoede. *NGTT* 45/2 (supplementum), 180-196.

Smit, DJ 2004/2007. On the impact of the church in South Africa after the collapse of the apartheid regime. In Dirk J Smit: *Essays in public theology. Collected essays I.* Stellenbosch: Sun Press, 57-74.

Smit, DJ 2005/2007. On social and economic justice in South Africa today. A theological perspective on theoretical paradigms. In *Essays in public theology. Collected essays I.* Stellenbosch: Sun Press, 343-357.

Smit, DJ 2007. What does public mean? Questions with a view to a public theology. In Len Hansen (ed.): *Christians in public. Aims, methodologies and issues in public theology.* Stellenbosch: Sun Press, 11-46.

Terreblanche, SJ 2002. *A history of inequality in South Africa 1652-2002.* Pietermaritzburg: University of Natal Press.

Terreblanche, Sampie 2009. The second meltdown of the ideology of market fundamentalism. *Reformed World,* volume 59(1), 3-17.

Terreblanche, Sampie 2014. *Verdeelde land. Hoe die oorgang Suid-Afrika faal.* Cape Town: Tafelberg.

Terreblanche, Sampie 2014a. *Western Empires, Christianity, and the Inequalities between the West and the Rest 1500-2010.* Johannesburg: Penguin.

The new growth path. 2011. Pretoria: Economic Development Department.

The reconstruction and development plan. A policy framework. 1994. Pretoria: The Presidency.

Verhoef, Anne H and Rathbone, Mark 2013. Economic justice and prophetic discourse in the South African context – toward a dialogical mode of discourse. *JTSA* 145 (March), 92-109.

Villa-Vicencio, Charles 1992. *A theology of reconstruction. Nation-building and human rights.* Cape Town: David Philip.

SUBJECT INDEX

A

Accounting profession 169, 170-172, 182

African Union 140, 195, 196, 205

Apartheid 10, 11, 14, 18, 42, 49, 69, 70, 101, 107, 108, 113, 118, 124, 129, 160, 161, 164, 189, 212, 219-221, 226

   Post-apartheid 211, 215, 220, 221, 224, 227

C

Confessions

   Accra Confession (AC) 3, 123-126, 131, 142, 143

   Augsburg Confession 86, 87

   Barmen declaration 79, 85

   Belhar Confession 18, 48, 80, 84, 102, 123, 124, 128

Corporate social responsibility 144, 185, 186, 192, 193

D

Discourse

   Ethical discourse 125, 126, 128, 222

   Narrative discourse 125, 126, 128, 131, 222

   Policy discourse 128, 131, 143, 211, 222-224, 228

   Prophetic discourse 125, 128, 133-135, 141-145, 221, 222

E

Ecumenical

   Church 3, 5, 41, 50, 113

   Movement 22, 43

   Theologian 92

Economic policy 35, 39, 129, 201, 206, 211, 212, 215, 221-223, 225-229

Economy/economics 3, 6, 12, 21, 35, 37, 38, 47, 48, 57, 60, 61, 74, 97, 99, 101, 123, 125, 127, 129-131, 140, 150, 153, 155, 159, 163, 178, 192, 193, 195-198, 201-204, 206, 207, 211-215, 218-226, 228

Ethics

   Applied 39, 65, 149, 153, 155, 171, 172

   Biblical 96, 97

   Business 171, 172, 178, 180, 181

   Christian 96-99, 153, 154, 156

   Narrative 7

   Professional 97, 177

F

Fair (global) trade 36, 130, 139, 171, 195, 196, 198, 207

G

Globalisation 3-7, 9, 13, 15, 16, 29, 35, 56, 93, 125, 127, 170, 171, 195, 196, 202-204, 206, 211, 219, 221, 223

H

Happy/happiness 159, 160-165, 207

Hermeneutics 23, 25, 26, 72, 74, 75, 94, 95, 100, 107, 108, 129, 150, 161, 196, 222

Humanisation (and dehumanisation) 60, 117, 136, 154, 162

Human rights 31, 32, 34, 41-50, 58, 97, 128, 138, 153, 163, 164, 186, 187, 201, 217, 219, 223, 226

I

Ideological faith 107, 113, 114, 117

J

Justice

   Aesthetic 4, 13

   Cultural 3, 6, 10, 13, 15, 17, 18, 29, 33, 34, 38, 100, 136, 206

   Distributive 29, 30-32, 128, 130, 136-138, 207, 217, 223

   Economic 29, 38, 123, 126, 129, 133, 135, 136, 145, 151, 152, 156, 207, 211, 221-223

Partisan 21, 30, 35, 37-39
Prioritarian 206, 225

P
Post-apartheid theology 228
Poverty 23, 27-30, 35, 37, 38, 39, 50, 53, 118, 126, 128, 130, 135, 136, 139, 140, 149, 152, 162, 206, 211-213, 215-219, 222, 223, 227-229
Preferential option for the poor 21, 22, 24, 27-29, 34, 37, 39, 133, 135, 136, 138, 141, 145, 154, 207

R
Religious studies 69, 71
Responsiveness 92, 93, 99, 102, 185, 186

S
Scholarship 67, 91, 92-103, 107, 108, 116

T
Testament
   New Testament 3, 13-15, 17, 25, 68, 69, 82, 91, 93, 95-99, 107, 133
   Old Testament 25, 59, 82, 102, 111, 124, 133, 134
Theology
   Apartheid 49, 108, 117
   Liberation 22-27, 29, 30, 136, 141
   Lutheran 44
   Post-apartheid 227
   Public 53, 80, 93, 98, 99, 101, 103, 149, 156, 160, 220, 222, 228
   Reformed 43, 80, 81, 108, 118
Transparency 56, 173, 185-193

U
Ubuntu 46, 55-58, 162, 195, 204, 208

NAME INDEX

B
Barth, Karl 79, 80, 82, 84-88, 108, 114, 124, 153, 154, 171
Bedford-Strohm, Heinrich 4, 5, 16, 22, 37, 38, 39, 48, 128, 136, 206
Boff, Leonardo 23, 25, 27, 136

C
Calvin, John 80-83, 87

D
De Gruchy, John 60, 70, 108, 113, 155, 161, 220-222, 225, 226
De Villiers, Etienne 113, 117, 124, 125, 149-156, 220, 223, 226, 227

G
Gustafson, James 15, 39, 124-126, 128, 129, 134, 135, 141, 143, 144, 222-224
Gutierrez, Gustavo 21-24, 26, 44, 207

H
Habermas, Jürgen 76, 93, 94, 129, 219
Huber, Wolfgang 41, 42, 44-46, 152, 165

J
Jonker, Willie 25, 80, 81, 95, 96, 101, 108, 118, 161

K
Kant, Immanuel 30, 41, 46, 55, 163, 164, 208
Koopman, Nico 47, 221-225

M
Mbiti, John 55, 162, 208
Moltmann, Jürgen 27, 43, 46, 48, 99

N
Nürnberger, Klaus 221-224

R
Raiser, Konrad 3, 5, 16
Rawls, John 21, 29, 30-34, 36, 38, 56, 128, 135, 137-139, 153, 207, 209, 222

S
Smit, Dirk 7, 15, 18, 48, 53-56, 58-61, 81, 94, 97-99, 102, 108, 123-125, 154, 156, 159, 162, 163, 211, 219, 220, 222, 223, 225-228
Stiglitz, Joseph 21, 35-39, 129, 135, 138, 139, 195, 204, 205, 207, 208

T
Terreblanche, SJ (Sampie) 214, 218, 221
Tödt, Heinz Eduard 42, 44-46, 141, 142, 144, 211

W
Welker, Michael 3-6, 8, 15, 16, 87, 107, 118

www.ingramcontent.com/pod-product-compliance
Lightning Source LLC
Chambersburg PA
CBHW080439170426
43195CB00017B/2829